CONTENTS

Dave Thomas

JUSTICE

I the Lord love justice, I hate robbery ...

Isaiah 61:8

Copyright © 2003 Coltshill Publishing
95 Castle Road, Mumbles, Swansea SA3 5TA
d.thomas23@ntlworld.com

ISBN 0-9545733-0-7

Published by Coltshill Publishing

Typeset and edited by Mick Knight

Print production and cover design by
Bookprint Creative Services
P.O. Box 827, BN21 3YJ
Printed in Great Britain

PREFACE

AS A RETIRED Police Officer I have witnessed the devastating effects of crime, which invades every section of the community. Treasured items are stolen, homes are ruined, fear and uncertainty set in, peace of mind is lost, and the stress of the incidents is etched in people's memories.

In one of my cases the victim had all her jewellery stolen, which would be valued at £20,000 in today's prices. The items of jewellery were irreplaceable, as they were an inheritance from her parents. She was grief stricken, and felt as if something so dear to her had been wrenched away. I thought at the time, that for something so valuable she should have ensured it was more securely protected.

However, I caught the persons responsible and recovered all the property. I still remember the look of joy on the woman's face when she was once again able to hold the jewellery. Her rightful inheritance had been restored to her. Sadly, I discovered that some years later all the jewellery had again been stolen, and as far as I am aware has not been recovered. She had not taken the necessary action to prevent a re-occurrence of the theft.

There is a thief whose actions have an effect upon each of us in much the same way. The Bible refers to the devil as that thief, who seeks to steal, kill and destroy.

The purpose of this book is not only to show how to guard and prevent any of our spiritual inheritance from being stolen in the first place, but also how to take back anything that has already been stolen from our lives, and see God's justice revealed.

Dave Thomas, *December 2002*

PERSONAL TESTIMONY

For I, The Lord, love justice; **I hate robbery** ...
(Isaiah 61;8)

THIS BOOK was birthed from the above verse of Scripture. I had probably read that particular verse of Scripture hundreds of times before, but it was only on that day in 1998 that I truly understood the context in which it is contained, and which I will describe later.

I will confine my testimony to the circumstances that created a crisis in my life, and the subsequent revelation that has brought me release and a new start.

In June 1996 I collapsed in work as a result of suffering a complete physical and mental breakdown. I was 46 years old at the time. There were a multiple of factors that caused the collapse. They can be summarised as overwork and not taking proper care of my health. The Police surgeon formed the opinion that there was no prospect of my returning to work. I was pensioned off in 1997, two years before I was due to officially retire. I had completed 28 years service.

Following my retirement I descended into deep depression, as I considered myself a failure, both as a Christian and as a Police Officer. I felt like a marathon runner, who had run the first twenty-six miles, but had failed to complete the last half-mile. What made it worse was the fact that my early retirement was a result of my own actions, and not as a direct result of my Police work.

When an athlete injures a hamstring muscle, or over-stretches himself, the only things that he can do are rest and have restoration treatment to the injury. If he were to attempt to continue training, or enter competitions he would simply be unable to complete the race, and would in any case risk further injury. His recovery time would be extended. It could be said that our mind is like a muscle. If it becomes injured, or damaged, then the best treatment is rest and then restoration.

I have come to realise that life is like a set of scales. If you have a bad day, whether through ill health, stress at work and home, mental strain, or just running yourself into the ground, these days go into the balance. You can get away with it over the short term, but if you continue to have such days, eventually the scales will tip, as the bad days outweigh the good ones. There will inevitably be a consequence. There is a verse of Scripture in Ecclesiastes, which gives excellent advice on how to live a balanced life.

The man who fears God will **avoid all extremes**.
                                                    (Ecclesiastes 7;18)

You will notice that the above verse refers to **all** extremes. In my own case it was over-work, and stretching myself, both physically and mentally in too many directions when I was in ill health. It is also possible that my pattern of living caused some of the ill health in the first place.

I have been a driven person for most of my life. Driven people rarely understand God's Grace. Philip Yancey, in his book entitled *What's So Amazing about Grace?* states –

"There is nothing I can do to make God love me more, and nothing I can do to make God love me less."

These are wise words and put everything into perspective.

ONSET OF ILLNESS

Over an eighteen-month period I continuously had the following illnesses. Severe ear infections which resulted in me having about three hours sleep each night; migraines on a weekly basis which lasted for up to three days; high blood pressure; x-rays revealed that I had degeneration of my discs in a number of places causing considerable pain and restriction of movement; arthritis in my back, legs and arms; and continual infections and viruses affecting my chest and elsewhere. I had not previously suffered from these sicknesses, apart from the migraines.

Each of these illnesses is fairly minor. However, they all came upon me at more or less the same time. The main problem that affected me was the daily coping with lack of sleep, and the recurrent migraines over that eighteen month period. They had a debilitating effect. Looking back, it is clear to see that most of the sicknesses were symptomatic of a physically run down condition. I did not recognise this at the time. I thought that they were just a temporary period of ill health, and would pass.

My only purpose in mentioning the above sicknesses is to illustrate that serious things can develop from comparatively small beginnings, if left unchecked. Over the last few years I have met a number of individuals who have suffered breakdowns, and accompanying ill health. They have each said the same thing; namely that there was a gradual decline at first, and then an acceleration just before it happened. The signals, in hindsight, were abundantly clear. However, at the relevant time, they were either ignored or not properly recognised.

Unfortunately, even though my health was deteriorating I still continued my involvement in far too many activities, whilst trying to get by on a few hours sleep each day.

TOO CLOSE TO THE EDGE

I had led aid trips to Romania since 1990, following the revolution. The work was very fruitful and fulfilling, but involved a tremendous amount of time and effort. I came back from the trip in 1995 totally exhausted. It was not until a year later that I eventually collapsed. But when I came back from that particular trip, I felt a tiredness inside me that I had not previously known. It is difficult to describe. It seemed almost tangible. It did not pass.

Many people experience a number of times in their lives when they are close to the edge, but manage to avoid the drop. Unfortunately for some, they get too close one time too many, and tip over. We have all heard the expression – it is the last straw that breaks the camel's back. It can seemingly be the lightest of extra pressure that causes the collapse. The fall may happen in a day, but it can take months or even years to climb back up to where you were. It can be prevented.

Ecclesiastes 7;18 warns us to avoid all extremes, whether they are good or bad. The Lord wants us to live a balanced life. It was only at the age of forty-six that I realised the extent of my driven nature, and how much that I had lived off nervous energy and a natural strength and vitality. I discovered too late that there is no foundation to nervous energy. I had always been able to bounce back from difficulties. Unfortunately, you cannot bounce back when the foundation has gone. A rebuilding was required. This time it had to be on a solid foundation.

HOPE IN GOD

Psalm 42 is a good example of a person who is struggling with himself, and outside circumstances. He is in torment, and he knows it. In the midst of his suffering, these words rise from within him:

> *Why are you downcast, O my soul? Why so disturbed within me?* **Put your hope in God**, *for I will yet praise Him, my Saviour and my God.*   *(Psalm 42;5)*

The essence of Psalm 42 is that the Psalmist knew that there was something wrong, and he began to ask himself some searching questions, as he could not understand how he was not able to snap out of it. He asked himself two questions beginning with why: *why are you downcast?* and *why so disturbed?* You can almost feel the inner debate that he was having within himself.

Fortunately, he came to the right conclusion – **put your hope in God**. This will result in us having faith for the immediate, but also hope for the future. When we truly apply this principle, the timescale of our breakthrough does not develop into a major issue.

Owing to the degree of the physical and mental breakdown, my doctor who is a very kind and caring person, referred me to a psychiatric hospital, together with prescribed medication. I did not want to go down that route. I cancelled the hospital appointment and declined the medication. Although I was suffering mentally, and had entered deep depression, my faith stood firm. I still had hope that The Lord would deliver me.

I do not wish anyone reading this to feel condemned if they are receiving psychiatric help or drug treatment. I have only included these things, as it is part of my personal testimony. In other words, it is pertinent and relevant to my personal circumstances. Some other person may quite rightly chose a different path, and obtain the help which is at hand to get them through a difficult period.

Taking medical treatment of any kind does not reveal, or imply, a lack of faith. God does not condemn, or cut someone off because they take the path of medicine, whether on a temporary basis or long-term. Condemnation only comes from one source – the devil. The all-abiding truth is that God continually loves us, and wants the best for us. His Grace is always there.

PHYSICAL HEALING

> *Praise The Lord, O my soul, and forget not all His benefits* – **who forgives all your sins and heals all your diseases**. *(Psalm 103;2/3)*

I do not believe that any sickness comes from God. One of the Names of God in The Old Testament is Jehovah Rophe which means 'The Lord who heals'. (Exodus 15;22/26). Jesus fulfilled this Name in His life, and at The Cross. Isaiah prophesied of the forthcoming Messiah:

> *He was pierced for our transgressions – and* **by His wounds we are healed.** *(Isaiah 53;5)*

In The New Testament the Apostle Peter refers to this passage in Isaiah, when he testifies about Jesus. He uses words that are in the past tense, thereby showing that it is a finished act. Our sins and sicknesses have been dealt with. They are not part of our inheritance.

> *He Himself bore our sins in His body on the tree...***by His wounds you have been healed.** *(1 Peter 2;24)*

Scripture clearly shows that ill health can come upon people by various ways, some of which are as follows.

1) Is any one of you sick? *(James 5;14)*

The devil afflicts us with sickness and ill health. Scripture encourages the person who is unwell to ask others to pray, and anoint with oil. If sickness were from God, we would be acting against His will if we asked for prayer in respect of our healing, or took any form of medicine. It can therefore be seen that sickness does not originate with God.

2) Whoever eats the bread or drinks the cup of the Lord in an unworthy manner will be guilty of sinning ... That is why many among you are weak and sick.

(1 Corinthians 11;27/32)

If we treat the commands of God with disrespect, or step outside of His ways, then we obviously lay ourselves open to that which is harmful. Ill health can be one of the consequences.

3) "Neither this man nor his parents sinned", said Jesus, "but this happened so that the work of God might be displayed in his life." *(John 9;1-3)*

The blind person was **healed** in order to bring glory to God. You will notice that the sickness did not bring glory. It was the healing that accomplished this. If the sickness had brought glory, Jesus would have left him in the state that He found him.

I would add that I cannot explain the sicknesses in some people. All I know is that I respond to the heart of the Apostle John.

I pray that you may enjoy good health and that all may
go well with you, even as your soul is getting along well.
(3 John;2)

With regard to my own condition, I had basically
abused my body, and mind, by being a driven individual.
Although I may have prided myself on never having taken
drugs, smoked, or consumed excessive alcohol; I had in
fact abused my body in a destructive manner. I had not
looked after God's temple. The devil then took an opportune time to afflict me.

Don't you know that you yourselves are God's temple.
(1 Corinthians 3;16)

I believe that there is an appointed time for us to die,
after we have fulfilled God's plans and purposes for our
lives. However, by our own actions, or by allowing ourselves to be robbed, we can die before our time. Scripture
gives us the following warning:

Do not be a fool. **Why die before your time?**
(Ecclesiastes 7;17)

SPIRITUAL EMPOWERING

I will briefly describe some of the experiences that I
encountered on the road back to recovery.

In the middle of 1998 I was in a particularly low state,
both physically and mentally. During one night in this
period I was lying alone in bed when the room filled with
demonic activity. The bed was situated in the corner, and
it was the only place in the room that was not filled with
this evil presence. I can best describe it as spirits weaving
in and out of one another, with indistinct faces.

I then experienced a closing in on me, as my life was

being sucked away. My breathing became difficult, and I was forced more and more into the corner of the room. I can remember thinking to myself – " This is it. There is no escape." I was not on any medication; I was awake, and not hallucinating.

Like most Police Officers, I have come face to face with evil and terror. You get hardened, and are able to deal with most things. Very little fazes you. In addition to which, I have been a Christian since the age of sixteen, and have seen aspects of satanic influence. But I had never experienced anything like that night. I cannot suitably relate the sheer evil and terror of the experience.

When I was at the point of being overwhelmed I shouted at the demons – "In the name of Jesus". Immediately, the room emptied of all demonic activity, and a total peace and calm filled the room.

Peter made the following declaration about Jesus.

"You are The Christ, The Son of The Living God." *Jesus replied, "Blessed are you, Simon, for this was not revealed to you by man, but by my Father in Heaven* ... **I will give you the keys of the Kingdom of Heaven.** " *(Matthew 16;15/19)*

This same confession was made once again by Peter at Pentecost, after the disciples were filled with The Holy Spirit. He said to the gathered crowd:

"Therefore let all Israel be assured of this; **God has made this Jesus**, *whom you crucified*, **both Lord and Christ.** " *(Acts 2;36)*

Notice that Peter's confession is exactly the same on both occasions. When he made his first declaration The Lord told Him that He would give him the Keys, therefore meaning at a future time. That time came at Pentecost. Peter declared for the second time the revelation and confession of **Jesus as Lord**, **The Christ – The Anointed one**. Our use of the Keys is dependent upon the same revelation. (For a fuller explanation please refer to chapter twenty-nine).

I then knew with absolute clarity that on the night that I have just described I had used the Keys of the Kingdom, the revelation that Jesus is the Lord over everything. The devil saw this as an opportune time to afflict me. He tried to take advantage of my weakened state. But he was defeated because he had to withdraw at the Name of Jesus.

SIDE BY SIDE

Towards the end of 1988 I suffered a further setback to my recovery. I was beginning to lose the battle against deep depression. It was like wave after wave. I began to contemplate death as a release.

Although I have been blessed with many close friends, I did not share the mental and spiritual battle that I was encountering. I did not even tell my wife Irene, as I did not want to worry her. She had recently lost her mother through cancer.

It was at this point that I heard a voice saying, "Let me in". Even in my low state I knew that this was a demonic attack, and that the voice I heard was a spirit of suicide. I realised that this was another opportune time when the devil sought to take advantage of my weakened state. Over a period of three months, both night and day, I heard these voices. Each time I repelled them using the authority in the name of Jesus, the Keys of the Kingdom.

Dawn and Christine are close friends of Irene and I.

One morning Dawn telephoned Christine, and during the conversation, told her that she felt burdened to pray for me. They knew of my physical illnesses, but were totally unaware of the spiritual battle I was facing.

Christine then related a dream that she had during the night. In the dream I was standing in pleasant surroundings, but opposite me was a large number of faces, which were mocking and sneering at me. Other faces were lying in ambush for me. All the while, these faces were saying "We've got him now". Into the gap between the faces and me stepped Christine and Dawn, and looked directly at the faces. They spoke to the faces and said, "No, you are not having your way. We are standing against you in the powerful name of Jesus". The faces then retreated.

As soon as Christine finished telling the dream to Dawn they both knew that they had to meet immediately to pray for me. It is important to emphasise that Christine saw both her and Dawn standing side by side in the dream. As further confirmation, when Christine arrived at Dawn's house she saw that Dawn was wearing the same clothing as in the dream. What had seemingly been a chance telephone call turned into a most significant encounter.

Within the hour of first speaking they had met together, and prayed for my protection and deliverance. Just like the dream, Christine and Dawn stood in the gap.

Unknown to them, I was facing the climax to a sustained onslaught which, as stated earlier, had lasted for three months. I heard the voices most days, and I was in a very weakened state. I was standing against these spirits in the name of Jesus and knew that things were coming to a head. The crucial time was the morning that Dawn and Christine were praying. The victory and release came at mid-day. My sustained recovery began at that point in time.

Neither Dawn, nor Christine, mentioned this to me until a week after the incident. I had been unaware that they were at my side in the battle, and they did not know what was taking place in my home. I regret to say that I still did not tell anyone about the full significance of what had occurred. It was only some time later that I felt able to disclose the state I was in.

OPPRESSION AND POSSESSION

Many of you will be asking at this point – Can a Christian be overtaken by a demon? I do not believe that a Christian can be possessed, but I believe he can be oppressed, which are quite separate states. Allow me to explain my reasons from Scripture.

It is first necessary to understand that each of us comprises of three distinct parts, namely spirit, soul, and body.

> *May your whole* **spirit, soul and body** *be kept blameless.* (1 Thessalonians 5;23)

The body is our outer shell; the soul is our mind, emotions, heart, conscience, will, and intellect; the spirit is our inner being, the very centre of our life. We will look at this subject in greater detail in chapter eight. I will just briefly mention a few points for clarity purposes, as part of my personal testimony.

The essence of being born again is that we accept Jesus as Lord of our life, and in so doing, The Holy Spirit takes up residence in our spirit. At our conversion we were born again of The Spirit. Our spirit, which we have had since birth, is re-born. It experiences a metamorphosis, which means a marked change in character. A fundamental and radical change takes place. The Lord Jesus, by His Spirit, occupies our inner being (spirit). He dwells in our spirit, the very centre of our lives. The Lord Himself is seated in Glory, but He abides in us by The Holy Spirit.

Flesh gives birth to flesh, but **The Spirit gives birth to spirit**. *(John 3;6)*

If Jesus, by His Spirit occupies our spirit, then it is impossible for the demonic to move Him from that place, and He is certainly not going to share that place with any one else. The reason we can know for sure is explained by the Apostle John.

The One who is in you, is greater *than the one who is in the world.* *(1 John 4;4)*

Therefore, if Christ is dwelling in us, He is greater and more powerful than anyone else who would seek to gain entry to our spirit, and He has also promised never to leave nor forsake us. He has made a covenant with us. We can therefore be completely confident that, as born again believers, we cannot be possessed by the demonic.

Never *will I leave you,* **nor** *forsake you.*
(Hebrews 13;5)

But, for someone who is not truly born again of The Spirit, the situation is completely different. Just as The Lord dwells in our inner being (spirit) by His Spirit, so the demonic, who are also spirit, seek to dwell in a person's spirit. The reason for this is that spirit relates to spirit. This is how someone, who is not a Christian, can be both oppressed and possessed. A spirit oppresses their soul, or even takes up residence in their spirit. Jesus explains this to a crowd of people, after He had delivered a man from a demon.

When an evil spirit comes out of a man, it goes through arid places seeking rest and does not find it. Then it says, " **I will return to the house I left.** *" When it arrives, it finds the house swept clean and put in order.* **Then it goes and takes seven other spirits more wicked than itself, and they go in and live there**. *And the final condition of that man is worse than the first.* (Luke 11;24/26)

DELIVERANCE

When someone has been delivered of a demon, it is so important that they accept Christ as his or her Lord and Saviour as soon as possible, and thereby become born again of The Holy Spirit. If this does not happen, the person's spirit that has been swept clean is open to be filled again with many more demons. The above verses in Luke vividly illustrate what can happen.

But if a person commits his life to Christ after being delivered, then The Lord dwells in that person's spirit. The demonic cannot then enter that place. He is safe. Notice that the verses reveal that the demonic look for a home. Our spirit is meant to be occupied by The Lord, and no one else.

God gave a warning to Cain. I do not know if the account of Cain is an example of demonic activity. All I know is that the verse of Scripture graphically describes the principles involved. It crouches at the door, looking for an opportunity to get in, desiring to control our actions.

Sin is crouching at your door; **it desires to have you,** *but you must master it.* (Genesis 4;7)

To avoid such encounters, it is wise not to open ourselves up to patterns of thought, or behaviour, which open the door. Keep the door firmly shut, and do not take foolish risks. This was the advice given by God when He told Cain that he must master it. In other words, take complete authority over it, and do not allow it to come through the door. A Christian has that authority in Jesus.

Greater is He who is in us, than he who is in the world.
(1 John 4;4)

Cain opened the door to the thief, who came in to plunder. He then killed his brother Abel. This is unfortunately the pattern of things. People let unhealthy feelings and attitudes take root. The scene is then set to open the door to something even worse.

The thief comes only to steal, kill, and destroy.
(John 10;10)

BALANCE

It is important to emphasise that we do not to get out of balance in this particular subject. A person can go through the whole of their life, and not consciously be affected by any demonic activity.

While it is necessary not be naive about demonic activity, it is equally necessary that we do not go over-board and attribute every sinful act to their influence. Some well meaning, but unfortunately misguided Christians, seek to deliver people from demons when they are neither oppressed nor possessed. It is just plain sin that is at the centre of the issue.

The vast majority of sin is committed through such things as disobedience, yielding to temptation, and having our own agenda in life etc. Nothing at all to do with demonic activity. We need to be wise, and have clear discernment and balance in this area. (Please refer to chapter thirty-three).

I know that some people feel somewhat uncomfortable even discussing such matters. There is a feeling amongst some believers that these things are best left alone. More often than not these attitudes can come from fear, and a lack of understanding of our spiritual authority in The Lord. I know that I was also in this category. It is therefore not my desire to sensationalise the subject, or cause offence to anyone. I am merely trying to encourage believers to have a greater awareness, and not be afraid to exercise authority in Jesus' name.

BATTLES OF THE MIND

The question remains – If a Christian cannot be possessed in his spirit (inner being), then in what area is he open to be oppressed? In order to answer this, it is necessary to look at the make-up of our soul. As we have already seen, the soul comprises of our mind, emotions, heart, conscience, will, and intellect. Consider for one moment, as to what part of us is prone to attack, and is the area that has doubt and fear?

The answer of course is our mind, heart, and emotions. These are the parts that are so often the battleground, and explains why it is so needful for our mind to get renewed, in the same manner as our spirit has been changed.

I now understand how my hope in The Lord remained intact throughout all the adverse circumstances. My mind, which is part of my soul, was in a very weakened and vulnerable state, but my spirit (inner being) remained strong, because it was continually being strengthened by The Holy Spirit. There is a verse of Scripture that encapsulates what happens.

> *I pray that out of God's glorious riches* **He may strengthen you with power through His Spirit in your inner being,** *so that Christ may dwell in your hearts through faith.* *(Ephesians 3;16/17)*

The demonic were attacking my mind, trying to convince me that all hope was gone. But in my spirit, I was continually being strengthened by The Holy Spirit, who was telling me to hold fast, put my hope in The Lord, and deliverance would come.

> *The Word of God penetrates even to* **dividing soul and spirit**. *(Hebrews 4;12)*

Our soul is the area in which we can be oppressed. Our mind is subject to fear and doubt, whereas our spirit which has been renewed, stands firm. Our salvation cannot be snatched away from us. We are safe and secure in The Lord.

> *My Father, who has given them to Me, is greater than all;* **no one can snatch them out of My Father's hand**. *(John 10;29)*

Real freedom, peace, and victory come when we get our soul in line with our spirit. From our spirit flows life and truth, because Christ dwells there by His Spirit. This sustains and empowers us. I can testify to this. Although it was a long haul, because of His wonderful grace, my soul began to get restored when it got in line with the truth that The Holy Spirit was revealing to me in my spirit.

The demonic know that they cannot snatch us out of The Lord's hands, because The Holy Spirit inhabits our spirit. They therefore seek to torment and unsettle our minds, which are part of our soul. The devil will use all manner of means to make us feel insecure, and will put fear and doubt into our minds. He is a thief and deceiver.

Our spirit is renewed at salvation. It therefore follows that if we also get our soul restored and renewed, we will have basically slammed the door in the face of the devil. He no longer has a point of entry. He is not only shut out, but he is also kept out by the fullness of The Spirit. When our spirit and soul are full of The Lord, there is no opening for anything demonic.

This does not cause complacency on our part, but encourages us to develop the heart of a watchman in order to prevent anything untoward, as we shall see later in the book. (Refer chapter twenty-three).

RECOVERY

Have you ever been through an experience, which may be of short or long duration, and you have wondered whether you would get through? It appears that everything within you has been pushed to breaking point. But you manage to pull through, seemingly against all odds. The world has a measure of this fortitude. It is commonly known as 'strength of character'. But a Christian also has The Holy Spirit strengthening and encouraging us from our spirit. We operate from the centre outwards.

I would like to say at this point that my relationship with The Lord, and my understanding of spiritual matters, has been totally transformed since I have had greater understanding of spirit, soul, and body. It all happened after asking The Lord for revelation concerning Ephesians 3;16-17.

I suddenly saw that my spirit is the centre of spiritual activity, and that my soul is no longer to have dominance. Faith, joy, peace, truth, grace and anointing etc. rise up from a believer's spirit, because that is where The Lord dwells, by His Spirit. His will and purpose is revealed in our spirit.

We can therefore see how it is important that we do not allow doubts in our mind to nullify faith, which rises in our spirit. This is why Scripture talks of the renewing of the mind. Such feelings as stress, doubt and anxiety do not come from our spirit. They originate in our soul.

The choice then has to be made. Do we live according to our spirit, or our soul? Truly victorious living occurs when our soul has been transformed, and is in harmony with our spirit. When we consistently apply this principle on a daily basis, a renewing and transformation takes place. It then becomes the normal way of living, to the extent that we no longer have to consciously think about it. It has become our new nature.

This revelation concerning the different functions of our spirit and soul has been the final piece of the jigsaw in my recovery. I have come to realise that all my striving, and driven personality, came from my soul. In order to live a transformed life I needed to live out of my spirit.

When I discovered this truth, I looked back over the previous years and saw the times when The Lord revealed truth to my spirit. My soul, which contained my mind and emotions, slowly but surely got in line with the rebuilding, restoring, and renewing process that was taking place within me. It started in my spirit, and worked outwards to affect my soul and body. As previously stated – **a Christian operates from the centre outwards**.

You will notice that the book is wide ranging, covering many aspects of the Christian life. My intention is to show that when the devil attempts to steal, kill and destroy, it is not confined to one particular area of our lives.

Although I was familiar with most of the Scriptures contained in this book, I can testify that during the last six years I have seen them afresh. Each of the chapters is relative to something new that The Lord revealed to me over these last few years. I personally discovered that a rebuilding, restoring, and renewing were required in a number of areas.

I am writing these closing words in December 2002. I am gradually involving myself more in The Lord's work, but at a pace that is suitable to a fifty-two year old. My physical and mental health has been restored. It has been a long haul, but by His grace I am still alive and look with confidence to the future.

THE SONG OF DELIVERANCE

I would like to bring my testimony to a close with a few verses of Scripture that have greatly helped me.

> *Praise be to The Lord, for He showed His wonderful love to me* **when I was in a besieged city**.
> *(Psalm 31;21)*

The Angel of The Lord encamps around those who fear Him, *and He delivers them.* *(Psalm 34;7)*

There are times in life when we feel just like the Psalmist. We are in a besieged city for a host of reasons such as sickness, mental or emotional strain, family upheaval, job difficulties etc. We look out of our city, and all we see are one or more of the above or similar situations. But The Lord has a word for us. He says – **look again. Take another look.**

Although these situations are there, and very real to us, He tells us that the Angel of The Lord encamps around those that fear Him, and He delivers them. The Psalmist tells of God's wonderful love while he was under siege. Whether a siege lasts for a short or long duration, deliverance is at hand.

> *You are my hiding place; You will protect me from trouble and* **surround me with songs of deliverance**. *(Psalm 32;7)*

Let us sing from the same song sheet as Heaven, and see deliverance continually come to pass in our lives.

PART 1

CRIME AND ITS CONSEQUENCES

*The thief comes only to steal and kill and destroy; I have
come that they may have life, and have it to the full.*
John 10;10

CHAPTER ONE

GOD'S ATTITUDE
TO CRIME

HAVE YOU ever considered what God's attitude is to crime?

> *For I The Lord love justice;* **I hate robbery**.
> (Isaiah 61;8)

This is a very emphatic statement. It is fair to say that such a remark about robbery must obviously relate to an incident where people have become victims of crime, and that something has been stolen. It must be in context with a message that is being taught. The passage of Scripture immediately before this statement is as follows:

> *The Spirit of The Sovereign Lord is on Me, because* **The Lord has anointed Me** *to*
>
> *Preach good news to the poor*
> *Bind up the broken hearted*
> *Proclaim freedom for the captives*
> *Release from darkness for the prisoners*
> *Comfort all who mourn*
> *Provide for those who grieve.* (Isaiah 61;1-3)

These verses contain a list of people who have been subject to robbery. They have had their peace and joy stolen; they are injured; captive to sickness, or prisoners to despair. This is why our Lord God refers to robbery immediately after this passage. Notice that the chapter begins with these words:

The Spirit of The Sovereign Lord is on Me because...
(Isaiah 61;1)

The word *because* is used to link two statements. A truth is stated, and an explanation of the purpose follows. The Anointing is therefore not meant only as a blessing. It is also given to enable us to take back that which has been stolen from our lives, and that of others. It is to restore God's Kingdom and justice into that situation. Each of the categories in the above list relates to people who have been robbed. The Lord was anointed to take action against this injustice. We also have the same commission.

ANOINTED TO SERVE

The heart of Isaiah 61;1-3 is to receive The Anointing in order to minister to others. It was this particular passage of Scripture that Jesus quoted at the beginning of His ministry, as recorded in Luke 4;17-19. The Apostle Peter also refers to The Anointing that Jesus received in order to minister.

God anointed Jesus *of Nazareth with The Holy Spirit and power, and* **He went around doing good** *and healing all who were under the power of the devil, because God was with Him.* *(Acts 10;38)*

You will notice that the second part of the above verse reveals the Anointing was received in order to confront the works of the devil. Isaiah 61;8 informs us that our Lord God loves justice. It is against His will when His people are robbed by the devil of any of their inheritance in Him. Jesus came and proclaimed justice. **By His authority we can take back that which the devil has stolen, and see true justice implemented.**

I will put My Spirit on Him, and **He will proclaim justice** *to the nations. (Isaiah 42;1 & Matthew 12;18)*

APOLOGY

A few years ago my parents had a burglary at their home. It was an opportunist theft, while they had their evening walk around the nearby park. They were only gone for forty-five minutes. A number of personal items, together with some silverware were stolen. The thief left a note on the table in the living room. It contained the solitary word "sorry".

I have dealt with some criminals who were sorry for their actions, and do show genuine remorse. Some cynics would suggest that they were only sorry because they had been caught. But there is one thing of which I am certain. That is, the devil does not show any contrition or regret when he steals from us. He does not show compassion, even for those who are weak, or vulnerable. When he steals from us he does not leave a note saying "sorry".

The legal definition of theft is as follows:

A person is guilty of theft if he dishonestly appropriates property belonging to another with the intention of permanently depriving the other of it.

By clear definition the devil is dishonest, and he has the desire to permanently deprive us of any part of our inheritance in The Lord. He knows that he is not the rightful owner, but he still persists in his quest.

When a person is a victim of crime, they are affected both mentally and emotionally. This is partly through the loss of the item, and also the shock of the incident. They feel shattered. It is the same with spiritual theft. But we receive The Anointing to bring justice, and restore that which has been stolen. We have the equipping and the commission to reverse the situation by rebuilding, restoring and renewing.

> *They will* **rebuild** *the ancient ruins.* **Restore** *the places long devastated.* **Renew** *the ruined cities.*
>
> *(Isaiah 61;4)*

PERSONAL EXPERIENCE

Luke 4;1-13 records The Lord's temptation in the desert. It gives a clear picture of how the devil attempts to steal, kill and destroy.

He tried to **steal** The Lord's confidence by asking Him a series of questions beginning with 'if'. *If you are The Son of God* (v.3). Secondly he tried to **destroy** Jesus relationship with The Father – *If you worship me (devil) it will all be yours* (v.7). Thirdly he tried to **kill** The Lord and prevent His earthly ministry – *If you are the Son of God throw yourself down from here* (v.9).

The Lord defeated the devil on each occasion. But it did not stop there, because Scripture records that the devil left Jesus *until an opportune time* (Luke 4;13). We will be looking at some of those times later in the book.

Luke 4;14-21 then gives the account of when Jesus got up in the synagogue in Nazareth, shortly after His desert experience. The Lord quoted directly from the prophet Isaiah.

> *The Spirit of The Lord is on Me to ...*   *(Isaiah 61;1)*

Jesus had just received first hand experience of the devil's attempt to steal something in His life. Therefore, when He got up in the synagogue, He could testify to the purpose of The Anointing, and the power of The Word of God. Jesus finished by declaring that which the people were going to see happen in their midst in the subsequent years. It can also be our testimony.

Today this scripture is fulfilled *in your hearing.*
(Luke 4;21)

CHAPTER TWO

THE THREE R'S

TEACHERS EMPHASISE the importance of the three R's of reading, writing and arithmetic in order that a pupil develops. Whether the student eventually goes on to take 'A' levels, a degree, or even a doctorate, the foundation of anything he does will be the three R's of reading, writing and arithmetic. The skills and gifts he develops are merely an expansion of the three R's.

As we have just seen in the previous chapter, there are three R's contained in Isaiah 61 that are of even greater importance. They are the three R's of rebuild, restore and renew.

> *They will* **rebuild** *the ancient ruins and* **restore** *the places long devastated; they will* **renew** *the ruined cities that have been devastated for generations.*
>
> *(Isaiah 61;4)*

Rebuild, restore and renew have the following meanings:

Rebuild – Build again or differently.

Restore – Give back to the original owner, make restitution; reinstate; bring back to dignity or right.

Renew – Revive; regenerate; make new again; restore to the original state; recover one's youth, strength.

Isaiah 61;4 speaks prophetically of the work that God's anointed people will accomplish. No matter how much we grow in ministry or gifting, the work we carry out for The Lord will always have rebuilding, restoring and renewing at its root.

The result of robbery is a taking away, but the work of rebuilding, restoring and renewing is the complete opposite of robbery. It produces a giving back.

Notice the verse that follows the work of rebuilding, restoring and renewing. There is a clear message that when God restores, He gives back more.

> *Instead of their shame My people will receive a* **double portion**, *and instead of disgrace they will rejoice in their inheritance; and so they will inherit a* **double portion** *in their land, and everlasting joy will be theirs.*   *(Isaiah 61;7)*

THE GOOD SAMARITAN

The story opens with the statement that a person was robbed.

> *A man was going down from Jerusalem to Jericho, when* **he fell into the hands of robbers**.
>   *(Luke 10;30)*

Whenever this Scripture is read, or preached upon, the emphasis quite rightly is placed on the actions of The Samaritan. However, a point that is often overlooked is the fact that the account begins with a person being robbed. This is what happens to people. They are on their way through life when they fall into the hands of the robber, who steals their peace, joy, family, health etc.

The Samaritan, during the course of his journey, encountered a person who had been robbed. He did not pass by, but stopped. He recognised the need and responded. He bandaged his wounds, pouring on oil and wine. He took him to an inn, cared for him, and informed the innkeeper that he would call again and reimburse any extra cost.

It could be said that the Samaritan poured in the oil and the wine from the anointing which was upon him. He bound up the broken hearted, rebuilt his confidence, restored his dignity and renewed him in strength. The Good Samaritan in us will always seek to **rebuild, restore and renew**. He had fulfilled the heart of Isaiah 61. The thieves had robbed, but he gave back. At the heart of the action by the Samaritan was the desire to see a life restored.

He was also wise in not becoming a crutch to the person who had been robbed. He let him find his own two feet when he was able. However, he gave a promise and a commitment that he would call again. We can do the same when we help people rebuild their lives. As they become independent of us, we can leave them gain confidence in their own walk with The Lord, but in the confident knowledge that we are keeping watch over them. This is what the Samaritan accomplished, and is also the essence of the shepherd's heart.

The Good Samaritan is aptly named because he did good. Our prime example of someone who continually did good is our Lord. He was anointed, and went around doing good.

God **anointed** *Jesus with The Holy Spirit and power, and how* **He went around doing good** *and healing*

all who were under the power of the devil, because God
was with Him. (Acts 10;38)

There are many recorded examples in Scripture whereby The Lord, just like the Parable of the Good Samaritan, stopped on His journey to meet the need of an individual. He freely gave from the abundance of His inheritance. Let us also be prepared to stop, and not pass by someone who has been robbed.

CHAPTER THREE

OUR COMMISSION

WHEN A POLICE OFFICER first joins a Constabulary he takes an oath of allegiance to the King or Queen. At the inauguration ceremony he receives his commission from the Lord Lieutenant of the respective county, and in so doing receives the power and authority to carry out his duties, and apply the laws of the land.

I can still remember my first day of joining in July 1969. It was a very warm summer's day, and a group of us had been kept standing outside in direct sunlight for a few hours, while we were waiting to go through certain administrative procedures. After a while I used one arm to lean against a wall. At that point a drill sergeant marched past, and gave me some intuitive advice, in the manner that is pertinent only to officers of that particular rank – "The wall can hold itself up".

The oath of allegiance was a gateway into a new world, which would provide challenge, adventure, fulfilment, and comradeship. I had no idea at the time of my joining what would lie ahead. It proved to be far more than I could possibly have imagined. If someone had told me in the beginning what I would personally accomplish, and confidently deal with in the future, I would have doubted their wisdom, as I had always suffered from a lack of confidence.

The same can be said about salvation. We commit our lives to The Lord, but little do we realise what we will encounter and overcome through Him. He has promised never to leave us, nor forsake us, and He has given us His Spirit so that we reach our full potential in Him. He also gives every believer a commission:

> *All authority in Heaven and earth has been given to Me.* **Therefore go and make disciples of all nations...teaching them to obey everything I have commanded you.** *And surely I am with you always, to the very end of the age.* *(Matthew 28;18)*

A Police Officer is commissioned to obey and enforce the laws of the land. **Christians are commissioned to obey the laws of God, and establish His will on earth.** Each of them entails an establishing of justice.

A Police Officer has law books to remind him of his authority and power. We have the Word of God.

AUTHORITY

When someone has had some possession stolen, the Police seek to gather information as to the identity of the person responsible, and return the stolen property to its rightful owner. As Christians, it would be good to have the same attitude. We can then stand alongside those who have been robbed, and recover that which has been lost. In so doing we will see the person rebuilt, restored and renewed.

Once the Police discover the thief's identity, a search warrant is used to enter premises and recover the stolen property.

A warrant gives the Police:

1) The power and authority to enter
2) The ability to seize and remove property.

A comparison can be made between the powers of a Police officer in the natural realm and those of a Christian in the spiritual realm, namely the authority, power, and ability to restore. Praise God we do not have to just accept theft. **Our Heavenly Father is concerned with restoration, by returning that which has been lost to its rightful owner.**

As Christians we know where to look when something has been stolen from our lives, such as our peace, joy, relationships, health etc. As with the Police, knowing something is not enough. Something has to be done about the loss.

If the Police do not do their duty, or do not use their authority and power to bring offenders to justice, the public quite rightly feels aggrieved. Likewise, the world is looking for the church to take a stand against unrighteousness and evil. Are we aware of the power that we have in the spiritual realm? For we have been given His Spirit as the power, and His Word as the authority.

Just like a Police officer who uses a warrant to enter and recover property, we also have the power and authority to go to the devil and take back that which rightfully belongs to others and ourselves.

But even better, do not be robbed in the first place.

PRESENT IN THE WORKPLACE

In addition to the spiritual aspect of what I have just stated, I also have known the Lord's help in solving criminal cases, and recovering stolen property.

One of the cases involved the theft of a large amount of

cash in bank notes. It was one of those internal thefts that could have been carried out by any one of a hundred people. The case involved extensive interviewing, with no leads forthcoming. As the weeks went by it began to look as if it would be an undetected crime.

My wife Irene and I began to pray into the situation. Within a short time, anonymous information was received as to the identity of the persons responsible. The arrests were made, admissions gained, and the majority of the money recovered.

On the day of the theft, the company had provided us with an office to start the investigation. It was a large organisation, and we saw a considerable number of employees that first day. No formal interviewing took place. We concentrated on getting an overview of the situation, and eliminating certain avenues of enquiry. We believed that it was going to be a protracted enquiry.

During that day, for some unknown reason, I took note of one person. He was not interviewed, as nothing at the time pointed to his guilt. He was simply one of the employees. His face just happened to register in my mind, although he was a total stranger, and did nothing to arouse suspicion. There was also nothing strange or distinctive about him that would draw someone's attention.

He was not even interviewed in the following weeks, as he was at the bottom of the list of possible suspects. But as soon as he was arrested, I immediately recognised him from that first encounter. I have often thought about that enquiry, and wondered if The Holy Spirit was prompting me to interview him that first day. It would have saved a tremendous amount of work in the subsequent weeks.

I mention this, as I believe that The Holy Spirit aids

and helps us in whatever work we do, because he is interested in all of us, and in every aspect of our lives. There are no separate compartments as far as He is concerned. Our respective area of employment is the same as our family and church activity. It is all part of our life.

The Lord does not leave us as we enter our place of work, and wait for us to emerge at the end of the working day. He stays with us continually, and wants us to succeed in everything we tackle. Therefore, let us be aware and responsive to The Holy Spirit giving us ideas of how we can affect, and improve the environment in which we work. Then have the boldness to implement it ourselves, or approach our employer. It could provide the breakthrough that he had been waiting or praying for.

This sort of answer to prayer occurred on other occasions. We would pray, and information would be received, or there would be some other breakthrough. Some people may quite rightly suggest that what I experienced during my Police career were mere coincidences, and not answers to prayer. I cannot offer any proof to refute such a claim, apart from an inner conviction and certainty. All I can add is that there comes a point in time when the amount of answers to prayer outweigh the possibility of them being coincidences.

There is no doubt in my mind that it is The Lord's desire to bless us, whether it is in our family, homes, or work. Would you agree that we so often take so much for granted, and neglect to see the handiwork of The Holy Spirit in our lives? We accept so much of our lives to be coincidence or chance, and are thereby robbed of opportunities.

APPOINTED TIMES

I recently studied 'times', 'appointed times' and 'seasons' in Scripture. It is very enlightening, and makes you think twice about coincidences. I would encourage you to use a Concordance to follow these themes through The Bible, and I can promise you that not only will you be greatly blessed, but it will also create an increased sensitivity to the leading of The Holy Spirit.

Have you suddenly met a person that had been on your mind for some time or a conversation with a friend, or stranger has taken a particular course? After leaving these people you make the remark, "That was strange how I met them," or "It's amazing how that conversation went". I would suggest that many of our chance meetings with people are actually appointed times, and are an integral part of our commission.

Recently, whilst on a hospital visit, I saw a retired police officer whom I had known for all my service. He had led a self-destructive life, abusing himself with alcohol, chain smoking, and harmful living. When I saw him sitting in the waiting area he looked ill and desperate. His physical condition had deteriorated considerably as a result of the excesses of his life.

Although we had never worked together, we had always stopped and talked if we met. He had a number of good points, and he had helped me earlier in my service. I had a clear prompting in my spirit to approach him and witness to him about The Lord before it was too late. To my shame, I convinced myself not to bother at that particular time, and that I would see him again. He had not seen me across the foyer and I passed through the area unnoticed.

I never had that other opportunity that I so readily convinced myself would come my way, as he died within a few weeks. The Apostle Paul gave this command to Timothy:

> *Teach The Word;* **be prepared in season and out of season** *(2 Timothy 4;2)*

We do not always feel in season, and as a result of not being prepared and willing, we miss those appointed times. Opportunities and encounters in service for The Lord can be robbed from right in front of us if we fail to open our eyes to see the situations that He leads us into.

The prophet Jeremiah spoke these words from The Lord to the people of his time. They have the same relevance to us today.

> *Even the stork in the sky knows her* **appointed seasons,** *and the dove, the swift and the thrush* **observe the time** *of their migration. But my people do not know the requirements of The Lord.* *(Jeremiah 8;7)*

These verses challenge us to recognise and understand appointed seasons and times. This applies to those situations we encounter on a daily basis, and in respect of wider issues.

What a difference it makes when we are sensitive to appointed times. On one such occasion I met an old friend that I had not seen for a number of years, at a seemingly chance encounter. He was a Christian, but had not been in church for a long time.

As we were talking, The Holy Spirit gave me a short, but clear word. As a result of which, I said to him, **"Don't let the seed within you die".** He thanked me for the word and we parted. I knew that the word The Lord had given me would produce a positive result.

My Word that goes out from my mouth will not return to Me empty, but **will accomplish what I desire and achieve the purpose for which I sent it**.

(Isaiah 55;11)

He later told me that the word spoke directly to him, and caused a response. He subsequently rededicated himself to The Lord, and returned to church. It was not my friendship that caused the turn-around in his life. It was an appointed time set by The Lord, and into which He gave a life-changing word.

Sometimes we can lose contact with people for a variety of reasons, but The Lord never loses touch. He will engineer circumstances, so that we meet people, seemingly out of the blue. Thankfully, on this occasion I was obedient to the prompting of The Spirit.

How good is a word in season.

(Proverbs 15;23 King James version)

STEAL NO LONGER

During the years in the Police I would witness of my faith to my colleagues when opportunity allowed. Unfortunately, the Police Service is a very macho organisation, and not given to submitting themselves to God. They view submission as weakness. However, I saw truth come out even in humorous ways.

One such time was a theft case I dealt with, involving a businessman who was stealing from his customers. He was a well-respected man and it initially seemed inconceivable that he could have committed the thefts. There was no direct evidence, only circumstantial. I interviewed him, but he firmly denied any involvement.

Police Officers can get hardened and cynical very quickly, as we see the worst side of life. There is a presumption in English Law that a person is innocent until proven guilty. Police officers work from the opposite direction. They presume someone is guilty until they prove to the officer that they are innocent. This attitude unfortunately comes from dealing with such hard and unscrupulous individuals who do not know the meaning of truth.

Having said that, each of the officers on my group knew the person I had arrested, and took the uncharacteristic step of believing him to be innocent. I believed him to be the person responsible, but owing to his standing in the community, and listening to others, I also began to have doubts about his guilt. It can be very frustrating when you are unsure. You want to have that inner certainty if you are charging someone to court.

Some weeks went by, and I accumulated all the possible evidence. There was considerable circumstantial evidence, and a number of interlocking pieces. The sergeant on the shift decided to call all of us together in order to take an objective view from as many officers as possible. Although there was now no doubt that he had committed the thefts, we were still unsure as to whether there was sufficient evidence to sustain a conviction.

Situated on the wall alongside where we were seated were a number of yearly calendars. They ranged from the explicit, to the 'Gospel Gems' that I would bring in each year. For those of you unfamiliar with this particular calendar, the respective days of each month contain a verse of Scripture. They have given encouragement to millions throughout the years.

After a lengthy discussion we had not reached a firm conclusion. The Sergeant, who was not a religious man, got up from his chair and said to us in a joking way, " Let's see what the verse is for today. Perhaps we will get some inspiration". He could not believe his eyes. The verse for that day was the following:

He who has been stealing must steal no longer.

(Ephesians 4;28)

Immediately upon reading out the verse to us he exclaimed in an excited manner, "That's it. He's guilty". Everybody fell about laughing.

I submitted a file of evidence, and he was convicted. He did not appeal. His guilt was settled.

CHAPTER FOUR

DETECTING OFFENCES

EACH OFFENCE in law has a legal definition. In order to pursue a prosecution the evidence must contain the necessary ingredients of the definition in order to prove that the individual concerned has committed the offence. There are many legal definitions of criminal offences that have a parallel in the spiritual realm. I have already referred to theft, and robbery.

In a spiritual court of law it can be seen that the devil, who continually seeks to steal our inheritance, is guilty as charged with the additional two offences.

Deception (Legal definition):
It is an offence to dishonestly obtain property belonging to another by *any deception in words or conduct*, with the intention of permanently depriving the other of it.

In chapter thirteen we will be looking at the character of God. His truth remains truth. It does not vary, or change. Therefore, our first priority is to know the truth. This prevents us from being deceived. He gives us this commitment about Himself and His Word:

I The Lord do not change. (Malachi 3;6)

A person cannot be deceived if they know that a lie is being told. Take, for example, a thief who steals a cheque book and debit card from someone, and then goes into a store to buy goods with the stolen items. If the cashier knows the name of the thief, and his real identity, the person cannot be deceived. They will therefore not part with the goods in question. An attempt deception has been made. But the completed act could not take place because the truth was known, and the lie rejected. Jesus told us to be aware of the lies of the devil:

There is no truth in him. When he lies, he speaks his native language, for he is a liar and the father of lies.
(John 8;44)

The devil looks for an opportune time to steal. Deception is part of theft. The times that we are the most vulnerable to becoming a victim are obviously in times of adverse circumstances. When we are in ill health, do we allow ourselves to believe the lie that only certain people are healed, or that miracles only happen in certain parts of the world? When we are in financial need, do we believe the lie that only a few people receive provision?

A deceiver relies on someone believing a lie. He cannot achieve his objective if the truth is known, and acted upon. This illustrates the importance of having a thorough knowledge and application of Scripture. However, it is a real tragedy if someone knows the truth, but is prepared to accept a lie, or does not act upon the knowledge that he or she possesses.

Someone once said, "The biggest deception of all time

has been committed by the devil. He has managed to convince people that he does not exist."

Another aspect of this subject is the act of **self-deception**. By engaging in this pattern of thought we become the authors of our own misfortune. Many people believe the misconception that everything will turn out all right on the night, no matter what we think, say or do. This is a clear act of deception. The above legal definition refers to deception being committed by word and conduct. It is wise not to be naive about the effect our words and conduct can have both upon others and ourselves.

> *Do not be* **deceived***: God cannot be mocked.* **A man reaps what he sows***.*   *(Galatians 6;7)*

Burglary – (Legal definition):
The offence of burglary is committed by a person, who having entered a building as a trespasser, steals or attempts to steal anything therein, or inflicts or attempts to inflict grievous bodily harm on any person therein.

The following verse of Scripture gives an accurate description of the activities of a burglar – someone who prowls around. The devil enters as a trespasser and seeks to steal and inflict injury upon us. He goes where he knows that he has no right to be.

> **Be self-controlled and alert***. Your enemy the devil* **prowls around** *like a roaring lion looking for someone to devour.* **Resist him***, standing firm in the faith.*
>   *(1 Peter 5;8/9)*

I have dealt with professional burglars whose entire life consisted of entering other people's homes and stealing.

They had convictions stretching from their teenage years all the way through into their sixties. It was more than just a sideline to get property. They were consumed with stealing from others. They were not always planning for the 'big job'. It did not even matter that on certain occasions the rewards were comparatively small.

It is the same with the devil. He continually seeks to steal, kill and destroy. It is not a side issue to him. He has given himself over completely to this course of action. This is why as Christians we are to be alert and aware of the devil's intentions, but without any fear on our part. It is against The Lord's justice when Christians or unbelievers experience theft in their lives. He has anointed us to take back that which the devil has stolen.

> **Greater is He that is in you,** *than he who is in the world.*
>
> *(1 John 4;4)*

If a home owner discovered someone trespassing on their property they would obviously eject him. Positive action would be taken. Similarly, if there is anything in our lives that is having a harmful effect upon us, it could be said that it is committing the offence of trespass. It has no right to be there. We have the authority in The Lord to evict anything in our lives that is not of Him, such as sin or sickness. We are to guard our inheritance in Him. Figuratively speaking, let us put up a sign in our soul stating 'trespassers will be shot on sight'.

DEAD DRUNK

Talking of firearms, a certain Police station, which shall remain nameless for obvious reasons, had a novel way of using their firearms to good effect.

It was the custom some years ago to have the Courthouse attached to the Police Station. During one summer's evening a drunk was arrested, and placed in the cells at the beginning of the night shift. The officers were tired of arresting this particular person, who was a constant nuisance and time waster. They decided to teach him a lesson.

In the early hours, the drunk was awoken, and taken into the Courthouse, where one of the officers was dressed in civilian clothes, and seated behind the Magistrates Bench. He told the drunk that he was fed up with his continued bad behaviour, and that he was sentencing him to death. He would be shot at dawn. The drunk was returned protesting to the cells.

At dawn the officers awoke him, removed him from the cells, and placed him against a wall in the exercise yard of the Police station. The officers were in possession of unloaded firearms that they had taken out of the property store. Another officer was behind the wall in the exercise yard, with two metal dustbin lids in his hands. When the command to fire was given the officer brought the two lids together with a loud bang. The drunk fainted, and fell to the ground. They returned him to the cells, and let him sleep.

When the morning shift woke him at 9 am the first words that the drunk uttered were "I had the most awful dream last night. I dreamt I was executed". I believe it was one of the most sobering experiences of his life.

CHAPTER FIVE

EXECUTING JUSTICE

THE MEANING of justice is – 'the exercise of authority in the maintenance of right'. Our God continually maintains that which is right.

> **Righteousness and justice** *are the foundation of Your throne.* (Psalm 89;14)

Justice and righteousness in a society have a stabilizing effect. You only have to look at certain countries in the world, where these are absent, to see the devastating result. It can therefore be seen that the same principles apply, both in the spiritual and the natural.

Isaiah prophesied of the coming Christ, and how He would establish and uphold justice and righteousness.

> *Of the increase of His government and peace there will be no end. He will reign on David's throne and over His Kingdom,* **establishing and upholding it with justice and righteousness** *from that time on and for-ever.* (Isaiah 9;7)

Having given us a declaration as to His purposes, God also gives us clear instructions in His Word as to how we are to live out this purpose in our lives.

> *Do what is* **right** *and* **just** *and* **fair**. (Proverbs 1;3)

It is neither right, nor just, nor fair when people have their material possessions stolen. The world cries out for justice not only to be done, but also to be seen to be done. They call for the Police to exercise their authority in the maintenance of right. Likewise, in the spiritual realm it is neither right, nor just, nor fair when the devil steals from us. The question that has to be asked is – What are we going to do about it?

Are we going to make a stand, and exercise our spiritual authority to take back that which has been stolen, and prevent further theft occurring in both our lives, our families, and those around us?

For our struggle is not against flesh and blood, *but against the rulers, against the authorities, against the powers of this dark world and against the spiritual forces of evil in the heavenly realms.* *(Ephesians 6;12)*

The Police have lawful authority for a purpose. We have spiritual authority for a purpose. There is no point in having authority unless it is used for its rightful purpose! If the Police fail to carry out their responsibilities there will inevitably be an increase in crime. Likewise, if we as Christians fail to carry out our responsibilities there is an increase in spiritual crime.

Let us each make a commitment to see God's justice established on this earth in whatever way we are able. In addition to which, decide that we are no longer going to suffer theft, or stand by and see others robbed.

AUTHORITY TO ENTER

When a Police Officer first executes a warrant to enter premises there can be a certain apprehension. Some premises are difficult to enter, and sometimes force is required to break the door down. The Officer, who is new in his role, is embarking on something that he has never before encountered in his life. He has received his commission, and is aware of his power and authority. But there can still be a certain nervousness about actually embarking on that course of action.

We also can feel the same when we first start to take authority in the spiritual realm. We may understand our commission, and be aware of our power and authority in The Lord, but we are nervous about entering into new territory. But there is nothing to fear for the Police Officer or ourselves if we are acting in a lawful manner. As Christians our actions are lawful when we are in line with God's Word.

If a Police Officer were to act in his own authority he would be refused entry. However if he holds the warrant there is absolutely nothing that person can do to deny access to the premises. He is powerless. Doors that have to be forced open can range from being easy, to extremely difficult. But none of them are impenetrable. It is the same in the spiritual realm. **When we operate in God's power and authority the devil is powerless.**

However, I am referring purely to the fact that the devil cannot refuse entry to a Christian acting in God's authority. This is in contrast to a situation whereby The Lord Himself has closed a door, and wants us to take a different path.

A DOG'S LIFE

With regard to difficult premises to enter, there was one criminal I knew, who installed a defensive measure that tested one's nerve and resolve. He kept two huge Doberman dogs in his front garden, in order to deter

Police from visiting his home. Whenever I had occasion to visit the house I tried remembering the passage of Scripture in Genesis, where God told Adam that He had given him authority over all animals. It is not always easy to keep this at the forefront of your mind when you are staring down the throat of a wild beast.

Having said that, I will relate another mad dog story that befell me.

At 2.30am, after completing my evening shift in the C.I.D., I was walking home. My car was suffering from one of its periodic breakdowns at the time. The weather was fine, and I was enjoying the exercise. That is, until I passed a junction that joined the long steep hill I was ascending.

I noticed that there was a pack of six or more Alsatian and Labrador dogs rummaging through bins. They were approximately fifty yards along the side street. I hoped that they had not seen me, and that they would get their pleasure from ripping the bins apart, as opposed to ripping me apart.

I continued walking up the long hill, and occasionally looked to my rear in case the dogs had got bored with the bins, and were looking for some further excitement. As I was crossing the next junction I looked behind, and my worst fear was advancing towards me at a rapid pace. One of the Alsatian dogs had left the pack, and had gone in search of further adventure.

Unfortunately, I was the focus of his quest. He was racing towards me in a single-mindedness that left me in no doubt as to the intended outcome. For some reason, dogs often have an aversion to people in uniform, whether they are postmen, milkmen, or policemen. But I was in civilian clothing, and felt that the dog was not playing by the rules.

At this time I was halfway across the junction, so there was no wall I could climb onto. There were no other people on the road, and no passing traffic. I stood still, stranded in the centre of the junction. I knew that I could not outrun the dog, and in any case my running would only give him more fun in the thrill of the chase. I also did not shout at him, as I did not want to upset or rile him.

The Alsatian stopped racing towards me at a distance of about four metres. He then started to slowly encircle me, and while doing so, was baring his teeth, snarling, and crouching ready to pounce. I was astounded as to how calculated he was in his encircling action, as if he was looking for the best position to attack. To say I was concerned would be an understatement. I was in one of those situations where there was no escape route. I could not use charm, nor reason. As you will well appreciate, I prayed.

I then made a conscious decision to exercise authority over the animal. It was not an act of desperation, but a genuine act of faith. I told myself that it was not right to be in such fear. I then said to the dog, " Go," and pointed back down the road. I neither shouted, nor spoke in an aggressive manner. I simply issued the command.

A remarkable thing then happened. The Alsatian, who had his eyes firmly fixed upon me, and was on the point of pouncing, suddenly got up from his arched position, cowered away from me in fear, and then raced at a fast pace back down the hill. I do not usually put fear into dogs. It is normally the other way round. They look upon me as easy pickings.

I looked down the road and could not see any of the other dogs. No traffic had approached, and neither had any other people entered the vicinity. There was no logical explanation for the dog's sudden change of behaviour.

There is no doubt in my mind that it was a direct answer to prayer, and then my taking a step of faith.

I walked the remainder of the journey with renewed confidence, praising God for His deliverance, and not fearing to look over my shoulder. It also taught me a lesson in how we need to confront evil. When a Christian is faced with an attack in their own life, or coming to the aid of someone else, the situation demands that someone takes authority. We can either back away and suffer defeat, or be bold in the power of The Lord, and see victory come to pass.

ZERO TOLERANCE

Where criminal behaviour is concerned, if people do not make a stand, their neighbourhood becomes a no-go area, and descends into a ghetto, where people have lost hope. The same applies in the spiritual realm. If we just let the devil continually steal, then our lives can become spiritual ghettos where we have given up hope. You have to be tough on crime.

In America they are having great success with their policy of zero tolerance. They have cracked down on even the pettiest of crimes, as they have found that if you do not tolerate such actions you create an environment where small crimes do not escalate into larger ones. As Christians we ought to have a zero tolerance in our lives towards sin and theft of any nature.

However, it has to be said that there is also a satisfying aspect to forcing your way into a thief's home, and recovering stolen property. You have the ability to completely ruin the thief's day in the same manner that he ruined the day of the person he stole from. **The devil has ruined enough of our days. It's about time we started ruining his days.**

When a thief is caught he is charged, and taken before court, where he is on full display before the judge, legal representatives, the victim, and any member of the public who wishes to attend. An open display is made of his wrongdoing, and it is made public that he has lost the items that he has stolen. He is then sentenced.

The same principle has already occurred in the spiritual realm. Following His Crucifixion The Lord went down into hell and made an open display of the devil, emphasising that he had been defeated, and thus had lost the keys of death and hell.

> *And having disarmed the powers and authorities,* **The Lord made a public spectacle of them**, *triumphing over them by the Cross.* *(Colossians 2;15)*

The devil is currently on a deferred sentence. He will be fully sentenced when The Lord returns.

BOLDNESS

Someone reading this may say to themselves, " I lack boldness. I do not have the confidence to tackle such matters." Take heart, you are in good company. Acts 4 describes how Peter and John had been brought before the High Priest, and other leaders. They were warned against any further preaching, and performing miracles, and then released. They returned to the other disciples and reported all that had been said, and everyone raised their voices in prayer.

> *Now, Lord, consider their threats and* **enable your servants to speak Your Word with great boldness**... *After they prayed the place where they were meeting was shaken.* **And they were all filled with**

The Holy Spirit and spoke The Word of God boldly. *(Acts 4;29-31)*

Notice that the disciples request was to have greater boldness. God answered them by filling them with His Spirit. When we ask The Lord to give an increase in a particular area He answers by filling us with His Spirit. It therefore follows that if we seek to be continually full of His Spirit we will experience a harvest in all areas of our lives.

The end result of the Anointing that came upon the disciples ministry can be seen in the following chapters of Acts. They received the boldness they desired, and their ministry expanded. They were equipped for whatever came their way. The same principle applies to us today.

Be strong and courageous. *Do not be terrified; do not be discouraged, for* **The Lord your God will be with you wherever you go**. *(Joshua 1;9)*

CHAPTER SIX

TRAINING

DURING A POLICE Officer's career he will attend various courses, which develop and equip him to tackle a wide range of issues. Those who avoid such courses invariably remain unaware of the full range of their powers. In addition to which, they do not develop fully either in knowledge or ability, and therefore do not reach their full potential.

One of the instructors on a C.I.D. course I attended continually used the phrase "knowledge is power" throughout its ten week duration. There is a Biblical principle to learn from this quote. How much knowledge do we have of the Word of God, and do we understand the spiritual authority we have through Him?

Usually there is one or more poignant moments on a course that stay firmly fixed in one's memory. I remember being on a driving course, which included speed driving along narrow lanes during darkness. There were four of us in the vehicle. I was seated in the rear with one officer, and the supervisor was in the front alongside a young police officer under instruction.

We were travelling along a single-track lane at a fast speed with no other lighting except our headlights. The lane was covered in overhanging trees, and everything around us was in darkness. One of the purposes of the course is to push you to the limits, in order to test your nerve and skill.

Unfortunately, the officer behind the wheel did not notice an impending sharp bend in the lane until it was too late. He hit the brakes and the vehicle went into a horrendous skid. We had already received instruction on the skidpan, so this training came in very useful for the current dilemma. The driver frantically tried to control the vehicle which was weaving from side to side, while fixed in the headlights of the vehicle was a wall of trees which were getting too close for comfort. At this point we all thought that this was going to be our final drive, because our time was up.

Miraculously, we slid around the sharp bend in the road, and the vehicle came to an abrupt halt as the lane joined a major road. If we had entered the road into the path of an oncoming vehicle my side would have taken the direct impact. The instructor, after drawing breath, shouted at the young officer – " You stupid boy," and at the same time hit him. None of us talked much on the journey back to the Training Centre.

STAYING AFLOAT

When I joined the Police in 1969 the philosophy at the time was to throw you in at the deep end. If you stayed afloat for the first year you would probably last the distance. The training you received was literally 'on the job'. There were only a few courses, and little emphasis on personal development. You basically reacted to what was facing you at the time.

At the end of an afternoon shift on the week-ends there was the opportunity to work four hours overtime, on what was commonly known as the 'meat wagon'. This was a van that attended disturbances in the city, and also responded to assistance calls from officers. Prisoners were unceremoniously thrown into the rear of the van and transported to the nearby police station, where they sampled the delights of a free bed and breakfast. They were then formally charged with the offences they had committed, and released on bail or kept in custody.

The combination of the alcohol, and a hot curry, did not assist the prisoners face a greasy breakfast from our Police canteen in the morning. As they languished in their cell, their meal was served to them on plastic plates, which were probably more edible than the food they carried. Our cooks were not noted for their cuisine. I am sure that many prisoners thought that eating one of their breakfasts was part of the punishment.

An officer working with me gave this request to the canteen staff – " I would like my bacon burnt to a crisp, my fried egg to taste like rubber, my sausages to be almost raw, and my fried bread to be swimming in fat." The staff member replied, " I couldn't possibly give you a breakfast like that." He replied, " Well that's what you gave me yesterday".

THE FIGHTING IS ONLY ON THE OUTSKIRTS

The training on the meat wagon gave officers the opportunity of dealing with multiple acts of violence. You can read about it, and listen to others instruct you in how to deal with such matters, but there is nothing like the real thing to train you.

In the late sixties a number of foreign restaurants opened in the area. For the weekend revellers, these restaurants were the last port of call, having consumed large amounts of alcohol during the course of the evening. Invariably, things would get out of hand, either through people trying to run from the restaurant without paying, or through fights with the waiters. Over a weekend you would attend numerous such incidents in these restaurants alone.

A colleague reminded me of one such incident we attended. The scene inside the restaurant was like a Wild West saloon in a cowboy film. Tables and chairs were upturned, objects were flying through the air, and everybody was fighting. The complete front of the premises was a mass of broken furniture and bodies. The only person missing from the incident was Clint Eastwood. Perhaps he was sorting out some other town that particular night.

In the midst of the bedlam inside the restaurant, one of the waiters was standing at the entrance door. He continued inviting other potential customers inside; using the phrase " There is room at the back." In order to get there, the customers would have to negotiate the surrounding chaos. I do not know whether he was inviting them in for a meal, or for ringside seats to the boxing match that was taking place.

It reminds me of an advertisement that appeared in the newspaper in the closing stages of the Vietnam War. Saigon was surrounded by North Vietnamese troops, who were closing in on the capital at a fast rate. Quite amazingly, a travel firm was still advertising holidays in the city. In an attempt to encourage customers, who quite rightly would feel somewhat nervous about such a 'holiday', the advertisement carried the reassuring words; "The fighting is only on the outskirts." Perhaps the waiter from the restaurant had a brother in the advertising business.

TRAINING COURSES

There are occasions when The Lord puts us on a training

course, because He wants to expand and strengthen our faith, or to enable us to overcome some issue. Here is an example of how God gave certain of the Israelites an opportunity to learn and develop in ways that hitherto they had not known.

> *These are the nations* **The Lord left to test** *all those Israelites who had not experienced any of the wars in Canaan.* **He did this only to teach warfare** *to the descendants of* **the Israelites who had not had previous battle experience.** *The Philistines, Canaanites* **... were left to test the Israelites to see whether they would obey The Lord's commands.**
>
> *(Judges 3;1-3)*

It can be clearly seen that various tribes were left for the specific reason of training the Israelites in warfare. These particular Israelites did not have any battle experience, and it was vital for their future welfare and security that they learnt such techniques. What do you think was going through the minds of those Israelites?

I am sure that many Israelites wished that God would have cleared the land before they arrived, and all they needed to do was settle smoothly into their individual piece of pasture. This would have been idyllic. We can all feel the same about so many issues in life. We ask the question – "Why can't things go according to plan? Why have all these difficulties arisen all of a sudden?"

The answer to these questions is "Yes," plans can come to fruition, and present difficulties can be overcome. In the process of tackling them we will learn something, and our faith and hope will be strengthened.

I know that I could not understand what was happening in my own life. I had planned to retire in 1999 after completing 30 years. I was already involved in a number of projects, but I also had a number of other ideas that I intended to commence close to my retirement, so that I could step straight into them upon completion of my service. All of these plans came crashing to the ground after I collapsed in June 1996.

It is only now, at the end of 2002 that I am beginning to see them start to take shape, but in a revised form. Although the last six years have been difficult, I can genuinely say that I am now better equipped to proceed as a result of what I have experienced.

However, I must point out that I am not saying that it was God's will that I had a physical and mental breakdown, coupled with illness. It happened because of a combination of my own recklessness, and the devil taking an opportune time to further afflict me. But The Lord has turned it around, and in so doing trained me in areas that I had not previously experienced.

But we do not have to wait for tribulation to be trained. He always looks for ways to train and equip us. The key is to recognise those times when God is training us in a particular area, and comply with what The Spirit is teaching us. At other times we seek His training as we grow in Him, or prepare for a specific work. While on other occasions He will use a set of circumstances that have befallen us, but which He will turn around for our good.

MISCONCEPTIONS

Some people believe the misconception that God brings sickness and disaster upon us in order to teach or train us in something. Affliction and ill health are not part of His inheritance for us. These sorts of experiences are quite separate from the training that the Lord Himself provides.

In all things God works for the good *of those who love Him.* *(Romans 8;28)*

In other words even the bad things that happen to us He will turn around for our good. He will use the circumstance to train us. In the course of which He will teach us more of Him. But it is always important to remember that He did not bring the bad things upon us in the first place. Because of His love and faithfulness He will turn anything around for our good.

One of the reasons why people encounter Him in sickness is because they usually seek after Him more at such times. If someone is lying in bed they are no longer racing around, and they consequently pray, read, and meditate more than normal. They mistakenly believe that because they hear from God in the situation He must have caused it. Whereas, the truth of the matter is that sometimes He has to wait until we are flat on our back before we take time to listen to Him.

The tragedy is that The Lord is always there, seeking to reveal more of Himself to us. Therefore, we do not have to wait for tribulation to know His nearness.

The Holy Spirit is continually looking for ways to equip and lead us into further truth. If He sees a lack in a certain area, He sets about finding ways to strengthen us in those parts that are weak. **The important thing to remember is that the devil afflicts us for our harm, but The Lord trains us for our good.**

VOLUNTEER FOR A COURSE

Perhaps those particular Israelites, as mentioned in Judges 3;1-3, had not previously wanted to engage in the battles. They did not want to get involved, and managed to avoid confrontation with the enemy. There is a parallel with today. There can be some sections of the church that live like that. Do we prefer to have the safety of the cloistered settings of continual church services and meetings? Do we exist in an enclosed world of purely Christian friendships? Would we rather not get our hands dirty?

Notice that the tribes in the previously mentioned Scripture were left in order to test The Israelites, as to whether they would obey The Lord's commands. In other words, they were left in their midst, in order to confront them. They could either respond to the challenge, or take the conscious step of refusing to take action. There was no middle ground. Could it be said that there are issues in our midst that we consciously choose to ignore?

There are also the simple everyday problems that we face that can be good training material. For example, have you ever wondered why you always end up with a boss whose type of personality you most dislike? Why does a particular relative, or member of the church, always seem to raise or remind you of an issue from the past that has not been dealt with?

Let us never forget that God loves us, and He wants the best for us. Therefore, when He puts us into a situation, it is for our benefit. He is not out to harm us. God knew what the Israelites would face, and what was needed to meet that challenge.

The same principles apply to us today. How would we have reacted if we had been faced with a situation like the Israelites? Would we have grumbled, and questioned why we had to go through such difficulties? Would it be fair to say that we all wish to live in a comfort zone? Be adventurous – ask The Lord to give you a new training course!

As you are reading this, can you think of some area in

your life that needs to be overcome, or a step of faith that you have continually put off from tackling? Sometimes we encounter situations in life that keep repeating themselves. Perhaps we simply need to stand still and ask ourselves the question – " What is really happening here?" Could it be that The Lord is putting me through a training course?

I know from my own experience, over the past six years, that having learnt something new, an incident or set of circumstances would follow soon afterwards, whereby I would have the opportunity to implement it. In addition to which, I have also encountered refresher courses, which test whether truths have really taken root.

For example, I am now more able to recognise those opportune times, when the devil seeks to steal. (We will be looking at this topic in chapter fourteen). As a result of The Lord putting me through training in this area, I am more able to deal with such situations at the outset, rather than let them develop. It has also enabled me to help others.

TRAINED IN WARFARE

God wanted all the Israelites to be trained in warfare as they took possession of their inheritance in The Promised Land. He knew that it was vital for everyone's safety and security.

What would you say was the average Christian's experience in spiritual warfare? Are each of us able to stand our ground, in order to confront and overcome what faces us? Do we see real breakthrough, both in our own lives, and that of others? I am sure that The Lord wants each of us trained in spiritual warfare in order to come into the full inheritance that He has provided for us.

Not all are called to the particular role of an intercessor.

But we are all encouraged to engage in intercessory prayer.

*I urge, then, first of all, that requests, prayers, **intercession** and thanksgiving be made for everyone.*
                                                    (1 Timothy 2;1)

We can confidently take authority in His Name. This is why in Ephesians 6;10-17 The Apostle Paul encourages all of us to put on the whole armour of God. We can then be fully equipped and trained at all times, so that we stand firm against anything which is not of The Lord.

*So that when the day of evil comes, **you may be able to stand your ground**, and after you have done everything, to stand.*   *(Ephesians 6;13)*

There is a danger in thinking that spiritual warfare is the territory of the 'prayer warriors' in the church. In the early years of my Christian life I had little knowledge of such matters. However, in recent years there have been occasions when a group of us have fasted and prayed over specific issues. When we met together it was with purpose, and as a result of taking authority in His Name we saw breakthrough.

I now realise that these occasions have unfortunately only been isolated examples, and not a continual experience. I am presently seeking to rectify this situation. Surely we are not meant to have just a few testimonies of such matters by the end of our lives. We should regard this vital part of ministry as normal, and not out of the ordinary.

The principles involved in spiritual warfare are not purely for the 'really serious' issues. The reason I say this is because we are in a constant battle, and we need the whole armour of God on a daily basis. This, coupled with a greater sensitivity to the leading of The Holy Spirit, will enable us to take up an offensive position as opposed to defensive. Looking back over my life, I can see how easily I allowed myself to be robbed because I was not trained in warfare, and unsure of spiritual authority.

Therefore, when The Holy Spirit presents us with a training course, whether it is brand new, or an old course that we failed to finish in the past, we ought to praise God for His patience and goodness towards us. Then complete the course.

Sadly, Scripture records that the particular Israelites who were given this opportunity in warfare failed, and continued living amongst the tribes, with tragic consequences. Let us not make the same mistake.

DISCIPLESHIP TRAINING

Although I have sought in this chapter to emphasise the value of training, I do not want to give the false impression that we need to be extensively trained before we are equipped to step out in faith, start a specific work, or move in gifting. For example, the same day that a person becomes a Christian, he or she is able to lead someone else to The Lord, lay hands on the sick, or see a miraculous answer to prayer. We are not in a probationary period, or have to attain a certain level before anything can happen.

In the first ten chapters of Luke's Gospel there are two recorded incidents where Jesus sent out His disciples. The first is recorded in Luke 9 when He sent out twelve. The second occasion occurs in the following chapter in respect of seventy-two. I am no Biblical scholar, but I would estimate that the first disciples were sent out sometime between six months and a year of being with The Lord.

It is very enlightening to examine the early chapters of

The Gospels and see what the disciples knew at the point in time when they were sent off on their own. Jesus had only just begun to transform their thinking. But it was all they needed to make an impact in whatever environment they entered. He taught them such things as having new wineskins for the work of The Spirit, seeking first His Kingdom, His words as their foundation upon which to build, being motivated by love, and eliminating traditional thinking.

Shortly before Jesus sent out the twelve He told them the Parable of The Sower. I would suggest that He was preparing them for what they would encounter. It is the heart of the sower that every bit of seed bears fruit. But unfortunately this does not always happen. He did not want them to get disappointed or disillusioned, but to press on. He took such care to prepare them.

When they returned, Jesus continued to train and equip them for the next time that He sent them out. They received further revelation of Him, and He tackled such issues as pride and unbelief. Immediately before the seventy-two left, He taught them about the cost of being a disciple. He was again preparing them for the difficult situations that they would face.

The Lord had a clear strategy. He progressively gave them further revelation about Himself; while at the same time gave them teaching, training, and equipping. It can also be seen from the Gospels that He even returned to certain subjects, in order to ensure that they had grasped the issues being taught.

During the time that this was taking place He gave them opportunities to put their training into practise. When they returned, He would go over what they encountered, and then give advice. This was a continuous process. The Lord did not hold them back until He had taught them everything.

There are only two recorded times of when He sent out His disciples. However, as the Gospels record, we have only a snapshot of what took place.

Jesus did many other things as well. *If every one of them were written down, I suppose that even the whole world would not have room for the books that would be written.* (John 21;25)

I would suggest that there was an ongoing pattern of discipleship involving revelation, teaching, training, and equipping, followed by a sending out. He was giving them experience in preparation for the time when He would physically leave them. The Lord empowered and released the potential within the disciples. He has done the same with us. He has given us 'wings to fly'.

The point I am endeavouring to make is that we do not have to gain a huge amount of knowledge or training before we step out in faith. The disciples had only been with The Lord a comparatively short time before He sent them out. The teaching and training is ongoing throughout our life as we continue to mature in Him. But He does not want us to put things on hold until we acquire great knowledge or experience. He simply wants us to 'get on with it'.

It is also important to say that there is a need to have a balanced approach in this matter of being radical and stepping out in faith. We obviously need to exercise wisdom in what we tackle. When necessary, seek the counsel of older men and women in the faith, who can help and guide. That is all part of being joined together in the Body of Christ. But let us each release the potential within us, and not by words or conduct, disqualify ourselves because of age or experience.

TEACHER OR PUPIL

The Christian life is all about relationship. Doctrines, teaching and gifts are obviously important. But we do not need endless teaching programmes and seminars before we feel able to step out. We are essentially deceiving ourselves and believing a lie if we say, "I don't have enough knowledge yet. It will be some time before I am ready".

Our effectiveness is not based on knowledge – it is dependent upon relationship with The Lord. Some people believe that knowledge will lead to relationship, whereas it is relationship that causes a thirst for knowledge.

In some parts of the world new believers are leading housegroups after only being saved for six months. They readily take this responsibility, because they know that The Holy Spirit will continue to give them revelation about The Lord, as they teach and train others. In the West, Christians seem to devote too much time to theory. In the East they simply get on with the practical, and get results. There ought to be no difference between the east and west, because it is the same Spirit who raised Christ Jesus from the dead, and who is at work in each of our lives.

> *In fact, though* **by this time you ought to be teachers,** *you need someone to teach you the elementary truths of God's Word all over again.* (Hebrews 5;12)

The above verse was not written exclusively to elders, potential leaders, or those involved in a specific teaching ministry. The words were addressed to the whole church.

It concerned everyone, because every believer ought to be able to teach. This does not mean having the ability to get up on a platform, or some other public venue. It is about being able to teach another individual or group about what has happened in our own lives, since we met The Lord.

Studies have shown that 70% of Christians come through personal evangelism. If every new believer was then adopted by a spiritual parent, who would teach and disciple them, can you imagine the impact that this would have?

I well remember a married couple that Irene and I befriended, and who soon got saved. They had a tremendous thirst to know about The Lord. Their questions stretched us. We therefore had a choice to make. We could take the easy option as I had done on other occasions, and refer them to the pastor or some leader. Alternatively, we could take the responsibility ourselves. Their thirst produced growth in us.

The writer to the Hebrews was obviously concerned that their faith had remained elementary. Very direct words were used: **by this time you ought to be teachers.** Unfortunately, they still required teaching on simple truths. They are described as living on milk, and not solid food. The reason is explained:

> *But solid food is for the mature,* **who by constant use have trained themselves ...** *(Hebrews 5;14)*

The mature are described as taking the responsibility to train themselves, and not rely on others. It is not spasmodic training, but by constant use. The reason for these key words of counsel and direction is given in the following chapter. They are addressed to each person:

*We want each of you to show the same diligence...***We do not want you to become lazy**. *(Hebrews 6;11/12)*

The first day that a person becomes a Christian they can teach. This is explained by the fact that they are able to tell someone else about encountering The Lord, and what this means. If we understood this in a purely simple form, it would help eliminate a lot of the fear that some people have regarding witnessing, and discipling others.

The depth to which we continue to teach others will relate to our own desire to be taught by The Holy Spirit. The above verse is an encouragement to remain diligent, and not become lazy. We feed ourselves, not rely on others. Although it is important to listen to the preached Word of God, and hear other peoples revelation and testimonies, it is clear from Hebrews 5;14 that the main way to mature in The Lord is to **constantly train ourselves.**

SELF TRAINING PROGRAMME

After Paul became a Christian, he informs us in Galatians 1;17 that he went out into the desert. Have you ever considered what took place out there?

He was a naturally talented and intelligent individual with tremendous drive. What was needed was for these talents to be harnessed for The Lord's work, together with the other gifts that The Lord would give him. Paul needed to die to himself. A retraining took place. The Paul that emerged from the desert was a different person. He was trained in the ways of The Lord.

I have been crucified with Christ and **I no longer live, but Christ lives in me**. *(Galatians 2;20)*

Paul was given incredible revelation of The Lord. He

was already well versed in the Old Testament Scriptures, but after his encounter with Jesus on the Damascus Road, he suddenly saw the Scriptures in a different light. He discovered Jesus on every page, and how they prophesied, and led up to His coming. Paul did not want to waste or let slide any of the revelation he received, and he was continually hungry for more.

He understood that there was a process involved in discipleship. Jesus mainly trained His disciples as they went from place to place. Although there were such occasions as the Sermon on The Mount, predominantly it was simply being in His Presence. They heard Him speak concise teachings on a daily basis. It was this continual discipleship of hearing words of truth that subsequently transformed their minds and actions.

Paul had learnt the value of living a trained and self disciplined life. Therefore, he placed great emphasis on training in his letters. He knew that the most vital part of training is to get immersed in Scripture. Paul gives this important advice to Timothy:

> **All Scripture** *is God-breathed and is* **useful for teaching**, *rebuking, correcting and* **training in righteousness**, *so that the man of God may be* **thoroughly equipped** *for every good work.*   *(2 Timothy 3;16-17)*

When Paul spoke of dying daily it is obvious that this was not something that he learnt overnight. He subjected himself to a self-training spiritual programme, which did not end after a few months. It was a continual process. Notice that the words he used to the church are in the present tense:

> *I beat my body and make it my slave.*   *(1 Cor. 9;27)*

This was not some teaching that was the flavour of the month that he could add to his spiritual CV.

Paul trained himself, and then trained others, such as Timothy and Titus. He knew that effective training in the ways of The Lord will not only help us become more like Him, but it will also enable us to face anything we encounter in life. We will remain calm, and not panic. Paul gave the following advice to Timothy:

Keep your head in all situations.   *(2 Timothy 4;5)*

CHAPTER SEVEN

A NIGHT ON THE BEACH

IN THE PREVIOUS chapter I explained how training could help us keep calm and composed in traumatic times. Having said that, I well remember a situation that I got myself into, which put this principle to the test. It was one of those times when from deep within you a loud shout develops – "Oh no. What have I done? How did I allow this to happen?".

You feel that you have jumped out of an aeroplane, and have forgotten to take your parachute. You are in free fall, and the ground is getting closer by the second. I can now look back with laughter, but for a long time after, it sent shivers down my spine.

It all began on a warm night in the middle of summer 1973. I was working an area car on my own. The weather was beautiful, and there was no need of a jacket or outer clothing. Everything had calmed down by 3am and I was looking forward to sorting out some paperwork, and getting everything up to date.

At 3.30am I received a message to attend one of the local beaches, where a car had got stuck in the sand, and was in danger of being covered by the incoming tide. The driver had returned to his vehicle, and I was asked to simply relay a message to him that the breakdown truck was en route.

When I arrived I met a young man accompanied by two females. They were about twenty years of age. The man explained that he had borrowed a car from a friend, and the three of them had gone down close to the tide-line to enjoy the moonlight. It sounds rather romantic, but it all came to a sad end when his wheels sunk in the soft sand, and owing to his excessive revving to free them, they had sunk deeper. I informed them that the recovery vehicle was on its way. Dawn was breaking, and it was quite light.

Unfortunately, as the expression goes, 'time and tide wait for no man'. The advancing sea was starting to cover the wheels, and it would not be too long before the car was engulfed. The man was very concerned, as the car was borrowed, and only a week old. He waded fully clothed into the sea, and attempted to push the vehicle out of the water. The two females and myself stood at the water's edge for a few minutes watching his desperate attempt to move the vehicle. It looked a lost cause.

I then did something for which I do not fully understand to this day. I stripped off all my clothes and shoes, down to my underpants. I handed all my clothing to the two females, and asked them to look after it while I entered the water to assist their friend. My clothing also contained my radio and car keys.

I do not know if it was the beautiful summer's morning, the warm lapping tide, or the simple act of an idiot that was the root cause of my actions. All I can say is that it happened before I was married, and became sensible, mature, and boring.

As we were struggling to save the vehicle one of the young ladies informed us that they would walk back up the beach to once more telephone the breakdown service, as the situation was getting critical. Back then, the telephone box was situated up a hill leading to the beach. Rather than leave my clothing on the wet sand, they carried it with them, and disappeared from view.

After a short time we were literally up to our necks in the water, and we realised that our efforts to save the vehicle from its impending fate were fruitless. We walked up the beach to meet his friends. When we reached the top of the beach, they had not returned, so he told me that he would walk up the hill to find out what was happening.

The telephone kiosk was situated around a bend, and up a slope, so they were completely out of our vision. As I have already mentioned, he was fully clothed, while all I was dressed in were my underpants. I then stood alongside my Police vehicle, to await their return.

Suddenly, the full weight of what I had done began to dawn on me. My Police vehicle, which was locked, was parked on the main road with me standing naked beside it. It was now fully light. All manner of scenarios went through my mind. What if they decide not to return? What if they just dump my clothing? What if I leave my vehicle to get help and they decide to take it for a lift home? What if my Inspector arrives?

Young children often have dummies, or a particular teddy bear that help them through traumatic times. They keep them close, in order to bring re-assurance and comfort in particular times of need. I found myself having the same emotions towards my Police car. Although it was locked, and as such of no real use, I stood as close as possible to it. I may have lost everything else, but at least my car remained intact. The vehicle was my only piece of comfort in a rapidly deteriorating set of circumstances.

I thought of walking up the hill to meet them. But what if a motorist were to stop, and question what I am doing walking along the road dressed in underpants at 4am? What would I say? "Everything is okay. I'm a Police Officer. My car is over there, and my uniform is up here somewhere."

I looked out to sea, and saw that the vehicle was now fully submerged. I began to think that my career was going in the same direction.

Up until now many of you have probably gone to sleep at night, safe and secure in the knowledge that there is a professional, highly trained, and responsible Police Force protecting you. I am sorry to disillusion you.

After about fifteen minutes, but which seemed like an eternity, the three of them returned. I have never felt such pleasure in putting on clothes in my entire life. They had not been able to contact the recovery firm, but it was too late in any event. I gave them a lift back into civilisation, and returned to my normal duties.

The owner of the vehicle called at my station the next day to thank me for my assistance. He informed me that he would not get any insurance money for his vehicle, as the company classed the actions of the driver as an "unnecessary risk." I thought these words would be the epitaph written on my career.

PART 2

CRIME PREVENTION

Free yourself, like a gazelle from the hand of the hunter,
like a bird from the snare of the fowler.
Proverbs 6;5

CHAPTER EIGHT

SPIRIT (of man)

YOU WILL remember from the personal testimony at the beginning of the book that my recovery began when I read Isaiah 61. That chapter of Scripture commences with a prophetic exhortation regarding The Anointing, which is followed by a list of people who are to be rebuilt, restored, and renewed by the power of that Anointing. The reason for their predicament is explained in verse 8 of that chapter – **they had been robbed**.

The middle section of the book will now look at ways to prevent theft occurring in the first place. In order to accomplish this, it is first necessary to understand our make-up, and the areas of our life that are vulnerable.

May your whole **spirit, soul and body** *be kept blameless.* *(1 Thessalonians 5;23)*

The Word of God tells us that we comprise of three distinct parts, namely spirit, soul and body. The spirit is our inner being; the soul is our mind, emotions, heart, conscience, will and intellect; the body is our outer shell.

Notice the order in which they are placed. The spirit first, the soul second, and the body third. I would suggest that the intention behind this is to show their correct order of importance. We shall see from an examination of

Scripture that our spirit is the very centre of our lives, and from that place, life flows into our soul and body. In addition to which, our spirit and soul are of eternal significance, whereas our body will pass away.

RE-BIRTH

Permit me to ask you a question before we go any further. What is your perception of our inner being (spirit), and what is your understanding of what takes place there? In order to provide an answer, we need to have a clear understanding of what occurs at our salvation.

The essence of being born again is that we accept Jesus as Lord of our life, and in so doing, The Holy Spirit takes up residence in our spirit. Jesus told Nicodemus what actually takes place at our second birth.

> *"I tell you the truth, no one can enter the Kingdom of God unless he is* **born of water and The Spirit**. *Flesh gives birth to flesh, but* **The Spirit gives birth to spirit.**" *(John 3;5-6)*

Scripture states that our spirit is a distinct place on its own. This is clearly shown in the above verses by the fact that The Holy Spirit is given a capital 'S', while our spirit has a small 's'.

It is our spirit that encounters this re-birth. It is not our soul. The reason being is that our salvation is a completed act. Our spirit becomes perfectly renewed, because Christ dwells there by His Spirit. This is not the case in respect of our soul. Our mind, emotions, heart, will, and conscience enter a process of renewal.

Jesus told Nicodemus that he needed to be born of water, and of The Spirit. Being born of water is our natural birth, while being born of The Spirit is our spiritual birth.

Our spirit, which we have had since birth, experiences a dramatic change. Before that encounter with The Lord, our spirit had effectively been lying dormant. It then comes alive, and experiences a metamorphosis, which means a marked change in character. A fundamental and radical transformation takes place.

The Spirit himself testifies with our spirit *that we are God's children.* (Romans 8;16)

Prior to our salvation, our soul had the upper hand, and our mind and emotions ruled us. But after we are born again of The Spirit, the soul is no longer the dominant force. We have a new master, The Lord Jesus, whose Spirit occupies our inner being (spirit). Christ is seated in Glory, but He abides in us by The Holy Spirit. Our spirit becomes the focal point of our bodies. **Spirit relates to spirit**. Our salvation is complete and cannot be stolen from us. The Lord emphatically states this truth.

I give them eternal life, and they shall never perish; **no one can snatch them out of My hand**.

(John 10;28)

The devil knows this, but he attempts to put fear into us, in order that we believe to the contrary. He also tries to steal, kill and destroy in the areas that are vulnerable to attack, namely our mind, emotions, heart, will, conscience and body. We can see how it is so vitally important to be strengthened in these parts, so that we do not experience theft.

A FULL MEASURE

I pray that out of God's glorious riches **He may strengthen you with power through His Spirit in your inner being,** *so that Christ may dwell in your* *hearts through faith...*   *(Ephesians 3;16-17)*

It can been seen from these verses that the whole of the Godhead is affecting our inner being; The Father from out of His riches strengthening; The Holy Spirit empowering; Christ taking up residence. Notice the two words *'so that'*, which link the two parts of the verse. When such words are used, it is to show that the former part is used for a definite purpose, namely to achieve a result. The empowering by The Holy Spirit is so that Christ may dwell.

The Old and New Testament refer to the heart as comprising of such things as thoughts, emotions, will, conscience, and reasoning. These are aspects of our soul. The Lord already lives in our spirit following our salvation, but He also seeks to dwell in all parts of our soul.

We can therefore see from Ephesians 3;16/17 that we are filled in our inner being (spirit) by The Holy Spirit, Who then flows into, and affects the remainder of our person, *'so that'* Christ may dwell in our hearts. He does not want to be a temporary and spasmodic feature of our thoughts and emotions. He wants to inhabit us totally.

In the natural our heart has a continual pumping action. There is a spiritual parallel. What therefore pumps out of our mouths is determined by the health and composition of our spiritual heart. Jesus explained this in the following manner:

"Out of the overflow of the heart the mouth speaks."
            (Matthew 12;34)

UNBROKEN LINE

God has raised us up with Christ and **seated us with Him in the Heavenly realms**.   *(Ephesians 2;6)*

When we are born again, there is an unbroken line created between our spirit (inner being), where Christ dwells by The Spirit, and His throne in Heaven. We are joined. Just think of that for one moment. There is no gap whatsoever between our spirit and His throne. This occurs because The Holy Spirit is in our spirit, and we are therefore joined to Heaven.

Since I have understood more about our spirit and soul, my relationship with The Lord has been transformed. I have always found delight in God's Word, but it has come alive even more.

Because of that unbroken line we are already raised up by our Heavenly Father, and seated in Heavenly realms. Not only that, but The Holy Spirit also brings Heaven into our earthly lives. Jesus told His disciples about the work of The Spirit, who continually seeks to reveal more of The Lord and His purposes to us. All we have to do is be receptive.

He will bring Glory to Me by **taking from what is Mine and making it known to you**. *(John 16;14)*

Close your eyes for a moment and picture an unbroken line between Heaven and your spirit. Then imagine all the activity that is taking place along that line, as The Spirit is taking revelation from The Lord, and then revealing it to us. This is our line of communication, our access to the Throne of Grace, and our power supply. Hallelujah!

What is absolutely amazing is that not only does The Lord come to save, and take up residence in our spirit, but He also comes to empower that inner being. From that inner place, where Christ reigns, comes the fullness and overflow of The Holy Spirit.

Jesus said, "Whoever believes in Me, as the Scripture has

said, **streams of living water will flow from his innermost being. By this He meant The Spirit,** *whom those who believed in Him were later to receive.*
(John 7;38/39 Amplified version)

Notice that the verse states that The Holy Spirit flows out from our innermost being. It can be further seen from Revelation 22;1 that the *'river of the water of life'* is flowing from the Throne of God. This represents the continual flow of The Holy Spirit. The flow comes from the Throne, along that unbroken line into our spirit. Jesus tells us that The Living Water then flows out of our inner being (spirit). It floods not only our spirit, but also our soul, and body, so that we are saturated in Him.

Our spirit is the place where God directly communicates with us. This is where our Lord reveals truth, whether it is spoken or visual. It is birthed in our spirit, and released into our soul in order that we dwell upon the word or image. But it is not by reasoning or a working out by our mind that we will find the meaning. The Holy Spirit leads our understanding from our spirit, and into our soul.

DREAMS AND VISIONS

Part of our communication with Him is the receiving of dreams and visions. These are received in our spirit. Visions usually occur when we are awake, while dreams occur when we are asleep, but this need not necessarily always be the case. The feature that distinguishes them from normal images is that they stand out, and do not simply evaporate, coupled with the fact that there is a rising or leaping in our spirit.

Our soul is subject to all manner of thoughts, emotions,

and prejudices which can greatly affect our dreams. But a Christian's spirit is uncontaminated because it has been changed and renewed by the Presence of The Holy Spirit. We can therefore see that if we want to have the correct interpretation of dreams, visions, Scripture, spiritual gifts, or anything from The Lord it has to be Spirit led.

> **The Spirit searches all things, even the deep things of God.** *For who among men knows the thoughts of a man except the man's spirit within him? In the same way no one knows the thoughts of God except the Spirit of God.* (1 Corinthians 2;10-11)

This Scripture reveals the inherent weaknesses in psychology and philosophy. Both of these subjects deal exclusively with the soul. They provide a human interpretation of the workings of the mind, emotions, heart, conscience, will, and intellect, which are composites of our soul. Although these sciences are of some value, they fall far short of the real truth that can only be discovered by spiritual discernment.

> **The Man without The Spirit does not accept the things that come from The Spirit of God,** *for they are foolishness to him, and he* **cannot understand them,** *because* **they are spiritually discerned**.
>
> *(1 Corinthians 2;14)*

Paul warned The Colossian Church against relying on human reasoning.

> *See to it that* **no one takes you captive** *through* **hollow** *and* **deceptive philosophy,** *which depends on* **human tradition** *and the* **basic principles of this world** *rather than on Christ.* (Colossians 2;8)

Paul, who was a very well read and intelligent individual, knew the dangers of taking a purely philosophical or psychological approach to issues in life. He cuts right through to the core, and points out their limitations. Notice the words that are used – *hollow, deceptive philosophy, human tradition, basic principles of this world.*

By examining the verse you will see that Paul is not saying that all philosophy is wrong. He highlights **deceptive philosophy**. He is basically advising the church not to be unduly influenced or governed by human reasoning, based on worldly principles. This is because they originate in the soul. You will recall that Paul warned the Roman church not to follow the pattern of this world.

> *Do not be conformed any longer to the pattern of this world, but be transformed by the renewing of your mind.* (Romans 12;2)

Our minds can be explored, stimulated, and expanded by the human sciences, but they cannot be renewed by them. This can only be done by the Holy Spirit instructing us in The Word of God.

It has also to be said that there are many eminent Christian psychologists and philosophers who contribute immensely to our understanding of issues. But the great difference with these men and women is that they are Spirit led, as opposed to soul led. They know that human reasoning is of value, but has its limits.

There may be a science for the interpretation of dreams that originate in the soul, but a dream or vision from God, which is birthed in our spirit, can only be discerned by The Holy Spirit. The mind and intellect of a human cannot fathom the mysteries of God. It is only with the help and guidance of The Holy Spirit that this can be achieved.

In Joel 2 it is prophesied about the increase in dreams

and visions when we are filled with The Holy Spirit. Have you ever wondered why God speaks in such a way? There is that well known expression 'one picture paints a thousand words'. The Parables used by Jesus were visual. He knew that the people would remember these images, and those who sought God for their meaning would find enlightenment.

The question that many people ask is – How do I know it is from God? I would suggest that a dream and vision from our Heavenly Father is a direct message from Him, and therefore it is prominent and clear, not hazy. It does not matter how initially strange it may appear, if it is of God it will contain a Scriptual meaning and application. It will contain a truth which lines up with God's Word.

The same principle applies in respect of the gift of prophecy or a message in spiritual tongues. Although the actual words or interpretation may not have direct Scriptural words, if it is of God they will always have their root in The Word of God.

If we seek after Him, The Lord will give us the interpretation of the dreams and visions that He gives us. Alternatively, He may use someone else. Obviously, the more messages we receive in this manner, the greater will be our sensitivity to the leading of The Holy Spirit, so that we get to a point where we instinctively know when it is from God.

Some years ago my wife Irene and I went to a meeting in another church, and a total stranger from another country prophesied separately into our lives. He confirmed things that we had individually been praying, which no one else knew. He then called us together to share a vision he had from The Lord for us both. The first part of the vision was fulfilled within a few weeks, while the latter part is now happening years later.

I mention this, because I believe that we need to continually remember dreams and visions in the same way that we hold onto other words from God. Some take immediate effect, while others develop over a period of time. The more we function from our spirit, the more we will remember the words and promises that The Lord gives us.

LEAPING

What causes you to leap? Luke 1;39-41 gives the account of when Mary, who was carrying Jesus in her womb, went to the home of Elizabeth, who was pregnant with John.

When Mary came near, John leapt in his mother's womb, and Elizabeth was filled with the Holy Spirit. The same thing happened thirty years later when John was baptising in the Jordan River. When Jesus approached, John exclaimed to those around:

> *"Look, The Lamb of God, who takes away the sin of the world."*   *(John 1;29)*

Once more John's spirit leapt. What caused him to leap in his spirit? It was the nearness of The Lord.

Do you encounter a leaping inside you when you suddenly get a revelation from Scripture? Have you ever considered what is literally taking place inside you at that particular moment? The Holy Spirit, within your spirit, is leaping with joy at the further revelation that you have received. He is zealous for truth to be revealed, and when it happens, He responds accordingly.

THE QUIET PLACE

I have recently discovered an aspect of intimacy with The Lord that was previously lacking. It arose out of a clearer understanding of the presence of The Holy Spirit in our spirit (inner being).

Ephesians 3;16/17 informs us that we are strengthened in our inner being (spirit) by The Holy Spirit. As we have already seen, our spirit is the very centre of our lives. Christ dwells there by His Spirit. It is therefore a place of great intimacy.

> *Deep calls to deep.* (Psalm 42;7)

Scripture encourages us to enter His gates with thanksgiving, and His courts with praise (Psalm 100;4). We also bring our requests before Him on behalf of others, and ourselves (Philippians 4;6). Both of these aspects are right and proper, and are part of our fellowship with The Lord.

But can I ask you – How often are we silent before Him? Give yourself a simple test. At the end of a week, add up the amount of time you were silent before God, by simply waiting, and listening to Him. I would venture to say it would be a small amount.

> **Be still, and know that I am God.** *(Psalm 46;10)*

Many people find it difficult to cope with silence. An awkwardness develops within them, and there is a compulsion to say or do something. Churches also find this a particular problem area. We seem to be afraid of silence. We somehow find it threatening. If a pastor says to the congregation, " Let's just wait upon The Lord," I guarantee that within a few minutes someone will pray, or start a chorus.

THE TABERNACLE

Consider the layout of the Tabernacle in The Old Testament, which consisted of the Outer Court, Inner

Court, and Holy of Holies. The Outer Court was where the sacrifices were made for forgiveness of sins; the Inner Court was the place where The Lord was ministered to in worship; the Holy of Holies was the place of intimacy where God spoke. The High Priest was the only person who was able to enter that most intimate of settings.

Although every born again believer can now enter that inner place because of The Lord's sacrifice, I would like you to keep in mind the picture of the entire tabernacle, and the different functions that took place in each area. An analogy can be made between its layout and our relationship with The Lord. Are we basic, close, or intimate? Where do we spend most of our time with Him – in the outer court, inner court, or place of intimacy?

Are our prayers basic, mainly surrounding our own needs? Do we simply ask forgiveness and only pray about situations that concern us, or family and friends? Do we remain mainly in the outer court?

We may, however, have a sensitivity in our prayers, and also know the joy of having praise in our heart, with worship spontaneously rising within us. We move freely between the inner and outer courts. We are fruitful and fulfilled in prayer, and in addition to which may also know the closeness to The Lord as we minister in worship.

But how often do we consistently reach that point of intimacy in the inner court where we are simply in His Presence? A place where we have learnt how to be silent before Him, where we do not ask or expect anything. There is no doubt in my mind where He desires us to be. We have only to read The Song of Songs to have an insight into His longing for intimacy with us.

What took place in the outer and inner courts was important, but they were simply a route to the place

of intimacy.

I would encourage each of us to learn to be still and quiet before Him. Empty our mind of any requests, be silent, and dwell on Him. I must emphasise that this is not in any way to be confused with any religion where they empty their minds, or enter into some form of meditation, simply to strengthen the mind. The purpose for a Christian is to give time to our Lord, who will fill us in our spirit (inner being), in order that we become like Him. We come empty to be filled. What I am trying to convey is best illustrated by Solomon.

> *Guard your steps when you go to the house of God.* **Go near to listen** *rather than to offer the sacrifice of fools, who do not know that they do wrong.* **Do not be quick with your mouth; do not be hasty in your heart to utter anything before God. God is in Heaven and you are on earth, so let your words be few**.
>
> *(Ecclesiastes 5;1/2)*

In other words, guard our relationship with our Heavenly Father by coming to Him in order that we might listen to Him, as opposed to us continually speaking, or having a set routine and formula. The Scripture instructs us that our words ought to be few in number. Have we ever simply gone through the motions in our time with The Lord, and not spent any time listening? Solomon describes this as the sacrifice of fools. Let us approach Him with a humble heart that seeks to listen.

LEARNING TO LISTEN

Sometimes the silence is unbroken. When that occurs, do not be confused and believe that nothing has happened. Other times, The Holy Spirit may reveal more of the character of God, or direct you to a Scripture from which He wants to reveal some truth, or to a person to whom you can uphold in prayer, or to encourage and guide you.

The purpose of such encounters is to focus on Him. We encounter His Presence. The key to these times is not to go to Him seeking a word, or having prayers answered for you, or others. It is simply to be with Him, without having any agenda. Allow The Lord to dictate how long He wants you to be quiet. Let me challenge you – **Be adventurous in The Holy Spirit.**

Would you agree that so much of our time is stage-managed? That is to say, we have our set routine of how, and what we pray for, a structured Bible reading, and a particular way of using our spiritual or natural gifts.

It is right to continue in prayer about an issue until the breakthrough comes, and also to study The Word systematically. But I also believe that we need to break free of a mentality that likes the safety of repetitive routine. Although there is a need for order and stability in our thinking, there is equally a need to rid ourselves of tradition.

How much of our time is truly led by the Spirit? The Lord may want to reveal something to us from His Word. Does He have to wait until we get to that particular Scripture in six months time? Allow The Holy Spirit to break into our agenda.

> *Here I am!* **I stand at the door and knock**. *If anyone hears My voice, and opens the door, I will come in and eat with him and he with Me. (Revelation 3;20)*

This verse shows His heart in wanting us to have fellowship together. It means to have a conversation. Many evangelists regularly use this Scripture to give a gospel message, and encourage people to seek salvation. We would all agree that it is a very challenging verse that has been greatly used. But it was actually written to the church. It is a message to believers. The Lord comes knocking. He wants fellowship with us, and in so doing wants to talk.

A desire to listen is an aspect of consecration. Something tangible takes place when we consecrate ourselves. We are preparing our soul. The place is then prepared for The Anointing, which is The Presence of God saturating our lives in Him.

CHAPTER NINE

SOUL

HAVE YOU ever wondered why our faith and determination to accomplish something gets diluted, or we are unable to remain focused? Why do doubts and worries occupy too much of our thinking, and we appear to be governed by our feelings and emotions? The answer is found in the different aspects of soul and spirit.

The dictionary informs us that the soul has *'the capacity for intense and uninhibited emotional feelings'*. It therefore has the ability to change our direction based on pure emotion or thought pattern.

But when our spirit has been strengthened and renewed by the infilling of The Holy Spirit, we come under a totally different driving force in our lives. A conflict then arises between the soul and the spirit (of man). Scripture informs us that The Word of God can divide the soul and spirit (of man). We have free will, so that we can make a conscious decision.

> *For the Word of God is living and active. Sharper than any double-edged sword, it penetrates even to* **dividing soul and spirit**. *(Hebrews 4;12)*

If you often feel a conflict taking place inside you, do not get downhearted, because you are in good company. The Apostle Paul went through exactly the same thing. He vividly describes it.

> *For what I do is not the good I want to do ...* **For in my inner being I delight in God's law***, but I see another law at work in the members of my body.*
>   *(Romans 7;18-23)*

He revealed the struggle that can occur between our inner being (spirit), and our mind and emotions. Notice that he explains that it is in his inner being (spirit) that he delights in God's ways. The reason being is that it is the place where The Holy Spirit resides. **The zeal and motivation to live a Godly life initially comes from our spirit.**

This means that if our soul, which includes our mind, heart and emotions, is thinking negatively, but in our spirit there rises faith and hope, we have to decide which path to take. This explains how The Word is able to divide between the soul and spirit of man. Out of our spirit will rise Scripture, because The Holy Spirit and The Word of God work in harmony. The Spirit is therefore able to cut a clear line right between that which is real truth, and that which is error of thought, or action. He uses The Word of God to accomplish this.

PEACE OF MIND

Everyone in the world wants peace of mind and happiness. Many people consider them to be illusive issues, which only occur momentarily throughout their lives. They have a few happy memories, but no lasting peace. The main reason for such inner turmoil is that the soulish part of us is seeking to have superiority over the spirit. Peace in our mind and emotions comes when our spirit and soul are in harmony.

The way to experience this on a consistent daily basis is for the soul to come in line with a renewed spirit.

The mind controlled by The Spirit is life and peace. *(Romans 8;6)*

The loss of peace in our minds can occur as a result of a sudden set of circumstances or as a gradual build-up over a period of time. We may not realise what is taking place until it has happened. We then confess to ourselves, or even to others, about the loss. Our confession can even cause our mental state to deteriorate further.

But did you know that it is impossible for a Christian to lose their peace? This may appear to be a dramatic statement at first sight, but allow me to explain.

But now in Christ Jesus you who once were far away have been brought near through the blood of Christ. **For He Himself is our peace.** *(Ephesians 2;13-14)*

You will notice that our peace is not dependent upon a state of mind, or emotional feeling. It is all about the person of Christ – **He Himself is our peace**. We know from Deuteronomy 31;6-8 and Hebrews 13;5 that He will never leave us, nor forsake us. Therefore, our Lord is with us continually, and since He is our peace, we can never lose it.

Some may say at this point – What happens when I simply do not feel at peace? The answer lies in understanding what is taking place in our soul.

The soul is the place where we dwell on thoughts in our mind and experience emotional 'feelings' of the heart. It is therefore plain to see how that at times we do not feel at peace. In those situations we have a straightforward choice: we can either dwell on our mental or emotional state, or we can draw from Christ, our peace, who resides in our spirit by The Holy Spirit.

The Spirit will either bring about peace from The Anointing of His Presence, or reveal words from Scripture to encourage, counsel, or convict. At other times He may change circumstances, or enable us to be sustained by the peace that passes all natural understanding as we go through difficult circumstances. There is a multitude of ways in which The Holy Spirit operates. But we have been given free will to make a choice in the matter. We can either comply with His leading and direction in our spirit, or we rely on feelings in our soul.

The principle that I have just explained in respect of our peace is also the same in respect of our joy and righteousness. This means that although we may at times feel sad or do an unrighteous act, the fact remains that our joy and righteousness can never leaves us, because Christ is our joy and righteousness. We have received The Kingdom of God in our spirit.

> *The Kingdom of God ...is of* **righteousness, peace and joy** *in The Holy Spirit.* (Romans 14;17)

Our peace, joy and righteousness are not about something which is intangible, or which can be here one minute and gone the next. It is permanent, because it is all about a Person, our Lord Jesus Christ. We receive all this at our salvation, and it is for our entire earthly life, and then into eternity.

A GOOD NIGHT'S SLEEP

A peaceful mind enables us to be more receptive to hearing from God. This not only applies to when we are conscious, but also during our sleep. Each night, while we are sleeping, many thoughts and images swirl around in our sub-conscious. They mainly relate to good or bad experiences of the previous few days, or even some worry or long term issue which remains unresolved. It is generally accepted that we only remember a fraction of these dreams, and then only the most vivid. All this activity takes place in our soul, because it concerns our mind, heart and emotions.

Of course, we may also encounter Godly images that originate in our soul, which are a blessing and to be savoured. These increasingly occur as we get our minds and emotions renewed in The Lord. We will then create the foundation for minds that have peaceful days, together with a good night's sleep. If we have disturbed sleep, nightmares, or a general feeling of unease during the night, it means that our soul is not at rest.

King David knew that there was a link between having a rested soul, and a quality sleep. He knew that when his heart was joyful, he would be able to sleep in peace.

You have filled my heart with greater joy *than when their grain and new wine abound.* **I will lie down and sleep in peace**. *(Psalm 4;7/8)*

By way of contrast, David also experienced times of worried thoughts and emotions. The end result of this state of affairs is dramatically described.

My soul is in anguish...I am worn out *from groaning; all night long I flood my bed with weeping.*
(Psalm 6;3-6)

It is fair to say that he was not having a very good night's sleep. The key to the situation is found in verse 3, where he states that his soul is troubled. This subsequently caused his unrest at night.

Because The Word of God is able to divide between the soul and the spirit (of man), then we are able hear clearly from God in all situations. The soul part of us, which includes our emotions, will say such things to us as " God is far from me. I cannot reach Him." The inner man, who has been strengthened and empowered by The Holy Spirit, will have a different confession.

"He will never leave me nor forsake me."
(Deuteronomy 31;6)

EMOTIONAL PEACE

I will give another example of how our decision process is affected by our spirit and soul. Have you ever felt offended, or someone has taken advantage of you, or perhaps you have felt a victim of injustice by an organisation or employer? Inside you, there rises up a feeling of indignation and you want to see 'justice' done.

Unfortunately, as so often is the case, our justice is merely a mask for revenge. We want to see the other person reap their rewards in a negative manner. We start off with one thought, which then leads onto another, and we find that minutes turn into hours as we dwell on the issue. We have all manner of excuses to justify our reaction.

The crux of the issue is that these feelings come from our soul, which feels such depth of emotions. If our inner being has been renewed in accordance with Ephesians 3;16/17, by being strengthened by the work of The Holy Spirit, and the indwelling Christ, then what pours out of our spirit is grace and forgiveness. The reason for this is that Christ dwells in our spirit (inner being), and He desires that we become like Him in every part of us.

We therefore have a choice to make. Do we react and allow a conflict to arise between our spirit and soul, or do we respond to The Lord's ways, and get the soul in line with our spirit. When that occurs the revenge that our soul initially wants, gives way to grace, forgiveness, and mercy. This does not mean that we become pushovers, weak or insipid. God does not intend that for us. His heart is that everything is done in a righteous and just manner. But it is in accordance with His way, and not merely as a means for us to vent our feelings.

Please do not think that I am suggesting that our soul is an evil place, whose agenda is our downfall. Quite the contrary. As we have seen, it is a place that contains our mind, emotions, heart, conscience, will and intellect. God gave us these when He created us. If they are God-given and then they are for our benefit, so that we can live a full and abundant life.

But it is when these different aspects of the soul come under the influence of the indwelling Christ that they find their true purpose and stability. Psalm 23, perhaps the best known of all the Psalms, states in verse 3 – **He restores my soul**. This reveals the heart of God. He wants our soul to reach its real and full potential, with every characteristic fulfilled.

In the previous chapter we looked at our spirit, and saw that when we are born again, our Heavenly Father sees us as perfect in Christ. Our spirit is transformed, and made new. But what happens in our soul, which is essentially our individual personality and character, is also of eternal significance.

It is not that we have to get our soul perfect in order to be with Him, because our salvation is already complete. We have been born again of The Spirit. It is simply that He wants our soul to come into its inheritance in The Lord while we are on earth. In Heaven this will not be an issue, because our mortal side will have taken on immortality as Paul describes in 1 Corinthians 15. We will be with The Lord.

SECOND NATURE

When a pattern of thought, or behaviour, is practised to the extent that it becomes adopted into our way of life, the world says it has become second nature. There is an aspect of deeper truth in this expression, because it aptly describes what happens when we continually get our soul in line with our spirit. When that occurs we do not have to question ourselves as to what is taking place, because it has become second nature to us. It literally means that we are consistently putting off the old nature, and partaking of our new nature in Christ.

> *You were taught, with regard to your former way of life,* **to put off your old self,** *which is being corrupted by its deceitful desires;* **to be made new in the attitude of your minds; and to put on the new self,** *created to be like God in true righteousness and holiness.* (*Ephesians 4;22*)

What do you operate out of, and are ruled by, for the majority of your average day? Is it your soul or spirit?

It is so important that our soul, which includes our minds and emotions, is renewed by the work of The Holy Spirit. It all starts by getting the inner man strengthened and renewed, and from there to overflow into the soul, so that it also is re-shaped. As this process continues, we will find that the battles that can often rage within us have started to lessen. This is because our soul is coming in line with The Word of God, and is being renewed by The Holy Spirit.

What initially seemed like a huge effort and struggle, progressively becomes a part of our new nature. The old nature is passing away. We begin to experience real change on the inside, which has an effect upon our thoughts, speech, and actions. Our soul and spirit are at peace with one another. We do not become complacent, or boastful in this, but we keep our eyes fixed on The Lord, and praise Him for His goodness in allowing us to become like Him. We are passing from the milk stage, and onto the meat.

For too long I had endeavoured to bring the soulish side under control, and had tried many different ways. I now realise that I had concentrated on the wrong part. I should have paid more attention to my inner being. From there, comes the strength and ability to influence the soul. **The change comes about from the inside out, as opposed to the outside in.**

Teaching, training, or formulas can be helpful in bringing about certain change. But a fundamental, life changing experience is accomplished by the work of The Holy Spirit operating from our inner being, so that Christ not only dwells in our spirit, but also in every part of our soul.

BRINGING THE SOUL IN LINE

Why are you downcast, O my soul? *Why so disturbed within me?* **Put your hope in God**, *for I will yet praise Him, My Saviour and my God.*   *(Psalm 42;5 & 11)*

You will notice that the Psalmist speaks to his soul, and tells it to put its hope in God. He is going through a difficult time, and the soulish part of him is speaking words of uncertainty and despair, which come as a result of outside circumstances, and a troubled mind.

The answer to this dilemma is for his soul to get in line with his spirit (inner being), where The Holy Spirit is at work, strengthening him by speaking words of truth.

From that place comes the certainty that his deliverance will come as he puts his hope in God.

He has a choice to make. Does he listen to his soul, or his spirit? He concludes the Psalm by once again repeating the above verse. He takes the positive step of speaking words of truth to his soul, which come from the inner conviction that his hope is in God. That knowledge of hope rises from his spirit. A poignant example of The Word of God dividing the soul and spirit (of man).

It could be said that the Psalmist was at a crossroads, and he had to make a decision as to which direction to take. The people of Israel in the time of Jeremiah were also faced with a similar situation, where an important choice had to be made. The Lord God gave an instruction through Jeremiah the prophet, which if heeded, would bring rest to their souls.

> **Stand at the crossroads and look;** *...ask where* **the good way** *is and walk in it, and* **you will find rest for your souls**. *(Jeremiah 6;16)*

In the following verse The Lord continues: *Listen to the sound of the trumpet.* The word trumpet is used in Scripture, amongst other things, to represent a summons by God. In other words, He calls our attention. The Holy Spirit will therefore call and direct us as to which way to go. We all encounter those crossroads decisions in life. When we listen to Him, we will take the right route, and in so doing will find rest for our souls.

FULLNESS

Paul knew that the fullness of Christ would have the effect of re-shaping our souls. When this occurs, we are steady and balanced. If we foolishly allow ourselves to become empty, we become unsteady and unbalanced. The reason is simple. We have a sure and solid centre of gravity when we are full of Him, and therefore we are not tossed back and forth.

That you become mature, attaining to the whole measure of the fullness of Christ. **Then** *we will no longer be infants, tossed back and forth ...*   (Ephesians 4;13)

As we have already seen from Scripture, The Spirit is able to divide between the soul and spirit (of man). The internal struggle that so often robs us of our peace and joy, and which can also affect our health, diminishes. We encounter the overflow from our spirit into our whole being. We are consecrated in thought and deed. From our inner being come not only the faith, but also the power to accomplish this. When that occurs we have a clear motivation:

Thy will be done on earth, as it is in Heaven
                                                  (Matthew 6;10)

Although I have made an attempt to put into words what I have seen about the subject I have to state quite honestly that I feel somewhat inadequate in trying to describe such matters.

But what I am able to say with absolute certainty is that I have discovered that a strengthened inner being, together with a renewed soul, will transform one's life. I am no longer robbed of my peace, joy, health etc., and I am far more aware of the circumstances that are conducive to theft occurring in the first place. I am encountering the inheritance that was there all the time, and I have an inner determination that I shall not be robbed of any of it anymore.

Where does that inner determination come from? It comes from a strengthened spirit (inner being), where Christ dwells, and a soul that is being renewed.

CHAPTER TEN

BODY

IN THE PREVIOUS two chapters we have seen the benefit of getting our soul in line with our spirit, so that they are operating in harmony. When this occurs, our body also benefits.

The medical profession informs us that a high proportion of illnesses are psychosomatic. In other words our mind and emotions are the root cause, or a contributory factor to the particular illness. Worry creates tension, which contributes towards high blood pressure, and can result in heart problems. Many arthritic conditions are attributed to the effects of worry. It is also an accepted fact that unhealthy emotions have an adverse chemical reaction in our body. They literally create juices that damage our organs and joints.

Where do worry, tension and anger originate? They certainly do not come from our spirit, because The Holy Spirit will not bring them into our life. Why do mood swings govern so much of peoples lives? I would suggest that the answer lies in the soul, which has not been renewed. It is therefore clear that if we allow our soul to be reshaped it will have a beneficial effect upon our body, and therefore our health.

THE BENEFITS OF FRUIT

I wonder if the Apostle John in his Epistle, writing under

the guidance of The Holy Spirit, saw the link between the soul and the health of our body.

I pray that you may enjoy good health, *and that all may go well for you,* **even as your soul is getting along well**. *(3 John;2)*

In Paul's letter to the Galation Church he informed them of the nature of the fruit of the Spirit. Each of these aspects of the fruit indicates that a believer is allowing The Spirit to shape their life.

The fruit of The Spirit is love, joy, peace, patience, kindness, goodness, faithfulness, gentleness and self-control. *(Galatians 5;22-23)*

Consider for a moment – what is the opposite of each of these attributes? These would involve hate, sadness, unrest, short temperedness, being miserable, calculating, lacking integrity, harshness, and lack of self-control. Now weigh up the effect each would have on our general well being. It does not take a person with a medical degree to come to the conclusion as to which is the healthier option. **God is our healer, but He also is the originator of preventive medicine.**

A cheerful heart is good medicine, *but a crushed spirit dries up the bones.* *(Proverbs 17;22)*

Laughter is an integral part of our emotions, and is described as good medicine in the above Scripture. I read of one man who was terminally ill, and had tried all manner of treatments, but had not been cured. He then heard that laughter produces juices that are healthy for our body. He decided to apply this principle to his circumstances, and watched comedy videos for at least an hour a day. He laughed heartily, his sickness departed, and he lived a healthy life.

It is also worth noting that the second part of the afore-mentioned verse warns us that a crushed spirit dries up the bones. It is a recognised medical fact that when we are depressed or bitter we create harmful juices, which lead to ill health. Because our Heavenly Father created us, He knows what is good for us. What the medical profession is now discovering, He wrote in His Word thousands of years ago.

There is a clear spiritual principle of sowing and reaping. At the age of forty-six I reaped the excesses of my thirties and early forties. I therefore have to ask myself the question – What do I want to reap in my sixties and seventies? The outcome is considerably influenced by what I sow in my fifties.

I am determined to pay close attention to all aspects of my spirit, soul and body, so that I am not only spiritually aware, but I am also mentally alert, and physically strong. Permit me to say to any young person who may be reading – Start paying attention to all parts of your spirit, soul, and body at an early age, because what you sow in your teenage years and twenties you will reap later.

LASTING CHANGES

When we are strengthened in our spirit by The Holy Spirit, His qualities take centre stage. From that place in our inner being, our soul is renewed by coming in line with the work of The Spirit. We will then live in the fullness of His peace, and are no longer at war within ourselves.

I well remember The Lord showing me that **prosperity comes from peace**. In order to illustrate the point; consider the effect of a country at war. It will not be long before it becomes a poor country. Its resources are being continually drained, and it will descend into weakness. It is the same with people. If a person is at war within himself, he will become drained and weak. He will feel debilitated for most of the time.

There is also another consequence. **A person who is at war within himself will invariably be at war with others.** The Lord placed great emphasis on peace. Some of the last words He spoke to His disciples before His crucifixion were on this subject. It was also the first thing He said to them after His resurrection.

> *I have told you these things,* **so that in Me you may have peace ...** *(John 16;33)*

> *Peace be with you.* *(John 20;19)*

The effect of our spirit and soul upon the general well being of our body is a vast subject, and I have only touched upon it in these few lines. However, it is vitally important that no one misinterprets what I have been saying. I am not suggesting for one moment that all ill health is linked to the state of our souls. I am merely stating that our health can be affected in such a way.

I can vouch from my own testimony, that a strengthened spirit, and renewed soul, will produce a healthier body. I believe that God heals miraculously. But I also believe that He wants us to remain in health. We can receive healing, but it would be good not to get ill in the first place. **Prevention is better than cure.**

In addition to all the healthier benefits, the outward appearance of our body will display the countenance of God.

Whenever Moses entered The Lord's Presence *to*

speak with Him, he removed the veil until he came out.
And when he came out *and told The Israelites what*
he had been commanded, **they saw that his face was**
radiant. *(Exodus 34;34-35)*

Have you noticed how those people who have an intimate relationship with The Lord have a radiance that
shines from their face? It comes from spending time in His
Presence. This occurs when our spirit (inner being) is full
to overflowing in Him, and the effect ripples through our
entire soul and body. We seek His face to reflect His Glory.

Those who look to Him are radiant; *their faces are*
never covered with shame. *(Psalm 34;5)*

CHAPTER ELEVEN

RENEWING OF THE MIND

PREVENTION is better than cure. It therefore follows that the wisest policy is to prevent crime occurring in the first place. It is fair to say that sometimes we get robbed through no fault of our own, but there are other times when our very actions and conduct invite the thief in. We become an easy target.

What is the most basic crime prevention advice that can be given? The first step is undoubtedly to close, and lock the front door to your property. A person who leaves his front door open invites theft. Once the thief gains entry he will steal at random. There is nothing sentimental or compassionate about a thief. What he wants, he takes. Nothing is sacred. It is the same with the devil in the spiritual realm.

What are the areas in which most people are spiritually robbed? I would suggest that it is in our mind and heart, which are parts of our soul. These provide rich pickings for the thief. In the previous three chapters we looked in some detail at the different aspects of our spirit, soul, and body. It may be helpful at this point to remind ourselves that the soul consists of our mind, heart, emotions, will, conscience and intellect.

Consider the layout of a dwelling house. Many different things can occur on a front garden path, and can be easily dispersed. But once something comes through the front door of a home it is a different matter.

The same can be said of our soul. The mind could be considered as the front garden path to the soul. In our mind we can have many different thoughts during the day. Some are fleeting, others we dwell on, while some we embrace and retain. However, once something gets through the door and gets embedded in our heart, it is far more difficult to eject.

We saw in an earlier chapter the importance of taking our thoughts captive. This means that we filter what we think. We exercise our free will, and chose what we wish to keep. Consider the consequences of not effectively dealing with a harmful thought, attitude, hurt, or sin in the mind. It travels along the path, and if unchecked and dealt with, it then enters through the door and takes up residence in our heart. It can so easily happen. Scripture gives us the necessary crime prevention advice:

Above all else guard your heart, *for it is the well-spring of life.* *(Proverbs 4;23)*

We are encouraged, even commanded, to protect it from anything harmful. In both the Old and New Testament, the word heart has the meaning of such things as our thoughts, emotions, will, conscience, and reasoning. Each of these is a composite of our soul. By looking at these different parts of the heart it is plain to see that they are the areas that we need to guard.

The word *guard* is used, as if to convey an image of an armed sentry standing at his post, and saying " Halt. Who goes there? Friend or foe?" Only that which is good is allowed to proceed further. The alternative is to allow the thief in to steal and plunder our mental and emotional peace and joy.

In order to emphasise the point of keeping watch over what enters, the Scripture states – **above all else**. If you examine the chapter in which it is contained, you will notice that a wide range of advice is given. But this is given top priority.

STOREHOUSE

Jesus revealed that the things that are stored up inside us are what we have allowed to come through the front door to our heart. He told us that good will come out of a heart that is good. The alternative applies in respect of a heart that stores up bad things.

> **Out of the overflow of the heart** *the mouth speaks. The good man brings good things out of the good* **stored up in him** ...   *(Matthew 12;34/35)*

When laws are made they are written down. Their application governs the conduct of citizens. A nation's laws are imposed from the outside of a person, to govern his conduct within. God does the opposite. His laws are written on the inside, so that a person's life is guided from the inside out, as opposed to the outside in.

> *I will put My laws* **in their minds** *and write them* **on their hearts**.   *(Jeremiah 31;33 & Hebrews 8;10)*

Jesus explained this when He was asked the question as to what was the greatest commandment. He replied as follows:

> *Love The Lord your God with* **all your heart** *and with all your soul and with* **all your mind**.
>   *(Matthew 22;37)*

At salvation The Lord takes up residence in our spirit by

The Holy Spirit. Therefore that part of us is given over to Him. What He is showing us in Matthew 22;37 is that He desires the remainder, so that the whole of our being is caught up in Him. When this occurs, there is no means by which a thief can enter and steal.

ROOTED

The Parable of the Sower, recorded in Matthew 13, is a story of how four different groups of people respond to salvation. But the principles involved in the account can also relate to our Christian walk as a whole. Whenever you hear directly from God, study the Bible, listen to a sermon, or read a book, how much of it becomes firmly rooted, and produces a good crop?

The challenge for us is to see as much as possible become fruitful in our lives. The alternative is to see it snatched away, or die, because of the lack of root or cares of the world.

Have you ever made new year resolutions to be more single-minded, more purposeful, have a clear direction in your life, so that by the end of the year you can look back and see the fruit of your achievements? At the end of the first week you have scaled down your expectations and resorted to plan 'B', and by the end of the month you have decided to wait until the end of the year to reconsider your resolutions. I am sure we have all seen birds come down and steal the planted seed before it has had any chance to sprout and produce fruit.

I recently heard of a professional study that discovered that 80% of conversation was negative.

As we know, our words are simply an expression of what has been taking place in our mind and heart. At the beginning of this chapter I used the illustration of a house with regard to our soul. We saw that thoughts travel along the front path, and if we dwell on them, we open the door for them to take up residence in our heart. This then shapes our attitudes and resultant conversation. Jesus explains this principle:

> *Out of the overflow of the heart the mouth speaks... For by your words you will be acquitted, and by your words you will be condemned.*   (Matthew 12;33/37)

If 80% of what proceeds out of our mouth is negative, can you imagine the figure in relation to our mind and heart? But it does not have to be this way. We have been given free will, so we therefore have a choice in the matter.

Is there an answer to this recurring problem? Can a mind be changed from inconsistency, so that it is not continually robbed? Thankfully, God's Word gives clear guidance. It not only gives the goal of a renewed mind, but also the means for its implementation.

SELF-EXAMINATION

Try this simple three-point test upon yourself. I have used it on myself and others, and can testify that it works.

Step 1 – Sit down and think about a specific worry you are currently facing, a bad memory or hurt from the past, or a relationship problem. In other words, find something to focus your mind upon which is specifically negative. Once you have decided upon the topic set a timer for 30 seconds, close your eyes, and let your mind run free concerning the issue.

During the allotted time, only dwell on the negative problem. At the end of the time, count up the amount of thoughts that followed from the first one. It will probably average about four or five.

Step 2 – Set the timer again for 30 seconds and close you eyes. This time, try and stop all thoughts entering your mind, whether good or bad. Within a few seconds some thought will enter you mind, even if it just the fact that you are sitting in a chair. But even with the simplest thought try and stop it from becoming a second thought. Erase it, and keep your mind blank. This is quite difficult at first.

Step 3 – Go back to the negative thought in step (1). Think of a Scripture that is pertinent to the issue, whether it is concerning the right heart attitude or instructions on how we are to deal with the situation. Set the timer for the same time as before, close your eyes, and dwell on the verse, or a word that The Lord has given you. See what follows from that verse or direct word as you meditate and allow The Holy Spirit to guide you. Don't pray. Just focus on the verse or word from God.

FEEDBACK

Let us now examine what took place. We first thought of something negative. We next practised capturing thoughts so that one thought did not follow on to another. Finally we replaced the negative with the positive, by meditating on The Word of God, or applying a Godly principle.

The purpose of step (1) is purely for the purpose of illustration, in order to show what can so easily happen to us daily. It is clear to see that the first negative thought can quickly develop into forty negative thoughts, in a comparatively short space of time. This is proved by the fact that we can have five such thoughts in only thirty seconds. Obviously, after trying step (1), do not continue using it. It is tried once in order to demonstrate how negative attitudes take root.

In the normal course of each day we would only apply step (2) and (3), in order to counteract any negative thought or attitude that may be filling our mind. Although it is virtually impossible to eliminate everything that is negative, there is no doubt that if we practise the last two steps each day, there will certainly be little room for anything negative to enter in the first place.

In order to clarify any misunderstanding about negative thought, I do not mean that we are to adopt an escapist approach, and refuse to think about or face a problem. It is obviously necessary to thoroughly think through difficulties or issues that we face at work, home or church. But it is how we approach these things that is important. Our mental and heart attitude will be deciding factors on the outcome.

This illustrates the importance of a renewed mind that is Spirit led. Not only will our mind, heart, emotions, and conscience be changed, but also our conversation will be transformed. When this occurs, The Holy Spirit increasingly influences our thoughts and resultant speech.

> **This is what we speak**, *not in words taught us by human wisdom but in* **words taught by The Spirit**, *expressing spiritual truths in spiritual words.*
> *(1 Corinthians 2;13)*

The Holy Spirit searches the thoughts of God and reveals them to us. We have received The Spirit to understand those things that are spiritually discerned.

THE MIND OF CHRIST

We have the mind of Christ.   *(1 Corinthians 2;16)*

Where do we have the mind of Christ? It is in our spirit,

because that is the place where He dwells by The Holy Spirit. That is the focal point from which we work. The goal is straightforward. **Our minds are to be renewed by the mind of Christ**. At the time of our salvation our spirit is instantly renewed. But it is a process in respect of the components of our soul, as we saw in the previous chapters.

Now return and examine what happened in the above test, and see how we can allow the mind of Christ to re-shape our lives.

In order to conduct the test in step (1) we purposely thought of something negative. This was done to illustrate what can follow from one initial thought in just a short space of time. An immense and wide-ranging amount of thoughts enter our minds each day. However, we have a choice to make. What do we immediately stop, and what do we allow to continue?

What resides in our heart is basically what we have deposited there. What proceeds from our mouth is an expression of what is taking place inside us. There is a circular motion continually taking place in our soul. A thought usually enters our mind either unconsciously or purposely on our part. In addition to this we respond to any one of our five senses, namely sight, hearing, touch, smell or taste.

The thoughts that we dwell upon are those that take root in our heart. These shape our opinions, attitudes, conscience and will. In addition to all this, add our emotions into the mixture. This recipe of ingredients mixes together to form what proceeds out of our mouth. It all starts from an initial thought.

UNDER NEW OWNERSHIP

At this point I would like to refer back to the illustration of the house that we examined at the beginning of the chapter. It has to be said that there is no point in trying to eject something unwelcome on the inside, if the front door has been left open. While all our energy is committed to the inside, more is entering all the time through the open door.

This is why it is so important that in the process of changing our heart attitude, we do not also dwell on other negative things in our minds, because they will then take up residence in our hearts. If this were to happen, it could be compared to us clearing a pile of rubbish with our right hand, while at the same time piling more on with our left hand. It would not make any sense.

Just think how much harm we can do to ourselves if we continue to dwell on negative thoughts. It is not only our mind that is affected. Doctors believe that there is a direct link between the state of our mind and our physical health, as we shall see in a later chapter.

In step (2) we eliminated all thoughts whether good or bad. This is not simply to achieve a blank mind as an end in itself. It is to train ourselves in capturing our thoughts. I must emphasise that the success of this step in the procedure is dependent upon the willingness to practise it on a daily basis until it becomes natural. As we saw in chapter nine on the soul, it becomes 'second nature'.

FITNESS PROGRAMME

How much are we prepared to train ourselves in Godliness?

The Apostle Paul likened it to someone competing in The Games. (The Roman Games were a prominent feature at that time, so people could easily relate to what Paul was writing). He states that everyone who competes in these events goes into strict training. He then compares this to the manner in which he conducts his spiritual life. He states that he does not run aimlessly, or beat the air.

I beat my body *and make it my slave ...*
                                  (1 Corinthians 9;27)

You will notice that he puts it in the present tense. It is not something that he did a couple of times in the past. It was an ongoing process.

By way of personal testimony I now practice capturing my thoughts on a daily basis. I do it with simple, general thoughts in order to continually train myself in this area. As a result of this, it has enabled me to be far more able to capture any negative thought before it expands. The purpose of training is that we are continually prepared and equipped, and ready for those moments when it really matters. By practising it on simple issues it has made it far easier to bring it into effect when a real test comes.

The Apostle Paul in his letter to the Ephesian Church explained the importance of putting on the whole armour of God. Four parts of the equipment concern preparation. The reason for the preparation is clearly stated:

... **So that when the day of evil comes**, *you may be able to stand your ground.* *(Ephesians 6;13)*

In other words, there is no point in scrambling about trying to be able to deal with something when it is upon us. We need to be in a state of readiness by our preparation, and equipping.

I would encourage you to start simply at first. Try and eliminate all thoughts for five seconds, then build up to fifteen. I am not suggesting that we keep practising this until we can reach five minutes purely as an objective in itself.

The point in all of this is not to have a blank mind, but to train ourselves in capturing thoughts.

Some Eastern religions empty their minds as an end in itself. But it is the total opposite for a Christian. Our motive is to be Christ-like. Therefore, we first capture a thought in our soul. This allows The Holy Spirit to replace anything negative, with the positive Word of God emanating from our spirit. It is all about Christ filling every part of our being.

> *We demolish arguments and every pretension that sets itself up against the knowledge of God, and* **we take captive every thought to make it obedient to Christ.** *(2 Corinthians 10;5)*

When that occurs we discover that we have the mind of Christ not only in our spirit but also in our mind, because our soul has been renewed in His image.

CAPTOR OR CAPTIVE

This brings us onto step (3), which is the replacing the negative with the positive. If we have successfully accomplished step (2), then something has to follow. If a vacuum is created it has to be filled with something. Capturing the thought is not an end in itself, because something will replace it, either good or bad. This illustrates the benefit of having a sound grasp of Scripture.

> *All Scripture is God-breathed and is useful for teaching, rebuking, correcting and* **training in righteousness, so that the man of God may be thoroughly equipped** *for every good work.* *(2 Timothy 3;16/17)*

If we do not take our thoughts captive, we will subsequently enter captivity. People are held captive to hurts, unforgiveness, anger, jealousy, and resentment to name just a few. These feelings are the result of emotions that have taken root in the heart. They swirl around and spring forth when someone presses the appropriate button. Is there a way of controlling and re-shaping the make-up of our heart? It all begins with capturing the thought. We have a choice to make. **Do we want to be the captor or the captive?**

Paul wrote these words to the Philippian Church:

Whatever is true, whatever is noble, whatever is right, whatever is pure, whatever is lovely, whatever is admirable – if anything is excellent or praiseworthy – **think about such things**. *(Philippians 4;8)*

This reveals a different sort of capturing. We learn to take captive and hold onto that which is true, right etc. The above verse states – **think about such things**. This is very challenging. What do we choose to think about each day? We saw earlier in the chapter that it will determine the health of our soul, and resultant conversation. It therefore follows that what a person thinks, will affect what they become.

Jesus said, " If you hold to my teaching, *you are really My disciples. Then* **you will know the truth, and the truth will set you free."** *(John 8;31-32)*

Jesus spoke a very straightforward message. When we continually apply His teaching to every part of our soul, we will not be held captive to anything. As we have already seen, our spirit is set free at salvation. Therefore, when our soul gets in line with the truth that is being revealed by The Holy Spirit, it also will encounter the same freedom. This brings our spirit and soul into harmony, and flowing in the same direction.

So if The Son sets you free, **you will be free indeed**.
(John 8;36)

When this consistently occurs, we find that very few negative thoughts and unbelief enter our mind because it is being continually renewed. We do not have to work up faith because it instantly rises from our spirit without any hindrance from our mind or emotions.

The world has a habit of saying, " There is no realistic hope." As Christians we have a different confession.

With man this is impossible, **but with God all things are possible**.   *(Matthew 19;26)*

CHAPTER TWELVE

CONFORM OR TRANSFORM

LET US NOW look at the particular Scripture which relates to the renewing of the mind, and as you read it, take careful note of the process that is revealed.

> *Therefore, I urge you, brothers, in view of God's mercy to* **offer your bodies as living sacrifices**, *holy and pleasing to God – this is your spiritual act of worship.* **Do not conform any longer to the pattern of this world,** *but* **be transformed by the renewing of your mind. Then you will be able** *to test and approve what God's will is – His good, pleasing and perfect will.* (Romans 12;1-2)

These verses contain four steps to having a renewed mind, not just a temporary blessing, but as a permanent feature.

1) *Offer* your bodies as living sacrifices.

God does not take. We are to offer. There has to be a desire and willingness on our part to change. Notice the apparent paradox in the words that are used. '*Sacrifice*' talks of death, while '*living*' talks of life. There is a putting to death of our own desires and agenda, which means a dying to oneself. This is meant to be the Christian experience throughout our lives, not simply at the moment of salvation.

The literal meaning of consecration is 'set apart unto God'. As we continually put to death the old self, something extraordinary happens. We come alive in Christ. It can be compared to a pulley system. When one weight is descending, the other is ascending. The key to this manner of living is found in the first word of the text – '*offer*'.

Paul explains this principle of being dead to sin and alive in Christ in his letter to the Roman Church.

We were therefore buried with Him *through Baptism into death in order that, just as Christ was raised from the dead through the Glory of The Father,* **we too may live a new life**. *(Romans 6;4)*

The following steps, in the renewing of the mind, will only have the desired effect when step one is enacted, because it is not meant to be a formula. It is a daily living experience with The Lord. In order to live a new life we have to die to the old one.

2) *Do not conform* **any longer to the pattern of this world.**
This goes far deeper than simply avoiding the outward sins that are obvious. Make it a matter of course throughout the day to ask yourself – What would Jesus do? This is step (2) in the test that we looked at in the previous chapter, where we considered how to capture our thoughts.

Before retiring to bed, consider how much of our attitude and conversation during that particular day has lined up with The Word of God. I would add at this point that I am not seeking to be legalistic, or bring anyone into condemnation. I am merely suggesting that each of us take a fresh look at our thinking in the light of this verse.

This Scripture has as much, if not more, relevance today as when it was written. You have only to consider the mountain of different ideologies that our young people have to face, coupled with the pressure by the media to conform to a particular image. God knew what we have to face, and He gave us the means by which we are able not only to survive, but also to overcome.

If we look back a few centuries at the figure of Martin Luther, we see a man who made a stand for truth. No doubt, there were many people who said to him, "Why can't you conform and be like the rest of us? Don't make waves". Or words to that effect. But he made a conscious decision not to conform to the pattern of thinking that was prevalent at that time. As a result of which, he changed the course of history.

Although we may never have such a dramatic effect, we can be sure that we can change the course of events around us when we make a stand for truth, and not conform to anything that is unrighteous. By having the courage of our convictions, we honour God, and may change the history in another person's life.

There are numerous testimonies from people who have responded to The Lord as a result of seeing a Christian make a righteous stand, and not conform to the pattern of thought, or behaviour around them.

Change Our Working Environment
The workplace can be a very challenging environment for a Christian, where it takes self-discipline, and courage not to conform. The almost inevitable criticism of 'the boss', or other departments, pervades the working environment.

So often, there develops a culture of negativity. Open criticism of others becomes an easy and lazy way to start a conversation.

In this sort of atmosphere it is difficult to opt out of controversy just to avoid giving an opinion. It is obviously necessary and right to display integrity in identifying bad working practise. But in expressing a view we also need the wisdom and courage to take the lead and correct matters ourselves whenever possible, coupled with showing grace towards those who may be concerned in the matter.

Paul gave this advice to the Thessalonian Church.

Make sure that nobody pays back wrong for wrong, **but always try to be kind to each other and to everyone else.** *(1 Thessalonians 5;15)*

In a further passage of Scripture which tackles how we relate to one another, this intuitive advice is given –

If it is possible, **as far as it depends on you,** *live at peace with everyone. (Romans 12;18)*

The key to this verse is found in the middle section – as far as it depends on you.

The reality of life is that we will not always see eye to eye with everyone, and sometimes friction will develop. But The Word of God encourages us to take the lead in the matter of inter-personal relationships. We are to do all that is possible to live at peace with all people. If the other person then chooses to take the path of disharmony, then it is their choice, not ours.

I wonder what would be the effect if these two Scriptures from 1 Thessalonians 5;15 and Romans 12;18 were placed on notice boards in work, or included as part of a firm's vision. This is not meant in any way to simply obey another rule, but for it to become a genuine heart response.

If we are serious about changing our working environment, we need to start at the root of relationships. The fruit from this will spread throughout the organisation. A happy atmosphere will create a more contented workforce, who will become more productive, and efficient. This will increase profitability. Everyone gains, because the firm uses the extra income to expand, thereby making existing jobs more secure, and also creating new employment. All this can come about from obeying a simple truth from Scripture.

Political Correctness

The central principle of not conforming to the pattern of this world has remained the same throughout the years. However, there are certain cultural and social changes that occur in different centuries that The Church ought to provide effective leadership by warning of the dangers of following a particular course of action.

The world currently promotes many issues under the banner of 'political correctness'. The people who propagate this idea would have us accept that their policies are the 'best practise' and the right way forward. They want everyone to conform to their ideology.

If the politically correct issue lines up with Scripture then this is obviously acceptable. But if it goes beyond, or conflicts with The Word of God, then we need to be careful that we do not consciously conform to untruth. As Christians, we have a duty to stand up for Biblical principles, and not conform to that which the world has us believe is acceptable.

I have highlighted just a few ways in which we can be sucked into a particular way of thinking, without even being conscious of how far we have conformed to the pattern of the world. I am sure that many more examples will come to your mind.

3) *Be transformed* by the renewing of your minds.

You will remember that the first step in the renewing of the mind involved offering, meaning a willingness to change. Step two made us aware of not consciously or unconsciously conforming to the pattern of the world. The third step provides the means by which we can achieve that change, namely by *being transformed*. (This is the application of step (3) in the previous chapter).

The dictionary meaning of transform is *'make a thorough or dramatic change in the form, outward appearance, and character'*. There is nothing in this world that can cause such a radical transformation in someone's life as The Word of God.

> **All Scripture** *is God-breathed and is* **useful** *for* **teaching, rebuking, correcting** *and* **training** *in righteousness,* **so that** *the man of God may be* **thoroughly equipped** *for every good work.*   *(2 Timothy 3;16)*

You will notice that this is not meant to be a theoretical exercise. The words *so that* are used to show that it is for a practical application. The teaching and training by The Word of God enables us to be *thoroughly equipped*. Jesus explained the work of The Spirit in this transforming process. He takes The Word of God and not only *teaches* us all things, but He also *reminds* us of everything.

The Counsellor, The Holy Spirit, whom The Father will

send in My Name, will **teach you all things** *and will*
remind you of everything *I have said to you.*
(John 14;26)

He does not want us to miss out on anything. He continually leads us on into further truth, while at the same
time reminding us of what we have learnt in the past. The
more we become Spirit led, the greater will be the impact
of God's Word in our lives, and we will be amazed at the
transformation of our minds.

4) *Then you will be able* **to test and approve what
God's will is.**
We all want to have a renewed mind whereby we instinctively know the will of God. In order to get to that point
we need to look closely at the word that begins the fourth
step, namely the word – *then.* We cannot effectively reach
the fourth point until we have put in place the first three
steps.
  If we are willing to offer ourselves as living sacrifices in
order to change, no longer conform to the pattern of the
world's thinking, and at the same time being changed by
The Word of God, *then* we will indeed have minds that are
transformed. This will result in us being continually more
receptive to The Holy Spirit as He reveals the will of God.
All of this is a continual process. **There are no short cuts.**
But there is wonderful fruit from a renewed mind.

**The mind controlled by The Spirit is life and
peace.** *(Romans 8;6)*

CHAPTER THIRTEEN

THE NAMES OF GOD

THE MIDDLE section of this book began with an examination of our spirit, soul, and body. We saw the need to operate out of our spirit, where Christ dwells by His Spirit. The next two chapters tackled the renewing of the mind, which is a part of our soul. We saw how it is possible to get our soul in line with our spirit, so that they are in harmony.

This present chapter is a follow-on, and integrally linked to these two topics. The reason being is that the Names of God reveal the character of God that is embodied in Christ our Lord. The Holy Spirit continually seeks to reveal the character of God in our spirit in order that our soul is restored. The renewing of our mind is part of this process.

The Spirit (of God) searches *all things, even the deep things of God...so that* **we may understand** *what God has freely given us.* *(1 Corinthians 2;10-12)*

He (The Holy Spirit) will bring glory to Me by **taking from what is Mine and making it known to you.** *(John 16;14)*

Scripture informs us that The Holy Spirit will input

truth about The Lord into us. It is received in our spirit. It will remain consistent. It will not vary, or change. It is at this point that we have a choice to make. Do we allow the truth in our spirit to renew our mind, or do we remain subject to emotional fluctuations and unbelief that occur in our soul?

TRUTH OR LIES

Jesus told the people about the character of the devil.

> *He did not hold to the truth, for there is no truth in him. When he lies, he speaks his native language, for he is a liar and the father of lies.* (John 8;44)

A deceiver relies on someone believing a lie. He cannot achieve his objective if the truth is known, and acted upon. Therefore, the more that we know about the unchanging character of our God, the more able we are to discern what is true, because He does not change. We can then reject that which we know to be false. This is part of the process of our minds being renewed.

We have all heard the expression 'what's in a name?'. It is normally used in conversation to convey the meaning that a name in itself is not important, because it is the person behind the title that matters. But with God it is different. We not only seek to know His Person, but the Names that He gives concerning Himself are an integral part of knowing Him. The Names that were revealed in The Old Testament are of the same significance today. The reason is very clear.

I The Lord do not change. (Malachi 3;6)

It is worth noting that this statement is recorded in the last book of The Old Testament. It is as if God was clearly stating that all the different aspects of His character that He had revealed throughout the centuries would continue. There would be no change. This statement in Malachi is very challenging.

THE NAME REVEALED

Jesus came as the embodiment of God in human form, and everything about God is revealed in Jesus.

He is the image *of the invisible God.*
(Colossians 1;15)

God was pleased to have **all His fullness** *dwell in Him.*
(Colossians 1;19)

For no matter how many promises God has made, **they are "Yes" in Christ**. *And so through Him the "Amen" is spoken by us to the Glory of God.*
(2 Corinthians 1;20)

In The Old Testament there are a number of occasions when God revealed Himself by a different name. Let us now look at some examples of how Jesus fulfilled those names.

When Abraham was about to sacrifice his son Isaac, God told Abraham that He Himself would provide the lamb: *Jehovah Jireh* – 'God the Provider'. *(Genesis 22;1-14)*

Jesus Himself is the lasting sacrifice who was slain once and for all for our sins and sicknesses. Because God sent Jesus, we can be completely sure that there is no limit to His provision. He was and always will be God the Provider. He does not change.

He who did not spare His own Son, *but gave Him*

up for us all – **how will He not also, along with Him, graciously give us all things**. *(Romans 8;32)*

Another example is where God outlines to Gideon His plan for the deliverance of Israel, in order that they may have peace. He revealed another name: *Jehovah Shalom* – 'The Lord is peace'. *(Judges 6;11-24)*

Just before Jesus was to be crucified He said to His disciples:

Peace I leave with you; My peace I give you.

(John 14;27)

Paul, writing to the Ephesian Church, informs them about Jesus –

He Himself is our peace. *(Ephesians 2;14)*

Once again we see how Jesus fulfilled a name that God had already revealed about Himself.

PRAYING WITH ASSURANCE

I can testify that a knowledge of all the Names of God will not only help renew the mind, but it will also transform one's prayer life. If someone is encountering a real battle, it is a great comfort and strength to know that you are praying to The God who is *Jehovah Nissi* – 'The Lord is my banner'. This was revealed when Moses was assisted to hold the staff aloft. The staff, the banner of God, brings victory. The Apostle John gave the same assurance to believers regarding our victory through Christ. He does not change.

Everyone born of God overcomes the world. **This is the victory that has overcome the world,** *even our faith. Who is it that overcomes the world?* **Only he**

who believes that Jesus is The Son of God.

(1 John 5;4-5)

When we pray, we do so in the name of Jesus. Although it is through Jesus, it is also important to keep in mind what is embodied in Him, and how He fulfils all aspects of the character of God. The characteristics that God revealed about Himself in The Old Testament have not changed. We then have the promise that Jesus Himself will also not change. There is complete continuity through Scripture. What is promised will be fulfilled.

Jesus Christ is the same yesterday and today and forever. *(Hebrews 13;8)*

I will do whatever you **ask** **in My Name***, so that The Son may bring glory to The Father.* *(John 14;13)*

SURE AND CERTAIN KNOWLEDGE

The problem that faces many Christians is that they only call on The God of Peace when they are in a troubled and anxious state. Of course He will respond to the cry of someone, and in His mercy and grace minister to their need. But it is far better not to wait for such times to encounter Him in such a way. Let me explain.

The time to know **the God of Peace** is when we are at peace. The time to know **the God who Heals** is when we are in health. The time to know **the Lord who is my Shepherd** is when we are allowing Him to lead us. This has the effect of us developing our relationship with Him, and really getting to know Him. It also prepares us for those occasions when we face troubled times, sickness, or the need for direction.

It means that we really know Him to be our *peace, heal-*

er, and shepherd. When faced with situations that we need His help in such a manner, it is not a big issue where we have to summon up faith, because we already are fully convinced that He is all those things. We already know Him in such ways. Once our minds are convinced about something, there is no longer a conflict.

Paul knew with absolute certainty that nothing can separate us from God's love. He did not wait to encounter situations before he was convinced. His heart was to get to know God, and in so doing he developed an inner certainty that enabled him to face anything.

> **I am convinced** *that neither death nor life, neither angels or demons, neither the present nor the future, nor any powers, neither height nor depth, nor anything else in all creation, will be able to separate us from the love of God that is in Christ Jesus our Lord.*
>
> *(Romans 8;38-39)*

In 2 Corinthians 11;23-33 Paul catalogues a series of difficult times. They included imprisonment, floggings, near death experiences, being stoned, shipwrecks, death threats, plus all the pressure of assisting churches. You cannot get through the circumstances that Paul encountered unless you know The God who is the following:

Jehovah El-Shaddai – 'God who is sufficient';

Jehovah Shalom – 'The Lord is Peace';

Jehovah Shammah – 'The Lord is there'.

When Paul was shipwrecked and spent a night and day in the open sea he did not think that God had stopped being *Jehovah Nissi* – 'The Lord is my banner'. He knew that God does not change, irrespective of circumstances. He was not rescued in the first hour of being in the sea. It happened after twenty-four hours. We also may not encounter deliverance for a lengthy period of time. But this does not mean that God has changed.

KNOW THE PERSON

Paul wrote these words to the Philippian Church –

I want to know Christ... *(Philippians 3;10)*

This verse begins with his passion in life – *'I want to know Christ'*. His chief concern was not what The Lord could do for him. He simply wanted to know Him. Everything else was secondary.

When a situation develops, that could cause worry or anxiety, it is unproductive for our mind to linger on the problem. It is wiser to meditate upon the fact that 'The God of Peace' is with us. As we saw in the previous chapter, we capture the negative thought, and replace it with the positive Word of God. The more we train ourselves in this manner, the easier it becomes, until it is second nature.

In fact, the more that our minds are renewed concerning the character of God, there is little room for the negative to form in the first place. It comes to the point where we instantly think of God's answer to the issue.

I would therefore encourage you to meditate upon these different Names, which I have chronologically recorded as they appear in The Old Testament. Study the Scriptures in which they are contained, and see for yourself how Jesus fulfilled each of The Names. In the below list I have given New Testament equivalents. These are only suggestions on my part. If you do your own Bible study, you will find many others Scriptures that reveal how Jesus embodies each Name.

Surely I am with you always. *(Matthew 28;20)*

OLD TESTAMENT

ELOHIM – God the Creator
Created the heavens and the earth
Genesis 1;1-13

JEHOVAH – The I Am – To be
actively present. Faithful and
unchangeable Genesis 2;1-7

JEHOVAH EL-SHADDAI
God who is sufficient – God the
Enough. What God has promised
He will perform Genesis 17;1-8

JEHOVAH JIREH
God The Provider
God provided Abraham with a
lamb in place of Isaac
Genesis 22;1-14

JEHOVAH ROPHE
The Lord who Heals
Exodus 15;22-26

JEHOVAH NISSI
The Lord is my Banner
The banner of God brings victory
Exodus 17;8-16

JEHOVAH QADESH
The Lord who Sanctifies
Israel to be set apart & holy
Leviticus 20;1-8

JEHOVAH SHALOM
The Lord is Peace

NEW TESTAMENT

By Him (Jesus) all
things were created...
Colossians 1;16

Before Abraham was
born, I am
John 8;58

No matter how many
promises God has made,
they are " Yes" in Christ
2 Corinthians 1;20

The Lamb that was slain
from the foundation of
the world
Revelation 13;8

By His wounds you
have been healed
1 Peter 2;24

God gives us the victory
through our Lord
Jesus Christ
1 Corinthians 15;57

Those sanctified in
Christ Jesus and called
to be holy
1 Corinthians 1;2

Peace I leave with
you; My peace I give

OLD TESTAMENT	NEW TESTAMENT
God gives His plan in order that they have peace Judges 6;11-24	you John 14;27
JEHOVAH ROHE The Lord is My Shepherd God is the good shepherd to His people Psalm 23;1-6	I am The Good shepherd; I know My sheep and My sheep know Me John 10;14
ADONAI Lord & Master Ownership, Lordship, Divine Authority Isaiah 6;1-13	Every tongue shall confess that Jesus Christ is Lord, to the glory of God Philippians 2;11
JEHOVAH TSIDKENU The Lord our Righteousness The Messiah is prophesied – our righteousness Jeremiah 23;1-8	This righteousness from God comes through faith in Jesus Christ Romans 3;22
JEHOVAH SHAMMAH The Lord is There No matter what we face He is there Ezekiel 48;30-35	Surely I am with you always, to the very end of the age Matthew 28;20

THE AUTHORITY OF HIS NAME

I will conclude with the same question that I asked at the beginning of this chapter – What's in a name?

> " *These signs will accompany those who believe.* **In My Name** *they will drive out demons; they will speak in new tongues...* (Mark 16;17-18)

> *Therefore God exalted Him to the highest place and* **gave Him the name that is above every name,** *that* **at the name of Jesus** *every knee should bow.*
> (Philippians 2;9-11)

Salvation is found in no one else, **for there is no other name** *under Heaven given to man by which we must be saved.* *(Acts 4;12)*

If there is anyone reading this who has not asked Jesus to be his or her Lord and Saviour, can I challenge you. **Get to know The Person behind The Name.**

What's in a name? In the case of Jesus – everything!

CHAPTER FOURTEEN

AN OPPORTUNE TIME

THIEVES carry out their deeds either in a planned or opportunist manner.

> *When the devil had finished all this tempting,* **he left Jesus until an opportune time.** *(Luke 4;13)*

Have you ever considered when those opportune times were? It is obvious that the above scripture is giving us some insight into the fact that there must have been many occasions when the devil thought that The Lord was in a vulnerable state, and tried to make use of the opportunity. Each time the devil was defeated, but he continued his relentless attempts to steal, because that is part of his nature.

In this chapter we will examine some of the other opportune times that the devil might have used. It will enable us to recognise similar situations in our own lives. If we are able to discern such times, we will be able to respond in the right manner, and thereby prevent adverse consequences.

Before we look at some of those 'opportune times' let us consider the humanity of The Lord.

> **Who, being in the very nature God...made Himself nothing,** *taking the very* **nature of a servant,** *being* **made in human likeness.** *And being*

found in appearance as a man, *He humbled himself and became obedient to death, even death on a cross!*
(*Philippians 2;6-8*)

Since God's children have flesh and blood, He too shared in their humanity *so that by His death He might destroy him who holds the power of death, that is the devil, and free those who all their lives were held in slavery by their fear of death.* (*Hebrews 2;14*)

It is sometimes difficult to comprehend that The Lord actually took on humanity, and lived a normal life in respect of eating, sleeping, working, having friends, visiting homes, getting tired, needing rest etc. He subjected Himself not only to the ordinariness of life, but also to all of the trials of everyday living. The Lord faced all of life's problems, from the minor to the major. Never let us think that we are facing an issue or problem in life that The Lord does not understand.

For our sakes He left His throne in Glory, and after being conceived in Mary by The Holy Spirit, underwent a normal delivery into the world as a baby, grew up in a family with a sister and brothers, and then entered His public ministry at the age of 30 (Mark 6;3).

During the course of the next three years, He continually lived amongst a wide range of different characters, faced fierce opposition from religious groups, but reached out with compassion to the masses. All the while the devil was looking for an opportunity to steal and injure The Lord's ministry. He faced all that we go through and much more, yet He was without sin.

Our Lord is completely in touch with the real world! In His humanity He faced all that we go through, and now

He is continually interceding for us, because He loves and understands us.

> *We do not have a High Priest who is unable to sympathise with our weaknesses, but* **we have one who has been tempted in every way, just as we are, yet was without sin.** *Let us then approach the throne of grace with confidence,* **so that we may receive mercy and find grace to help us in our time of need.**
>
> *(Hebrews 4;15-16)*

Let us now look at some examples that the devil would possibly have regarded as opportune times to steal something from The Lord. When you read the following Scriptures, try putting yourself in The Lord's place, and reflect for a moment on how you would have felt in such circumstances.

Although these Scriptures and experiences are unique to The Lord, He went through them in order that we might know Him, and also to have the sure confidence that He identifies with us in all ways. There is therefore something to learn from each incident.

DESERTION

> *Jesus said to them, "I tell you the truth, unless you can eat the flesh of The Son of Man and drink His blood you have no life in you"* ... **From this time many of His disciples turned back and no longer followed Him.**
>
> *(John 6;53 & 66)*

Jesus made this statement to a large number of His disciples who had been following Him for some time. They had witnessed miracles, and had heard Him preaching and teaching. When He sought to take His disciples a step further on, many became offended at the above statement by The Lord, and left Him.

Can you imagine what the devil would be saying to Jesus at that point? "Your disciples have deserted you – they are not real believers – they never really believed you." How would we have felt? Would it be true to say that a feeling of desertion would have flooded our thoughts? We would also have experienced rejection and failure. This would be an ideal opportunity to steal one's peace and inner security.

REJECTION

Isn't this the carpenter? *Isn't this Mary's son and the brother of James, Joseph, Judas and Simon? Aren't his sisters here with us?* **And they took offence at Him**.
(Mark 6;3)

These were the remarks made by the people of Nazareth when Jesus returned to His hometown. Imagine returning to the people who lived in the street where you grew up, or your school friends, and you wanted to just help and bless them. Upon your arrival, all you encountered were disparaging remarks.

In these circumstances I would suggest we would have felt rejected and angry and questioned whether it was worth the effort in making the trip. However, Jesus did not allow Himself to be robbed, and He continued to minister amongst them. Unfortunately, as a result of their unbelief only a few people were healed.

DISAPPOINTMENT

Let one of us sit at your right and the other at your left in your glory. *(Mark 10;37)*

James and John made this request to The Lord immediately after He had explained to them that He was going to Jerusalem where He would be put to death. The Lord had just told them of His sacrificial death, but all they could think of was the opposite, namely their self-promotion.

Have you ever spent good quality time with individuals, and given considerable care and encouragement? They then come out with a statement or attitude that leaves one thinking – Have I been wasting my time? How would we have felt if James and John had made the above remark to us? Would we have been disappointed and frustrated with their frame of mind? We might have thought – Why bother?

TEMPTATION

Many people spread their cloaks on the road, while others spread branches they had cut in the fields. Those who went ahead and those who followed shouted, "Hosanna." (Mark 11;8)

When Jesus was entering the outskirts of Jerusalem a large crowd greeted him, and they spread their cloaks on the road, and waved branches, shouting praises. It would have been quite easy to get caught up in the moment, and thought to oneself – "This is great – all the people are excited – this could be the platform for something wonderful".

This can so often happen to individuals, and churches. We can all be guilty of living for the moment, getting our fulfilment from a temporary emotional high. In the process we get robbed of our integrity. The Lord did not allow Himself to get caught up in the moment, but kept His eyes focused on The Cross.

LONELINESS

Then Jesus returned to His disciples and found them
sleeping. "Simon," He said to Peter, "Are you asleep?
Could you not keep watch for one hour?"

(Mark 14;37)

Words seem very inadequate when we try to describe what took place at Gethsemane. The Lord was going through a momentous and agonising time. Verse 33 records that He was deeply distressed and troubled. He had asked His disciples to watch and pray, for just one hour! He returned to them on three occasions, and found them asleep. Have we encountered times when friends, or possibly relations, have apparently gone to sleep on us? We had hoped for support, even a solitary hour.

Sadly, we can all be guilty of not recognising a need, even when it is staring us in the face. How would we have felt in Gethsemane if we were in The Lord's place? Would we understandably have felt alone and discouraged that our friends could not stand by us, for just a short space of time? Would you agree that this was an opportune time to be robbed of trusting others?

APPLICATION OF SCRIPTURE

Each of these occasions illustrates an opportune time that the devil could have used to steal The Lord's peace, joy, and direction in ministry. The devil does exactly the same to us in using opportune times when we appear vulnerable. He continually failed with The Lord, and he will fail with us if we understand what is happening, and go immediately to The One who fully appreciates what we are going through, and will help.

The above examples have illustrated how feelings of

desertion, frustration, rejection, anger, distraction, and discouragement could develop. We may have encountered such feelings. The Lord, in His wonderful grace and love for us, went through the same trials in life, but did not sin.

Scripture is very clear on how we are to deal with such circumstances. You will recall that we looked at this subject in chapters eleven and twelve.

We take captive every thought *to make it obedient to Christ.*   *(2 Corinthians 10;5)*

Be transformed *by the renewing of your mind.*
                                                    (Romans 12;2)

When we encounter similar circumstances in life, and feel such emotions, we have a choice to make. Do we let negative thoughts and feelings take root, or do we follow Scriptual guidance in how to deal with such situations?

In your anger do not sin. Do not let the sun go down while you are still angry.   *(Ephesians 4;26)*

Hebrews 4;15-16 describes The Lord as our High Priest who went through all that we encounter, but was without sin. This Scriptures reveals that our Lord experienced all manner of things on our behalf, and overcame them all without sinning. At salvation He took up residence in us by His Spirit, and in so doing we have access to His mind so that we need not sin when faced with life's problems.

We have the mind of Christ.   *(1 Corinthians 2;16)*

Daily living produces opportunities of rich pickings for the thief, but also opportune times to give life, and to the full. We have looked at the negative side of an opportune time. Let us now look at some examples of how The Lord used opportune times to positive effect, by either stirring people into action or revealing a truth.

The thief comes only to steal and kill and destroy; I have come that they may have life, and have it to the full.
(John 10;10)

HARVESTIME

Then Jesus said to His disciples, "The harvest is plenti-ful but the workers are few. Ask The Lord of the harvest therefore, to send out workers into His harvest field".
(Matthew 9;37-38)

The verses immediately before this scripture describe how The Lord went through towns and villages preaching, teaching and healing. Can you picture the scene? The disciples had seen the needs of the people and had also seen how The Lord met them. They then heard His request for workers. What was going through their minds at that time? Were they feeling safe seeing The Lord take the reins, and being content to be part of the experience with no responsibility? Or did they rise to His challenge and respond as the prophet Isaiah.

Then I heard the voice of The Lord saying, "Whom shall I send? And who will go for us?" And I said, **"Here am I. Send me**.*"* *(Isaiah 6;8)*

Immediately after Jesus challenge, the following chapter of Matthew begins with The Lord giving His twelve disciples authority to drive out demons and heal the sick. He then sends them out into the towns and villages. He had used an opportune time to use the illustration of the harvest to first challenge them, and also to show them what they could achieve when empowered by Him. The devil seeks to rob us of initiative, but The Lord creates vision and zeal.

INDIVIDUAL CHALLENGE

Large crowds were travelling with Jesus, and turning to them He said, "... Anyone who does not carry his cross and follow Me cannot be My disciple".

(Luke 14;25 & 27)

When you are in a crowd and mighty things are happening it is all too easy to be caught up in the excitement and fervour that a large gathering can generate. It is possible to hide in a crowd, and avoid facing difficult issues in one's own life.

Stories about good things that are happening in churches, different countries, or individual lives are encouraging and important to hear. But we cannot live off the testimonies of others. Jesus took this opportune moment to put everything in perspective, and speak directly to the individual, to take up their cross.

HUMILITY

*Jesus said to His disciples, "I tell you the truth, **unless you change** and become like little children, you will never enter The Kingdom of Heaven".*

(Matthew 18;3)

The disciples had asked Jesus who was the greatest in the Kingdom of Heaven? It would appear that the disciples were concerned about position and status. This was an ongoing issue. The Lord saw a child nearby, and called him over in order to illustrate humility. Notice the words used by Jesus, *'unless you change'*. The presence of the child provided an opportune moment to bring home a truth to the disciples.

There are opportune times in life where we can encourage, exhort and teach one another. The Lord showed us by example that it is achieved in a humble manner and always seeking good for the other person. The devil seeks an opportune time to steal and take away. **The Lord seeks an opportune time to transform and give.**

Make the most of every opportunity.

(Ephesians 5;16)

CHAPTER FIFTEEN

LITTLE FOXES

Catch for us the foxes, **the little foxes that ruin the vineyards,** *our vineyards that are in bloom.*
(*Song of Songs 2;15*)

WHAT DO YOU associate with the words 'major crime'? I would venture to say that the average person would say such things as murder, rape, bank robbery, serious wounding, drug trafficking, and company fraud. These are the types of offences that we read as headlines in our newspapers. The reality of life is that although these incidents occur every day, most people do not directly encounter them.

The crimes that mainly affect us are small-scale burglaries, thefts, and damage. They are classed as 'petty crimes'. They are the most prolific, and consequently have a demoralising affect on neighbourhoods, and places of work. These petty crimes are the same as the *little foxes* that are referred to in the above passage of Scripture. Although the foxes are small in size, they are still able to destroy on a large scale.

Picture the scene of a vineyard in bloom as in The Song of Songs. Then visualise it decimated, and bereft of fruit. It is caused by a number of little foxes that invade, and spoil the crop. **It is the small repetitive theft that quite often has the most devastating effect.**

What affects you most on a daily basis? What invades your thought life, and robs your mental peace and joy? Is it the large issue, or a combination of seemingly minor ones?

We all have to face major things at some point in our lives, such as the death of a parent or close friend, personal injury or sickness, loss of job, car crash etc. Although they are serious and distressing, we manage to summon up the fortitude and strength to face these events, and in the fullness of time we get through them. These occurrences have a temporary effect.

Although we will remember them throughout our life, their impact will have a diminishing effect as time proceeds. It is the repetitive small issues that occur on a daily basis that can so often have the most impact on our peace and well being.

Would you agree that the subject that can cause the most problem in people's lives is that of relationships? Television has its 'agony aunts', and newspapers-magazines have their 'problem pages'. The feelings of hurt, resentment, and frustration etc are quite often the little foxes that plunder our peace and joy.

QUESTIONS OR ANSWERS

Many people experience theft in the area of relationships. It appears that their peace of mind, and happiness, and fulfilment are robbed right in front of their eyes. They ask themselves – How did I let this happen? Why do I feel this way after all the time and effort I put into our friendship? How is it that our intimacy has not deepened? Why is there so little understanding between us? Am I wasting my time?

Relationships cause many questions to be asked. It is one of the causes of mental and emotional turmoil. But there is an answer.

In order to understand the working out of relationships, it is first necessary to have a clear understanding of our own make-up. If we want to live a balanced, healthy and fulfilled life with others, we need to ensure that we are in the right relationship inside ourselves. Is our spirit and soul in harmony, or is there conflict? If we are not at peace, how can we be at peace with others?

Take a few moments to think of any little foxes that are present in your life. Those small, yet destructive areas of our lives that rob your joy, and take up too many of your thoughts. Would you agree that in the majority of cases it will probably concern relationships, and our interaction with one another.

Notice that Song of Songs 2;15 informs us that the vineyards are in bloom. That is what God's heart is for us in all areas of our life, including relationships. He wants to see our friendships in bloom, producing fruit, in enjoyment and effectiveness. In the next chapter we shall look at some of the key elements in the success of relationships.

But before doing so it is important to say that the people themselves are not the little foxes. It is the emotions that are entangled, and spill out from our interaction with one another that causes the problems. The goal is therefore to prevent the little foxes from entering our vineyard and ruining the crops.

Prevention is the key.

CHAPTER SIXTEEN

INTER-PERSONAL RELATIONSHIPS

CONSIDER for one moment how much time in your life that have you spent trying to work out what has gone wrong with relationships with others, whether they are your married partner, relatives, girlfriend-boyfriend, or friends in general? If that amount of time were to be added up, it would be considerable. That time has been robbed. Is there an answer to this problem, and can further loss be prevented?

It is widely accepted that there are five levels of communication.

1) **Casual-cliche** e.g. "Hi" – "Good to see you" – "Have a good day."

2) **Informative-reporting facts** e.g. "We sold our house" – " I am changing my job." "We are having another baby" – "We are going on holiday to Spain."

3) **Sharing ideas-judgements-opinions-convictions** e.g. "The government should lower interest rates" – "Our church should get a bigger building."– "Our council is ineffective."

4) **Sharing emotions, feelings** e.g. "That message caused me to look afresh at my prayer life" – "I am looking for a new direction in life."– "My family is facing a real crisis."

5) **Intimate-honest-transparent** e.g. Nothing hidden from each other.

Take a few moments to study this list, then look at your relationships, and compare them with the above points. You will discover that as you head for number 5 the amount of friendships in each category will continue to diminish, until you reach the fifth and last section, which will contain only a few.

Psychologists of today believe that the maximum amount of people with whom you can have a close and intimate relationship is twelve. The Lord Jesus showed them this 2000 years ago with the amount of disciples He gathered around Him. Let us therefore consider what Scripture records about the numbers of people who were in varying degrees of close contact with Jesus.

FORMING FRIENDSHIPS

When He began to preach He soon gathered a number of disciples. Luke 6;12-16 records that after a while, Jesus prayed about this group with regard to whom He would designate as Apostles. He chose **twelve**. He spent the most time with these individuals, teaching the deep things of The Kingdom of God, and revealing Himself. Out of that **twelve** He took only **three** on particularly intimate occasions, such as His Transfiguration. These were Peter, James, and John.

Later on in His ministry, Luke 10;1 records how Jesus appointed **72** others to go ahead of Him into the towns and places He was to visit. He would not have appointed such people without first knowing them. Following His ascension, Acts 1 & 2 record that there were **120** believers gathered together for prayer, and were present on the day of Pentecost. These were probably the most committed, and had been with Him for some time.

Do you see the picture that is emerging? Jesus was showing us, in His humanity, that there are a wide number of people within the scope of friendship, but only a few will develop into a relationship of intimacy. I believe that when He was on earth He gave us a pattern to follow in the way that we are to relate to others.

His love for everyone was the same, just as it is now. However, He showed us that it is physically impossible to have an intimate relationship with a large amount of people, because the degree of intimacy with others is closely linked to availability of time, which as we know, is a precious commodity.

TIME RESTRAINTS

Now take another look at your relationships, and compare them with the manner in which Jesus went about his everyday living. We all yearn for intimate friendships, but The Lord revealed to us that it is only physically possible with a small number. Just think how much time it would have taken if He had spent an equal amount with the 120. Is there a lesson to be learnt from this? Are there any pointers to indicate that a friendship will develop into one of intimacy?

If you examine the most intimate of your friendships you will probably discover that they are the closest to you in spirit, soul, and body. It is also important to say that you may have that closeness with friends in only one or two of those areas of spirit, soul and body, which is perfectly fine. But the amount of relationships that fulfil all of the aspects of spirit, soul, and body, will be few.

Let us then take a realistic look at relationships, and hopefully come to an understanding of how to avoid the heartbreak, and misunderstanding that they so often bring.

At the risk of repeating myself I would suggest that it is in the area of inter-personal relationships that most people suffer anguish, and disappointment. If we allow feelings of disappointment, anger, and bitterness to prevail, they will subsequently take root in our heart. In doing so we have left the front door wide open, and the thief can walk straight in and rob us of our peace and joy, and many other things.

What are the basic ingredients of relationships? How do we get the most out of them? As we look at these, try and keep the communication list at the beginning of this chapter at the forefront of your mind.

Before going any further it is important for me to say that when I refer to intimacy in this chapter, I am obviously not referring to anything sexual, as this should only be in the confines of marriage.

SOCIAL FRIENDSHIP

Dealing first with our **body**, make a mental note of those friends with whom you share a love of the same activities, whether it is sport, cultural, or social. Those people with whom you would watch a football match, go to a music concert, visit a museum, attend computer courses, play sport, go jogging, a walk in the woods, or your children play together etc. You may also go out for meals or a drink and have a pleasurable time together, or even a lively discussion on sport, politics, religion or current affairs.

You have a shared passion for the same things, and you enjoy it together, or in a group. You value each other's company for the time you are together. Many relationships develop from this initial stage.

For some, this may be as far as it goes. When you are together the only thing you have in common is the shared interest. You may have made attempts to develop the relationship further, but somehow it just never gets to any depth, and you end up only talking about the one thing you have in common, or a few surrounding topics. It is safe ground, which is predictable and routine. This often occurs with work colleagues.

As time goes on you never get much further than discussing the usual topics of conversation, family events, holidays, or perhaps a general discussion on church activities. The conversation may broaden, but it still stays very much on the surface. It does not deepen, even after many times together. Do you have Christian friends who talk about Christian issues, but do not share directly about the Lord? Referring back to the list of the different levels of communication, it is probable that these sorts of relationships do not develop further than level three.

What do you think is at risk here? There is the danger that the friendship simply drifts apart, and you end up losing contact with friends that you would still like to share your common interest. Both parties can feel condemned. Could it have been prevented?

The answer is to be honest. If you know that your friendship cannot progress much further than your shared activity or general friendship, then be prepared to be honest with yourself, and possibly them. The alternative is to be robbed of precious time. True friendships cannot progress much if they are based on an attitude of 'going through the motions'.

It is important to say that all friendships are to be valued, irrespective of the depth of the relationship. What I am endeavouring to portray is the nature of our everyday interaction with one another, and how we can have truly fulfilling friendships on different levels, and make the best use of limited time.

SOUL MATE

We will next consider our **soul**, which as we have seen comprises our mind, emotions, heart, conscience, will and intellect. Bring to mind those relationships with which you find it easy to bounce off, have a shared sense of humour, think in a similar manner, and also have common purposes and aims. Even when you disagree on a subject there is a mutual respect and appreciation of the other person's point of view. Undoubtedly, there are some people that stimulate you in perhaps just one area, while others may fulfil on a wide plain.

We have all heard the term 'soul mate'. These are the people that you can so readily share feelings and emotions, and who respond to you in like manner. They give you great pleasure. You readily telephone them, always look forward to meeting together, or call at their home at any time without the need to first telephone or make an arrangement.

These are the sort of relationships that have reached level four on the list of communication, whereby you stimulate one another in spirit, mind, emotions, and intellect. Some of them will also progress to number five, where you are in full harmony of expression.

Although these sorts of relationships provide real companionship, they also render you vulnerable, because you share your emotions and feelings, and even real intimacy.

Can you see the potential for problems? Because you expose yourself, there is the danger of the other person(s) taking advantage of you, not responding in the desired manner, or possibly revealing a confidence to someone else. Many people have been emotionally injured by such things, and resort never to open themselves up to anyone else. They decide to keep friendships purely on the first three levels of communication. They regard this as their self defence mechanism.

Joseph Newton described what could happen in such circumstances, when he said, "People are lonely because they build walls instead of bridges".

What do you think has been robbed? Certainly their mental peace, trust, and confidence in both themselves and others. Some people who have been hurt this way by an apparent soul mate, believe that by retreating into themselves they will prevent further loss. Unfortunately, the opposite is true. By not understanding what has happened in one's soul, and not allowing it to be restored, the person allows resentment and bitterness to fester. They believe that they have closed the door to further theft, whereas they have actually opened the door for the thief to further plunder.

If anyone has experienced such a time, it may be helpful to refer back to chapter nine, which dealt with the restoration of the soul.

INTIMACY

Lastly, we will consider our **spirit**, which is our inner being. With how many friends do you have real harmony in spiritual matters, and with whom you are transparent? The soul mate has moved onto an even higher level.

The friendships with whom you continually feel akin. There is no need for prolonged time together before you reach intimacy of thought and expression. Whether in conversation, or prayer, there is a oneness of spirit, and when you part company you know that you have been blessed. The sort of relationship that remains sharp.

As iron sharpens iron, so one man sharpens another.
(Proverbs 27;17)

We may have many friendships that encourage us, and we may even view some as being very close confidantes. But how many have reached that stage of real intimacy? I would venture to say that these sorts of friends are very few in number. One of the reasons for this is that, just like our body and soul relationships, they all require time, which is in short supply.

Look back at the list at the beginning of the chapter that contains the different levels of communication. Now reconsider those friendships that you regard as the closest and most intimate. I am sure you will discover that they are the ones which fulfil you the most in spirit, soul, and body.

There are some relationships that are intimate purely in the spirit, while others may be a mixture of soul and spirit, or just body and soul, or other combinations. However, the closest friends are usually those who we regard as intimate in body, soul, and spirit. The ones who are constantly in categories four and five on the aforementioned communication list.

MARRIAGE

Permit me to speak to single people at this point. May I suggest that before you enter a serious relationship, or contemplate engagement, think carefully about your partner in respect of spirit, soul and body. How close are you in these separate areas? In respect of body – Do you generally enjoy the same things, or at least get pleasure from joint activities? With regard to your soul – Do you have a similar sense of humour, vision, and outlook, and the ability to communicate on most matters? Do you regard them as a true soul mate? Lastly, in respect of your spirit – Do you stimulate, and have an affinity on spiritual matters?

This does not involve seeking someone who is a cardboard cut-out of yourself, or indeed to only marry a person with the same nature. In fact, the different types of personality and character can contribute to a successful marriage, as they blend together to form a rich mixture. But the most successful marriages are usually the ones where the husband and wife are real soul mates. They instinctively identify and share with one another on most matters. The lines come in to together, as opposed to running parallel, or away from one another.

These are just a few avenues to explore before you make a decision to commit the rest of your life to someone. I do not mean that you should look for perfection, nor have a tick list. You must be in love to begin with. The key is to have a oneness as you grow together, while at the same time appreciate and respect the other person's individuality.

Unfortunately, one of the reasons for the breakdown of Christian marriages is that they were never suited from the beginning in spirit, soul and body. They loved each other and had a good friendship, but there was not the capacity for individual, and collective growth, or stimulation. In these situations, one outgrows the other, or they simply grow apart. The devil is out to destroy marriages. Why provide him with ammunition?

LEVELS OF FRIENDSHIP

Once we understand that our spirit, soul, and body are continually at work, then we will pay closer attention to the function of each, both in respect of our own self, and in our relationship to others. We will then develop a better understanding of how to develop those relationships that will satisfy our desire for intimacy, and an acceptance of friendships that are meant to remain just general. If we have the awareness and maturity to be realistic in this area we will both give, and receive fulfilment.

I am not suggesting that you make a list of your friends and categorise them. This type of action can be somewhat calculating, and can also have a negative effect, because friendships can fluctuate, and go through different seasons. A closeness can suddenly blossom with people that you have known loosely for years. I am therefore not trying to propose a rigid structure to relationships, merely an awareness of how we function together.

The fact that some friendships only reach a certain stage, and do not deepen, does not mean that either party has failed. It possibly means that it was never meant to go any further. The devil continually seeks to condemn, and make us attach blame to others or ourselves. The Lord wants us to live in freedom, having the peace and joy to appreciate one another, irrespective of the depth of friendship. As I mentioned earlier in the chapter, in His humanity He gave us an example to follow.

With regard to close relationships, an area of selfishness to avoid is becoming a clique with our intimate friends, to the exclusion of others. Relationships that become self-indulgent invariably stagnate, because by their introverted attitude they have sown the seeds of self-destruction. The devil wants us to live according to the flesh, because it provides rich feeding grounds for selfishness. But The Lord wants us to live according to The Spirit, which means life creating and flowing. These sorts of relationships are living, vibrant, and healthy. The fruit from their intimacy is reflected in their relationships with others.

Healthy relationships do not retreat behind the walls

of a castle, and become impenetrable. They leave the drawbridge down in order that access can be gained.

HOSPITALITY

Having discussed the value of intimate friendships, there is another aspect of relationship that is important to foster. It is the privilege of hospitality. Some people have an obvious gift in this area, whereas others find it more difficult. One thing, though, is for certain. If we view it as a burden we will be robbed of blessing.

> **Offer hospitality** *to one another* **without grumbling**.   *(1 Peter 4;9)*

> *Share with God's people who are in need*. **Practice hospitality**.   *(Romans 12;13)*

These include people with whom we may feel that we have very little in common, and we believe will not develop any further than simple friendships. There can also be certain aspects of their behaviour and character with which we feel ill at ease. However, this ought not to prevent us from showing them hospitality.

By mixing together, we help fulfil one of the functions of the body of Christ. If we neglect such an opportunity the devil merely succeeds in creating a selfish heart. The desire not to get involved with anyone else, or the fear of someone getting attached to us, should not be the determining factor regarding hospitality.

My brother-in-law, Jimmie, once told me these wise words. "There are only two things that we take with us from this planet – The Word of God, and people." Just think, we can take people (who we have seen born again) into eternity.

FAMILY

One area of relationships that continually causes problems is that of relatives. There is the mistaken belief that the family bloodline is a magical formula that creates an idyllic environment of peace and harmony. We are all familiar with the expression; 'blood is thicker than water'. This statement is meant to be the driving force that keeps families together, irrespective of any ill-matched personalities, different goals and ambition or obvious lack of cohesion between family members.

The only blood that effectively binds people together is The Blood of Christ Jesus. Simply belonging to the same earthly bloodline, or even having an extended family through marriage, is not enough. This is not meant in any way to devalue the importance of being in strong and united families, which is pivotal to the stability of society. But, I would suggest that it is only under The Lordship of Christ that relationships really reach their full potential.

The reason being is that His Blood covers all our sins, and His Grace enables us to forgive and accept one another under a covenant agreement. We are saved and joined together because of His Blood, and His Word gives us direction in how we can live together as His family in a unique way. This is not meant to sound elitist. It ought to encourage us even more to see all our family saved, so that we are together for eternity.

One day, when Jesus was talking to a gathered crowd, His mother and brothers came to visit Him, and wanted to speak. One of the people informed Him of their arrival and He gave the following response.

"Who is My mother, and who are my brothers?" Pointing to His disciples, He said, " Here are my moth-

er and my brothers. **For whoever does the will of my Father in Heaven is My brother and sister and mother."** *(Matthew 12;46-50)*

The Lord obviously did not say this to offend His earthly family. He did not seek to diminish the importance of family life, nor to make it look as if He was rejecting them in favour of others. He was simply telling all those who were present that the closest bond of all is the Heavenly family. We are joined together as part of one body; and we have the same Spirit at work in our lives. We have the same bloodline because of The Lord's sacrifice, and we are with one another for eternity.

This is one of the reasons why it is unwise for a Christian to marry an unbeliever. It is not simply the practical issues of going to church, different friendships, or how the children are brought up. It is all to do with our whole approach to matters in general. The governing desire in a Christian's life is – **Thy will be done on earth as it is in Heaven.**

YOKED TOGETHER

A yoke is a crossbar with two U-shaped pieces that encircle the necks of a pair of animals working in a team. We have taken The Lord's yoke upon ourselves, and we are joined together, working as a team. When anyone is saved, irrespective of whatever church they attend, they come under the same yoke.

Jesus encourages us to take His yoke upon us, and in so doing we will find rest for our souls. (Matthew 11;29-30). Paul warns the Corinthian church not to be yoked to unbelievers. (2 Corinthians 6;14-16). We can therefore see from these two passages that the yoking (connecting-

joining together) of Christians is unique. This does not mean that we become inward looking or a clique in any way.

Unfortunately, some sections of the church have used the term unequally yoked to justify a separation from the remainder of the body, or an excuse not to mix with the world. This is a clear distortion of Scripture. Just before The Lord was crucified, He prayed that all believers in Him would be in complete unity as a witness to the world. (John 17;23). We may be in different teams as regards different fellowships, but it is the same yoke that is upon us. He also showed us the necessity of going into all sections of society, and befriending all types. That is part of His yoke.

Therefore, if we say that we have taken His yoke upon us, it will become evident in how we view other fellowships and believers, and how we mix with the world to reach them for The Lord.

Being yoked together means that we are going in the same direction. The term unequally yoked therefore means that you have a different focus and want to head in different directions.

This explains how a Christian and an unbeliever can only go so far together before there inevitably follows a pulling towards separate ways. This does not mean that there must be a severing of the relationship. It simply means that their involvement together can only go so far. We are obviously meant to have close relationships with friends and family who are unbelievers. But although they can be rewarding and the people greatly loved, they do not have the potential distance that a Christian relationship can travel. There is that something between believers that cannot be put into words.

The outworking of unity and love, as contained in 1 Corinthians 12;12-27 & 1 Corinthians 13;1-13 is only fully appreciated within the Body of Christ. There can be great companionship, love and compassion with friends and family members who are not yet Christians. But there is a forgiveness, grace and love that The Lord gives, which is higher than anything natural.

CHRISTIAN FAMILIES

Even within families that are predominantly Christian, relationships do not always flourish and can even be unfulfilling at times. We have our faith in common, but unfortunately not much more. This can sometimes lead to self-condemnation, because we feel guilty about the fact that we do not consider these family members as real soul mates. Although we may be part of the same family, and also joined together in The Lord as part of His Body, we just do not have real intimacy with one another, irrespective of how often we meet together.

The reality of the situation, as we have seen earlier in the chapter, is that the people we regard as true soul-mates are those to whom we are the closest in spirit, and soul. We usually only reach real intimacy with those who fulfil these factors. Being of the same natural or even spiritual family cannot of themselves create intimate friendships. We all know that well known saying – 'you cannot chose your relatives, but fortunately you can chose your friends'.

I want to make it clear that I am not attempting to downgrade, or lessen the importance of family life. I regard it as pivotal to society. I have merely been trying to illustrate another aspect of spirit, soul and body and how it affects our everyday lives. In addition to which, I have attempted to hopefully bring relief to some of those people who suffer guilt as a result of poor family relationships, and cannot understand how they just seem to remain on one plateau, not progressing.

I would say, however, that if one finds those special soul mates within a family setting it is a wonderful blessing. But if this is not the case, and we have done all that is possible, then we need to accept the fact and not be robbed of our peace.

SUMMARY

Most of our days surround relationships. The positive and negative effects of these relationships occupy a part of our thought life. If we can take a candid approach to these relationships, and realise what is happening, we eliminate the risk of frustration, and hurts, and wasted time. I once heard a preacher say that spiritual meat for a Christian is the working out of relationships according to God's Word.

We need to be balanced in our approach to friendships by examining The Lord's example. He had twelve very close friends, and out of that number there were three with whom He most intimately shared. He also had close friends such as Lazarus and his sisters Mary and Martha. There was then a wide circle of others to whom He came in varying degrees of contact.

You will appreciate that I am not suggesting that we are to keep to these exact figures. I am merely suggesting that The Lord has given them as a guide, so that we are aware of what is possible in conjunction with time, and what will ultimately prove to be fruitful.

He knew that there were time restraints. Take for example the healing of the demon-possessed man in Mark 5. After his deliverance he asked to accompany Jesus, but He told the man to return to his family. The Gospels only give us a brief outline of the miracles performed by The Lord.

> *Jesus did many other things as well.* **If every one of them were written down**, *I suppose that even* **the whole world would not have room** *for the books that would be written.* (*John 21;25*)

Can you picture the scene? Imagine if even a small proportion of this number stayed with Jesus as He travelled. They would, quite naturally, want to be as near Him as possible. However, He knew the task that was before Him, and also the need to impart teaching about the Kingdom of God into the twelve disciples, who would then teach others after He had risen. Some people might have been offended, but Jesus used all His time wisely, and in so doing fulfilled His work and completed His task.

He loves and accepts everyone the same, but He took on humanity for our sakes, and thereby subjected himself to the physical restraints of time, and what was humanly possible to achieve with relationships.

Perhaps this would be an opportune time to re-evaluate our relationships, and realign them in the light of how Jesus lived on earth.

CHAPTER SEVENTEEN

FORMER THINGS

MOST OF US know, and can identify with the saying, 'procrastination is the thief of time'. While this is true, I believe that there is another thief of time, of which we all can be guilty at varying times in our lives. It is dwelling on the past.

We can be robbed of fulfilment in the present, because we are bound up with regrets from the past.

Missed opportunities, and past mistakes can plunder our peace and joy in the present, and future, if we allow it to happen. Just imagine for one moment if we kept a yearly total of the amount of time we wasted on dwelling on past issues, whether they are of our own making, or caused by others. The figure would astound us. Our time is stolen from right under our noses. Worse still, we are active participants in the theft. Is there a way of preventing this crime from taking place?

The Lord God, speaking through the Prophet Isaiah, had these very straightforward words for the people of Israel – He warned them of the futility of dwelling on the past.

Forget the former things: do not dwell on the past. *See, I am doing a new thing! (Isaiah 43;18-19)*

It is important to say at this point that I am not suggesting that we ignore unresolved issues, or sins, and simply skim over areas that need addressing. These are distinctly separate matters, and should not be confused with the issue under examination.

There is no doubt that the Apostle Paul achieved a phenomenal amount, whether it be in establishing churches, teaching and training, writing, or in the general care for the early church. He faced many trials, and endured many hardships, as described in 2 Corinthians 11. Try and place yourself in his shoes. What do you think was the content of his daily thought pattern? Do you think he dwelt on his past life before he met The Lord, or the mistakes he may have made after his conversion?

In addition to which, imagine the challenges of meeting thousands of people on his missionary journeys. The early church contained the same sort of personalities you find today. Human nature has not changed. He no doubt encountered 'the good, the bad, and the ugly', to quote a well-known phrase. Scripture records a number of examples of Paul's ill treatment at the hands of others. In these sorts of circumstances how do you retain peace of mind, and the zeal to continue? This is the advice that Paul wrote to the Philippian church.

One thing I do: forgetting what is behind and straining towards what is ahead, *I press on towards the goal to win the prize for which God has called me Heavenwards in Christ Jesus.* (*Philippians 3;13-14*)

Paul was no different from us. He had the same mind, emotions, and feelings like us, but he had also taught himself to forget anything that would impede his moving forwards. He had brought his soul in line with his spirit.

RELIANCE ON PAST BLESSINGS

Do you encounter people who are locked into tradition, and continually reminisce about former days? Although they may have been good days, it is not wise to continually compare, and remember such times in an attitude that breeds despair about the present or future. Solomon had a clear word of warning concerning such talk.

> *Do not say, "Why were the old days better than these?"* **For it is not wise to ask such questions.**
> *(Ecclesiastes 7;10)*

The danger of such words is that they imply that God was more faithful, powerful, gracious, and loving, in the past. This could not be further from the truth, as we know with certainty that He is the same yesterday, today, and forever. It is a wise policy to guard our attitudes and words. It is criminal to be robbed of blessing in the present because we are locked into the past, even though they were good times. Memories of the past will not see us through the present, or future.

A NEW DAY

By way of personal testimony, I still occasionally struggle with the fact that I completed 28 years service, instead of 30, although it is now six years after the event. Whenever I happen to meet former colleagues who have completed thirty years, I sometimes experience feelings of inadequacy and failure, during and after I leave their company. Although they never bring the subject up in conversation, it comes to the forefront of my mind.

It is a battle, but slowly and surely my mind is being renewed in this area. I may have failed, but I know that God does not see me as a failure. In addition to which, in the realms of eternity it is of no consequence that I was unable to complete my thirty years service. There is a need to keep things in perspective, forget what is behind, and get on with the rest of my life.

The Israelite nation had seen its fair share of troubled times. It had endured many conflicts, and had experienced the consequences of rebellion. Thankfully, our Heavenly Father is full of grace and forgiveness, and will always restore. He is the same God today. He is willing and able to forget our rebellion, mistakes, and troubles of the past, and will create something new.

> **For the past troubles will be forgotten** *and hidden from My eyes...* **The former things will not be remembered, nor will they come to mind**. *But be glad and rejoice forever in what I will create.*
>
> *(Isaiah 65;16-18)*

Therefore, let us take hold of His words. If we have truly repented and done everything possible to resolve an issue and put our past troubles behind us, it serves no point in bringing them back into the foreground. Although many fleeting thoughts go through our minds each day, to dwell on something or even occasionally remember an incident is a direct act of our will. We make a conscious decision. We therefore have a choice in the matter, as we saw in chapters eleven and twelve.

GOOD MEMORIES

The question arises – Are we meant to completely forget all that has taken place in the past? Quite the contrary. Joshua 4 records how Joshua instructed the Israelites to place twelve stones on the banks of the Jordan as a memorial to their crossing of the river, and entering the

Promised Land. They were to be a sign not only to those who crossed, but also for future generations that would ask their meaning. Joshua was aware of how a testimony from the past has relevance in the present, and future.

Paul wrote these words to the Philippian Church.

> *Whatever is* **true**, *whatever is* **noble**, *whatever is* **love-ly**, *whatever is* **admirable** – *if anything is* **excellent** *or* **praiseworthy** – **think about such things**.
>
> *(Philippians 4;8)*

These are the sort of things that are good to remember. They will not only engender zeal and determination, but they will also keep our mind at peace. We discover that the purpose of remembering past blessings is not just to have good memories, or for them to be used as a crutch to help you through the present time. They are part of the process of having our mind renewed, by meditating upon the ways in which God reveals Himself.

> **Remember the former things**, *those of long ago; I am God, and there is no other;* **I am God and there is none like Me**. *I say:* **My purpose will stand.**
>
> *(Isaiah 46;9-10)*

God was encouraging the Israelites to remember what had happened in the past, when He revealed Himself to them, and in so doing they saw that there was no other God besides Him, and that His purpose continued. He has not changed. Therefore, when we remember former things, let them be God-centred by seeing how His will has come to pass, and rejoice in the fact that He has included us in His plans and purposes. Our thoughts will then be productive, and we will not be robbed of precious time.

The former things will then add to the present, and not take away.

CHAPTER EIGHTEEN

PREVENTIVE MEDICINE

ONE OF THE NAMES of God in The Old Testament is Jehovah Rophe, which means '*the LORD who heals*'. (Exodus 15;22-26). Jesus fulfilled this title in The New Testament, when He was crucified for both our sins and sicknesses on The Cross.

> **He Himself bore our sins** *in His body on the tree, so that we might die to sins and live for righteousness;* **by His wounds you have been healed**. *(1 Peter 2;24)*

The issue of our healing is therefore settled once and for all. But what do you think is the better way of living – being healed from sickness, or remaining in health so that we do not get sick? Can ill health be prevented?

Doctors believe that the majority of sicknesses are psychosomatic, meaning that there is a link between the psychological (mind and emotions) and the physiological (body organs and functions). This means that our mental and emotional well being can have a direct effect upon our physical health, and vice-versa. It is a known fact that when we are worried, stressed, angry, or emotionally drained we create harmful juices in our body, which affect our organs and joints.

We saw earlier that our mind and emotions are composites of our soul. It therefore follows that the state of our soul can have a positive or negative impact upon our general health. This again illustrates the importance of getting our minds and emotions renewed according to The Word of God.

Just imagine the consequence for the Health Service if everyone paid attention to his or her soul. The doctors' surgeries and hospitals would be greatly reduced in numbers, and the financial resources could be diverted to solving other problems such as poverty in under-developed countries.

TEMPLE OF THE HOLY SPIRIT

The Lord also encourages us to respect our body because it is The Temple of The Holy Spirit. We are not supposed to abuse it. For example, if our diet consists of greasy food, which is high in fat and sugar, and we fail to take any exercise, can we complain if they cause an ulcer or heart disease? The best illustration is smoking. There is countless scientific proof about its harmful effects, and yet even some Christians continue with this habit.

Our Lord by His Grace will forgive us, and can heal us of the sicknesses that result from this harmful living. But I am sure that He would prefer that we obey His laws and the guidance in His Word, so that we prevent ill health developing in the first place.

It is also evident that there are occasions when we are afflicted by sickness, which entered the world as a result of Adam's fall. There is no doubt that the devil wants to bring harm to us as he seeks to steal, kill and destroy.

But I believe that we need to be wise and honest in this

whole area of ill health. How much of sickness is caused by the devil being actively present? Would you agree that quite a percentage of it is self-inflicted by our lifestyles? In some cases we do not need to call upon The Lord for His healing, or spend time rebuking the devil for bringing sickness upon us. We simply need to change our style of living. By having discernment in this matter we will save ourselves unnecessary grief.

The following verse is all about preventive action on our part.

> *The Lord said,* **"If you listen carefully to the voice of The Lord your God and do what is right** *in His eyes, if you pay attention to His commands and keep all His decrees, I will not bring on you any of the diseases I brought on the Egyptians, for I am The Lord, who heals you".*   *Exodus 15;26*

If we step outside of His ways and commands we essentially write our own sick-note.

CHAPTER NINETEEN

POSTCODING

THE POLICE continually encourage the public to post-code their possessions with their individual address as a crime prevention measure. This involves marking the property with the postcode and number of the house. It is a unique mark, so that no one else can claim legitimate possession. It is a seal of ownership.

When bicycles are postcoded, a hammer is used to imprint lettering onto the base of the frame. There is one point safe enough to withstand the blows from the hammer and metal lettering stamp.

I heard of one officer who was somewhat unfamiliar with the strengths and weaknesses of a bicycle's frame. He was also unaware of the force of his hammer blows. A young boy proudly presented his new bicycle to the officer to be postcoded. Unfortunately, the officer decided to postcode the centre frame, and reigned down a severe blow with the hammer. The bicycle buckled, and the boy left the station in tears. Appropriate action was taken.

God has put His seal of ownership on us, but He does not buckle or strain us in the process. He takes great delight in us, and it ends in joy not tears. We have been purchased with a price, which was The Lord's sacrificial death. In addition to which, the purchase comes with a guarantee.

Not only for this life, but also for eternity. **We have God's identification upon us, and we have the certainty that He will never relinquish ownership.**

> *He anointed us,* **set His seal of ownership on us,** *and put His Spirit in our hearts as a deposit,* **guaranteeing what is to come.** *(2 Corinthians 1;21-22)*

POSTCODE IN HEAVEN

We have been given a postcode that has Heaven as the address. It is not simply for the future, but also for the present. Therefore, we can look down on any situation from above in His authority, as opposed to looking up at problems and seeing them as giants.

> *And God raised us up with Christ and* **seated us with Him in the Heavenly realms** *in Christ Jesus.*
> *(Ephesians 2;6)*

We have a postcode with Heaven as the address; coupled with the fact that no one can snatch us out of His hand. On top of all that, He has given us an inheritance both now and in eternity. He also gives us His Spirit as a guarantee of our inheritance in Him. Who is entitled to claim an inheritance? Those who are heirs.

> **The Holy Spirit Himself testifies** *with our spirit that* **we are God's children.** *Now if we are children, then* **we are heirs – heirs of God and co-heirs with Christ.** *(Romans 8;16-17)*

When someone dies, an inheritance is left. But the person who is entitled to the inheritance has to do something. They have to take action. Although it is rightfully theirs, they still have to claim it. It is the same in the spiritual realm.

Through faith and patience we inherit *what has been promised.* *(Hebrews 6;12)*

Hebrews 11;1 states that *'faith is'* – meaning that it is present tense. Faith is always ready for the here and now. However, not all things come at once. That is why we are encouraged to have patience as well as faith. There is therefore a balance created. Faith for the present, but also patience so that we have hope for the future.

The full measure of our inheritance in Him will be fully realised when we meet The Lord in eternity. But He has already given part of that inheritance to us now. We can therefore claim our inheritance in Him now and enjoy all its benefits, or we can leave it unclaimed, squander it, or even allow it to be stolen. The question that each of us has to answer is – What are we going to do with our inheritance? If we show our value of earthly possessions by post coding them, how much more we should treasure our inheritance in Him!

However, if some part of your inheritance is lost or stolen, whether it is your peace of mind, health etc, do not just accept it. It still has your postcode, and it therefore rightfully belongs to you. Go and get it back.

PREVENTIVE MEASURES

When a Police officer attends the scene of a crime, it is possible to quickly identify how the crime has been committed. It is noticeable that some thieves could not believe the opportunity that they encountered. They were able to steal with the minimum of effort. The victim had made it so easy, that they might as well have put up a sign saying 'Thieves are welcome. Come on in. Take what you want.'

When crime prevention advice is given, it sometimes

falls on deaf ears, and it is not long before a further theft occurs. It is the same in the spiritual realm. From what I have witnessed in my own life, and that of others, I am entirely sure that by applying Scriptual principles contained in God's Word, we can prevent theft occurring in the first place. As I have said previously – **prevention is better than cure.**

The challenge for us is to know with absolute certainty as to the nature of our inheritance in The Lord. Then figuratively speaking, put our postcode on it, and have the determination that it is not going to be stolen.

Our God is the original Crime Prevention Officer. Let us take heed to what He says in His Word.

CHAPTER TWENTY

SPECIALIZATION

IN THE PREVIOUS twelve chapters of this middle section I have attempted to focus our attention on various ways that we can individually prevent theft in our lives. The remaining chapters in this section will deal with our collective responsibility in crime prevention, and how we function together.

In the course of a Police Officer's career it will become evident to his supervisors, and also to himself, that he is gifted in a certain aspect of Police work, which will result in him being transferred to the respective department where he will specialise. This has the effect of not only helping the officer to be fulfilled, but his expertise is of benefit to the Police Force and community as a whole.

He does not stop being a basic Police Officer, but he is put into an environment where he can achieve his full potential. Some of the specialised departments within the Police Service are the Criminal Investigation Department, Serious Crime Squad, Fraud Squad, Traffic, etc. They were created because some crimes require specialist investigation, and also so that their input and expertise can contribute to the overall fight against crime.

Generally speaking, the average traffic patrol officer does not deal with an involved fraud case, and neither does a fraud investigator deal with a fatal road accident. They do not possess the necessary skills to deal with complicated enquiries outside of their normal duties. If an officer discovers a crime that is outside of his experience, or ability, he will usually call upon the help of a department that specialises in such matters.

On some occasions the officer is attached to a particular department to complete the enquiry. This enables him to gain the necessary experience and confidence to tackle such a crime in the future. This does not reflect badly upon the officer concerned. He is merely being realistic. The main person to consider is the victim, so that there is a fruitful outcome to the investigation.

Officers can also be attached as an aide to a department for a period of six months. This greatly benefits the individual, and also enables the department to see if the officer has an aptitude for such matters.

One of the specialist departments in which I supervised involved preparing criminal files of evidence for summary and jury trial. There were twelve officers under my supervision. The work was very intense, and involved overcoming many difficulties. I would be in daily contact with each of the officers, and we had a great relationship.

When we first started the department, the officers would ask advice from me saying "I've got a problem with a particular file". I would light-heartedly joke with them saying "There is no such thing in life as a problem, merely an opportunity to prove God". Thereafter, they used to approach me saying "I have an opportunity for you and God".

GIFTS TO THE CHURCH

There is nothing new in specialist departments. God created them 2000 years ago, so that His Church could function properly, with every member being trained, fulfilled, and serving the body.

After a person has been a Christian for a period of time it may become evident to church leaders, and to the individual concerned, that he is gifted in one or more areas such as pastoral work, teaching, evangelising, or the ministries of apostle, and prophet. These are named ministries in Scripture, which are given as gifts to the church.

> *It was He who gave* **some** *to be* **apostles,** *some to be* **prophets,** *some to be* **evangelists,** *and some to be* **pastors** *and* **teachers, to prepare** *God's people for works of service,* **so that** *The Body of Christ may be* **built up**.
> *(Ephesians 4;11/12)*

Of course, these five named ministries are not to be regarded as the pinnacle of attainment, but parts of the whole body. There are also many other gifts and functions that contribute to the overall health of the body, as each member fulfils their part: stewardship, administration, counselling, to name just a few. Specialization has wonderful benefits but it is always intended for the Body of Christ as a whole, and not for individual gratification.

PERSONALITY CULTURE

It is important to point out that specialization can have a detrimental effect if it is handled badly. One of the main things to avoid is elitism. It happens in secular organisations, and sadly it also occurs in the Church. It always creates separation in the end, with a string of casualties along the way. The central teaching of Ephesians 4 is that the ministries were given to serve the church, not the church to serve the ministries.

There is one head to the body, namely Christ. All the other parts of the body are of equal importance and standing. If one of those parts is elevated above the remainder, either by self-promotion, or by the action of others, it will ultimately prove to be harmful. The Apostle Paul saw what was happening in the Corinthian church, and drew their attention to its dangers.

> *You are still worldly...there is jealousy and quarrelling among you...For when one says, "I follow Paul," and another, "I follow Apollos, are you not mere men?"*
> *(1 Corithinians 3;1-4)*

There is obviously a need for leadership and order within the church environment. But if someone is gifted in some specialised form of ministry, or in some form of leadership, this does not mean that they are in an enhanced role. They have the gift to serve the body, not themselves. Paul was so concerned about this particular matter that he refers to it on a number of occasions in the first few chapters of his letter. He informed the Corinthian Church of the reason for his obvious concern:

> *I have applied these things to myself and Apollos for your benefit, so that you may learn from us the meaning of the saying,* **"Do not go beyond what is written". Then you will not take pride in one man over another.** *(1 Corinthians 4;6)*

This is a clear Scriptual warning not to go beyond what is written. The manner in which some sections of the church were seeking to elevate individuals was wrong. Paul explained that he had applied these things to Apollos and himself as an example. He wanted them to know that the two men worked as a team, although they had visited the church at different times. There was no competition between them, and there was no desire to form any groups of followers.

> *I planted the seed, Apollos watered it.*
>
> *(1 Corinthians 3;6)*

Unfortunately, Paul had to return to the subject of the personality culture in his second letter to the Corinthian Church. Some people had fallen into the trap of calling some men *'super apostles'*.

> *I am not in the least inferior to the super apostles, even though I am nothing.* *(2 Corinthians 12;11)*

The same old thing had occurred. Either the individual apostle, the people who followed him, or a combination of both, had fostered the personality culture to elevate an individual. Paul had warned them in his previous letter that this sort of behaviour has pride at its root. You will notice that he refers to himself as *'nothing'*.

SERVING THE BODY

Paul recognised his calling, and had confidence in his leadership. But he never lost sight of the reason that he had such ministry and gifting. It was for the support of the body. Gifting and ministries are not meant to be the focal point. It is all about the body being strengthened, and The Lord glorified.

> ... **So that the body of Christ may be built up**.
>
> *(Ephesians 4;12)*

The Apostle Peter also mentions the same truth.

Each one *should use whatever gift he has received to*
serve others..so that in all things God may be
praised through Jesus Christ.   *(1 Peter 4;10-11)*

Notice the words *'so that'* are again used to emphasise
the point that gifts are given for the service of others, and
the Glory of God. All gifts, whether spiritual or practical,
are given for the common good.

Specialization is not about position. It is all about
servanthood.

Jesus called them together and said, "You know that
the rulers of the Gentiles lord it over them, *and*
their high officials exercise authority over them. **Not so**
with you. Instead, whoever wants to become
great among you must be your servant, *and who-*
ever wants to be first must be your slave, just as The Son
of man did not come to be served, but to serve.

                                    (Matthew 20;25-28)

CHAPTER TWENTY-ONE

SERVANTHOOD

IN THE PREVIOUS chapter we briefly looked at the importance of having ministries and gifts functioning within the church. If anyone is used in this way, it is vital that it is done with the right attitude and motive. Scripture gives very clear direction in these matters. By keeping an attitude of servanthood, pride and self-promotion will be prevented. The devil will then not have a foothold to steal, kill and destroy.

My history teacher in school was a self confessed cynic. He said, "Revolutions are all about the people who have it want to keep it; and the people who haven't got it want to get hold of it". Revolutions in the world usually surround power and influence.

But, as Christians we are involved in a totally different revolution. When we seek to influence or take the lead in any way, it is neither to displace another Christian, nor for individual gratification or self gain. It is for the good of the body of Christ as a whole. We are all involved in preparing a Kingdom that is fit for its King. We are getting the bride beautiful for the coming Bridegroom.

EXTINGUISH THE FIRE

There are a number of ways by which a fire can be extinguished. Stamping on it is dangerous, and can even make the fire spread. Deluging it with water creates a cloud of steam and hot air, which attracts attention. The two safest and gentlest ways of extinguishing a fire are by carefully removing the logs, and also by starving it of oxygen. They each entail a thoughtful gradual process, but will ultimately achieve the desired result.

This representation of a fire can be related to pride and selfish ambition, which are the complete opposites of servanthood. They are like fires that burn. The end result is damage and injury to the individual and others. Can it be prevented?

I would suggest that removing logs represent the practical, physical things that can be done, while the starving of oxygen addresses the issue of conversation and attitudes. Our prime example is how The Lord dealt with this issue. It is noticeable that He did not exalt or praise individuals. Is it because He knew the danger of inflating a person's ego? There are four occasions whereby He commends individuals.

Matthew 8;5-13 – Centurion.
Matthew 16;13-20 – Peter's confession of Jesus.
Matthew 26;6-13 – Woman anointing Jesus with perfume.
Luke 10;42 – Mary, sister of Martha.

He commended each of these persons not for who they were as people, but for the acts that they did and the revelation they received. **Jesus did not elevate the individual. He elevated the work of God in the individual's life.**

The Centurion for his faith.
Peter for the revelation he received.

The woman for her act of worship.
Mary for her spiritual hunger

NO PEDESTALS

Jesus did not hold any of His disciples up in front of the crowds as people to emulate. He always endeavoured to keep their feet on the ground. Take for example the account of the seventy-two that returned to Jesus after ministering in His name. (Luke10;17-20). The disciples were obviously excited about what had happened, which is very clear from the first words that they spoke to Jesus. They had already seen The Lord perform such deeds, but suddenly they were doing the same.

> *"Lord, even the demons* **submit to us** *in your name."*
> *(Luke 10;17)*

Jesus immediately informed them that He had seen satan fall from heaven. The reason he fell was because of pride, and the desire to be exalted.

Jesus began His response to the disciples with this statement about satan, which can first appear to be at cross-purposes to what they had just told The Lord. But it is not in any way out of context, because He knew that He needed to warn the disciples at the very outset about getting carried away with their own importance. He wanted the disciples to have a real grasp of the authority they possessed over anything in His name, but not to let it go to their heads. James in his Epistle also links selfish ambition with the devil.

> *If you harbour bitter* **envy and selfish ambition** *in your heats, do not boast about it or deny the truth. Such 'wisdom' does not come down from Heaven but* **is**

earthly, unspiritual, of the devil. For where you have envy and selfish ambition, there you find disorder and every evil practice. *(James 3;14-16)*

God gave the following warning to Cain.

"If you do not do what is right, **sin is crouching at your door***; it desires to have you, but you must master it."* *(Genesis 4;7)*

There is no doubt that down through the years the devil has found many churches easy pickings. The combination of leaders behaving in a dictatorial manner, individuals seeking power and influence for their own ends, and competition between fellowships, have all contributed to a loss of effectiveness. In fact, the devil did not really have to do anything. The churches themselves self destruct, with endless splits along the way.

NO FOOTHOLD

Jesus knew the disciples hearts, and from what emerged in conversation and attitudes, that the sin of pride and selfish ambition was crouching at their doors. The advice He continually gave them was to keep the door shut, and not to let it in. He told them to rejoice that their names are written in Heaven. This is because their names are there on account of the gift of salvation, and not by any achievement on their part. The Lord removed the log that represented self-importance.

The wonderful thing about the manner in which Jesus dealt with individuals is that when they did wrong, He did not crush the individual. He simply crushed the wrong attitude. The individual never felt battered, because Jesus administered life.

The disciples obviously had a problem with selfish ambition and jealousy. It is mentioned at least five times in Scripture. (Matthew 18;1-4: Matthew 20;20-28: Matthew 23;1-11: Mark 9;33-37: Luke 22;24-27). James and John even got their mother to approach Jesus on their behalf. If something is mentioned five times, it is fair to say that it must be an important issue that God wants us to be aware of, and address.

It is important to encourage individuals, but Jesus knew the difference between a word of encouragement, and the fuelling of egos. The Lord never added logs to the fires of pride and selfish ambition. He used the two means of extinguishing the fire, namely by removing logs and starving it of oxygen, as illustrated at the beginning of this chapter. He did certain practical/physical acts to remove the logs, and also used the right conversation to starve destructive motives of their oxygen.

LEADING BY EXAMPLE

On occasions, Jesus used visual means in order to influence the disciples thinking. The following are two such examples.

> *At that time the disciples came to Jesus and asked,* **'Who is the greatest in the Kingdom of Heaven?'** *He called a little child and had him stand among them. And he said, "I tell you the truth, unless you change and become like little children, you will never enter the Kingdom of Heaven. Therefore* **whoever humbles himself like this child is the greatest in the Kingdom of Heaven."** *(Matthew 18;1-4)*

> *After completion* (washing disciples' feet), *He said to them,* **"I have set you an example** *that you should do*

as I have done for you."   *(John 13;1-17)*

Not only did Jesus give the disciples visual images to focus upon, but also He continually brought servanthood into general conversation. He did not talk to His disciples about having a role or position. He continually reminded them of having a servant's heart. The following are some examples.

> *Jesus said to them,* "**If anyone wants to be the first, he must be the very last, and the servant of all**."
> *(Mark 9;35)*

> "**I am among you as one who serves**." (This occurred immediately after Jesus reveals the nature of His sacrifice in the breaking of bread).
> *(Luke 22;24-27)*

> "**The greatest** *among you* **will be your servant**."
> *(Matthew 23;11)*

The pattern of the world's thinking is that you do things to get noticed, cultivate the right friendships, do favours for the right people, name-drop, say the right things, and display loyalty to 'key' individuals. If you abide by these principles in the world you will generally get noticed and secure advancement.

Jesus' own brothers were caught up in this mentality and did not understand His ways. Their advice to Him is a perfect example of the pattern of the world's approach.

> *"You ought to leave here and go to Judea, so that your disciples may see the miracles you do. No one who wants to become a public figure acts in secret. Since you are doing these things, show yourself to the world." For even*

His own brothers did not believe in Him. (John 7;3-5)

It was this same sort of thinking that Jesus highlighted in respect of the Pharisees. Jesus made the following comment concerning their motives and actions.

"Everything they do is done for men to see."
(Matthew 23;5)

NO HIERARCHY

The reason that Jesus spent so much time removing logs and starving pride and selfish ambition of its oxygen is that He did not want his disciples to conform to the pattern of the world's thinking, but to be transformed in their thinking.

Do not conform any longer to the pattern of this world, *but be transformed by the renewing of your mind.* *(Romans 12;2)*

The pattern of the world's thinking is that leadership is about hierarchy. God's perspective is the opposite. Leadership in His eyes is all about servanthood. It means being prepared to take the lead in serving, humility, love, kindness, practical help, spiritual watchfulness over others etc.

The logs that Jesus removed from the fires that were burning in the disciples were their worldly perception of position, status, and leadership. Their ill judged views concerning status and position not only caused division and jealousy between themselves, but also affected their view of others.

"Teacher,"said John, "we saw a man driving out demons in your name and we told him to stop, **because he was not one of us.**" *(Mark 9;38-41)*

Jesus told John that he had acted wrongly. His response to the incident revealed how that He was inclusive, whereas John's attitude had been exclusive. This passage of Scripture illustrates how pride not only causes division within the immediate group, but also affects the relationship towards other individuals or fellowships.

Jesus continually starved the oxygen out of conversations that would enhance their egos. He confronted them with the clear contrast between conforming to the pattern of the world, or alternatively of having their minds transformed by His Word. Thankfully, this transformation eventually took place in the disciples lives.

Peter encourages the believers to *live as servants of God.* (1Peter 2;16)

He begins his letter referring to himself as *a servant and apostle of Jesus Christ.* (2 Peter 1;1)

James in his letter, *a servant of God and of the Lord Jesus Christ.* (James 1;1)

Jude begins his letter, *a servant of Jesus Christ.* (Jude 1;1)

Paul began a number of his letters as *a servant of Christ Jesus.*

TASKS

It was this understanding of servanthood that explains how 'position' or 'roles' are to be rightly viewed. Paul refers to them as tasks. 1 Corinthians 3 deals with divisions in the church. It basically surrounds the issue of people elevating individuals such as Peter, Apollos and Paul, which in their case was against their wishes. Whenever individuals are elevated, either by their own desire or by the ill-judged behaviour of others, cliques develop.

Once that happens, there inevitably follows jealousy and quarrelling, as Paul describes in 1 Corinthians 3;3. He refers to such behaviour as *infantile and worldly*. (vv 1 & 3). It again emphasises the warning in Romans 12;1 of not conforming to the pattern of the world. The key to understanding position, role, or office is found in Paul's letter to the Corinthian Church.

> *What, after all, is Apollos? And what is Paul?* **Only servants,** *through whom you came to believe* – **as The Lord has assigned to each his task.**
>
> *(1 Corinthians 3;5)*

It can be seen that Paul refers to '*tasks*' not position. The reason being is that when we view any role as a task we maintain a servant's heart. Once we view it as a position to be attained, it crosses the line into pride and selfish ambition.

Paul continues with this subject in 1 Corinthians 4 where he begins the chapter by repeating servanthood –

> *So then,* **men ought to regard us as servants of Christ.** *(v1)*

He did not want to be regarded in any elevated form. When he needed to exercise authority, or bring discipline, as in the case of the Corinthian church, it was through the anointing upon his life and ministry, not because he was admired or held in awe. Paul then goes on to explain why he has spent so much time on this subject.

> *Now, brothers,* **I have applied these things to myself and Apollos for your benefit,** *so that you may learn from us the meaning of the saying,* **"Do not go beyond what is written." Then you will not take**

pride in one man over against another.
(1 Corinthians 4;6)

Wherever pride exists, there is always the danger of going beyond what is written. Abuse of authority, and elevation of individuals are just two of the consequences.

REQUIREMENTS FOR LEADERSHIP

Paul wrote to Timothy about the characteristics required of an elder and deacon. He clearly emphasises that it was not to be regarded as a position, but a task. When the world is seeking individuals to hold a position of authority, they look for people with certain leadership qualities, who have a good education and experience in management and supervision.

Although these can be useful, the characteristics outlined in 1 Timothy 3 do not mention such things. The chapter begins with the essential ingredient of a servant's heart. The reason being is that a servant remains humble and views whatever he does as a task, not as a progression or step upwards.

If anyone sets his heart on being an overseer, **he desires a noble task**. *(1 Timothy 3;1)*

Paul explains that this quality of servanthood is required in respect of the ministries that are given to the church as described in his letter to the Ephesian Church. The ministries are referred to as gifts, indicating that they are something given, not earned or applied for. If the ministries keep this at the forefront of their minds it will prevent pride getting a foothold, and they will maintain a servants heart.

Be completely humble and gentle. *(Ephesians 4;2)*

SERVANTS OF ALL

Having described the manner in which ministry and gifting is to be viewed, Paul then brings the passage of Scripture in Ephesians to the conclusion and explanation of it all. It is to prepare each of us for works of service. We are each to have a servant's heart.

> **To prepares God's people for works of service, so that the body of Christ may be built up** *until we all reach unity in the faith and in the knowledge of The Son of God and become mature, attaining to the whole measure of the fullness of Christ.* *(Ephesians 4;12-13)*

Children will take on the character of their parents. Jesus gave His disciples a living example to follow. Paul and the other apostles were at great pains to continually tell others that they were servants, because they wanted their spiritual children to also have a servant's heart. The Lord wants each of us to reach our full potential, and be fruitful and fulfilled in whatever we do. But, it is not for the purpose of the individual being built up by himself or others. It is for each member of the body to have a servant's heart.

There is a balance that can be achieved between encouragement to grow and develop, while at the same time maintaining a servant's heart. There is no promotion in The Kingdom of God. Once we cross over into that mentality we are conforming to the pattern of the world.

> *For it is by grace you have been saved, through faith –* **and this not from yourselves, it is the gift of God – not by works, so that no one can boast**. *For we are God's workmanship, created in Christ Jesus to do good works, which God prepared in advance for us to do.* *(Ephesians 2;8-10)*

This is the starting point for each believer. It therefore follows that we ought always to adhere to the principles contained in these verses. Whatever we become in Him is a gift, so that no one can boast.

SOWING AND REAPING

In conclusion, I would suggest that Jesus never elevated the individual. Instead, He encouraged and paid tribute to the work of God in the believer's life. He never put extra logs on the fire of pride and selfish ambition. He never fanned the flames by talking of position, or role, but encouraged, and set an example of servanthood.

Whenever He sensed that pride and selfish ambition was entering into their thinking or conversation He would immediately starve the fire of oxygen so that it died down. He knew that if a fire is not dealt with, it could spread and even get out of control.

We ought always to encourage one another. But in so doing, to be aware of the difference between the beneficial effect of encouragement and the harmful implications of exalting an individual.

The health of our individual fellowships in five years time is linked to what we are presently sowing. 'Spiritual sons and daughters' will be the product of their parents. The question that therefore arises is – What can we do to encourage a healthy desire for self-fulfilment, while at the same time discouraging the harmful aspects of selfish ambition?

Whatsoever we sow we will reap.   *(Galatians 6;7)*

In this world it is impossible to completely extinguish pride, because it is unfortunately in the heart of man. However, I believe that it is possible to keep the fire as smouldering embers. By the wisdom of God we can remove the logs that may presently exist, and have discernment so that we do not add any more in the future. In our dealings with one another ought we to ask ourselves the question – "Is what I am saying, or doing, adding a log to the fire?".

In addition to which, by having our minds transformed in this area of servanthood we can be more conscious of how our conversation can either fan the flames or starve it of oxygen. By doing so, we can prevent the destructive effect of fires which burn out of control. Fires often start very simply. Preventive action can save injury and damage. It is a choice we each have to make.

> *Consider what a great forest is set on fire by a small spark.* (James 3;5)

CHAPTER TWENTY-TWO

COLLECTIVE RESPONSIBILITY

FILMS AND TELEVISION often feature a police officer as a hero who single-handedly cleans up an entire city. Whether it be detecting a murder, capturing a gang of armed robbers, or tackling a terrorist threat, he is portrayed as a person who operates on his own, and does not want any accountability to others.

The reality of life is quite the opposite, because the effectiveness of any Police operation will rely greatly on the quality of teamwork. Each officer is vital to the overall success, and it is therefore important that everyone sees himself as part of the whole, with individual and collective responsibility.

It would be irresponsible of a Police officer to work independently of others, or leave fellow officers carry the main burden. It is well to remember the saying of the legendary three musketeers – 'all for one, and one for all'. Similarly, within the Body of Christ we are all individuals. But we each have a responsibility to one another within that body. **We will be the most effective when we work collectively, with good teamwork.**

There is also the added advantage of protecting one another when we are close together. When someone is on their own, they are more vulnerable. There is a Scripture that warns of the risks of operating on one's own.

> *Be self-controlled and alert.* **Your enemy the devil prowls around like a roaring lion looking for someone to devour**. *(1 Peter 5;8)*

Notice that the verse says *someone*. It is in the singular, not plural. Have you ever watched nature programmes on television, when a lion is stalking a herd of wildebeest or zebras? He will try and separate one from the herd, and then pursue him relentlessly. If the animal remained with the others it would be safe. It is the same with us, we are not meant to exist alone. We are a body, with Christ as the head, and as members we are all joined together for purpose.

IN-HOUSE TRAINING

The Apostle Paul, who was instrumental in giving the framework to the early church, saw the advantage of collective responsibility, with each member seeing themselves as a vital part of the body. He knew the importance of including everyone, so that no one felt left out, either by age or gender.

He introduced a system of discipleship that was not formal, but a simple, natural way of Christian expression. In his letter to Titus he identifies four separate groups, namely older men and women, and younger men and women. Paul uses the word teach/train on eleven separate occasions in respect of these four categories, ten of which occur in chapter two. There was specific teaching for each group.

The older men were to be taught to exercise moderation and self-restraint, to be worthy of respect, self controlled, and sound in faith, love, and endurance. The older women were to be reverent in awe and respect, not slanderers, able to exercise self-control, and to teach what is good. The young men were to receive teaching in being self-controlled, having integrity, seriousness, and soundness of speech. The younger women were to be self controlled, pure, homemakers, kind, and respectful towards their husbands (Titus 2;1-8).

MID-LIFE OPPORTUNITY

The purpose of training the older age group is found in Titus 2;4 – *Then they can train the younger...* The older members were an integral part of the church structure. The world talks of mid-life crisis, but God's Word talks of mid-life opportunity. It is only a crisis if you feel lost, with no sense of fulfilment. If you know where you are going, it can be the most productive time of one's life.

Let me share a wonderful verse of encouragement.

You will come to the grave in full vigour, *like sheaves gathered in season.* *(Job 5;26)*

Just imagine that, reaching death in full vigour. We may not have the physique of a young person, but we can certainly be in full vigour in our zeal, and commitment for The Lord.

Don't let the devil rob the church of talents because of deceptive spirits, such as ageism. It is in the devil's interests to deceive middle-aged and older people that they are 'passed it', and that they now need to pass the baton on to younger people. This is contrary to what God has for these age groups as we can clearly see from Titus and other passages of Scripture.

If the early church regarded middle and older-aged groups as important, just think how much more relevant they are for today's society. The opportunities for discipleship are immense. It is not simply for those in the immediate care of fellowships, but also to outreach into communities. For example, you have only to look at the increase in the single-parent family to see one area where there is a crying need for help by mature men and women, who can provide the love and leadership to these young people.

Consider for one moment how many churches contain middle-aged or older Christians, who feel unused, unappreciated, and consequently unfulfilled. There is a wealth of untapped life lying dormant in our fellowships. This is totally contrary to the teaching of God's Word.

In addition to which, it is recorded in Acts that the early church went from house to house, and people who had possessions would help support the poorer members, so that no one was in need. Who were these people who were able to afford the time, and material needs? Predominantly they were the middle aged and older members of the fellowships.

A PEOPLE UNITED

The intention of identifying groups, and highlighting what they can teach-train, is for every person to reach their full potential. It is not to create separate groups or cliques, but to create '*a people*'. We have only to look at Acts 2;42-47 to see the fruit of a people with a common vision. When everyone is fulfilling his or her potential there is unity of purpose.

A people *eager to do what is good*   (Titus 2;14)

There was a clear purpose in each of Paul's instructions to Titus. In fact, the words so that/in order are used on seven separate occasions. Paul states:

> *I want you to stress these things* **so that** *they devote themselves to doing good.*   (Titus 3;8)

The words 'doing good' are used eight times. What is the best '*good*' you can do for a new believer? Surely the answer is to help develop that individual's relationship with The Lord, so that they in turn can disciple others. The Parable of The Sower in Matthew 13 tells us of the birds who come down to steal the seed. One of the reasons for discipleship is to prevent this theft occurring.

Churches often have the tendency to embark on training programmes. They are entered into with a good heart, but so often becomes merely an end in itself. Paul's instructions to Titus were not meant to be just another training exercise, but for it to develop into a way of life.

If the people could catch the revelation of training and discipleship as a natural lifestyle it would change their lives, and those around. They would automatically disciple, and support one another, and look for spiritual sons and daughters, who would then disciple, and have their own spiritual children. It would be a completely natural occurrence, and not something that is part of a training package.

DELEGATION

Paul also knew the need for a leader to delegate, so that the teaching-training reached everyone. Those in church leadership cannot reach every member, because of the limitations of time. A far better way is for everyone to 'take the lead'. It will also prevent leaders getting burnt out.

> *The things you have heard me say* ... **entrust to reliable men, who will also be qualified to teach others**. *(2 Timothy 2;2)*

In order to teach we have to be prepared to be taught. Teaching others also causes us to evaluate our own lives. I can think of one area of my life that I do not want either my natural, or spiritual children to follow. I am referring to my self-destruct button that I quite often press when I engage in feverish activity. It is important to distinguish between genuine zeal for The Lord, and driven activity. If it is of God it will be balanced and not lead to harm. For those of you, who are like me, I have a word of warning from Scripture.

> *Do not be a fool.* **Why die before your time?**
> *(Ecclesiastes 7;17)*

God has an appointed time for us to die, after we have fulfilled all the plans and purposes He has for us. Scripture instructs us to look after ourselves, so that we do not die before time. John 10;10 warns us that, amongst other things, the devil seeks to kill. Do we aid and abet him by our lifestyle? I think you would agree that it would be criminal to die prematurely because of our own stupidity.

A TIMELY VISIT

Moses was a wonderful man of God, but even he temporarily lost his clear sightedness, and fell into the trap of being a one-man band. Exodus 18;13-27 records how he was administering the role of judge for the people's disputes. He had taken full responsibility for the work, and was acting single-handedly. It was only when Jethro, his father-in-law, made a timely visit to Moses, that the error of his ways was highlighted.

After sitting with Moses for a full day as he fulfilled his work as the sole judge, Jethro saw that his actions were wrong, both for the people and Moses himself.

> *Jethro said to Moses,* **"What you are doing is not good.** *You and these people who come to* **you will only wear yourselves out.** *The work is too heavy for you;* **you cannot handle it alone ".** *(Exodus 18;17-18)*

Notice that Jethro had identified two issues, and how that one would cause the other. He saw that not only were Moses actions improper, but they would result in having an adverse effect upon his health, and that of others.

Jethro advised him to select capable men from among all the tribes, and appoint them as judges over set numbers of people. Moses would then judge only the most difficult cases. This is basically the same advice that Paul gave to Timothy in 2 Timothy 2;2. Jethro refers to selecting capable men, while Paul advises Timothy to chose reliable men. They both knew that a leader cannot carry the load himself.

> **"That will make your load lighter**, *because they will share it with you. If you do this and God so commands,* **you will be able to stand the strain, and all these people will go home satisfied".**
>
> *(Exodus 18;22-23)*

Moses had to learn the lesson of delegation and value of teamwork, while the other leaders and people had to learn the lesson of having collective responsibility. He and the people were later faced with a test as to whether they could apply the lessons learnt.

TEAMWORK

Numbers 32 records how the Israelite tribes of the Reubenites, Gadites, and half-tribe of Manasseh decided not to settle in the Promised Land, but to remain on the other side of the Jordan. Moses accepted their request, but informed them that it was still their responsibility to ensure that the remainder of the Israelite tribes came into their full inheritance. Their duty was to fight in the same manner as the other tribes.

It was also important that Moses did not let the wishes of a few tribes have an adverse effect upon the whole nation. Teamwork and collective responsibility were necessary for the task ahead. Moses had learnt these principles from his earlier experience. After outlining their responsibility, Moses said the following to the Reubenites, Gadites and Manasseh.

> **"If you fail to do this, you will be sinning against The Lord***; and you may be sure that your sin will find you out."* (Numbers 32;23-24)

The same principle can be applied today. There may be people in fellowships that do not wish to enter into all that The Lord has for them. They are content just to go so far and no further. It is their choice.

However, although they do not wish this for themselves, it is still their duty, as part of the body, to do everything possible whether by faith, prayer, encouragement, service etc. to ensure that the remainder of the fellowship enters into its full inheritance in The Lord. That is all part of teamwork, wanting the best for everyone in the team. It is to be hoped that when they see the inheritance that the others enjoy, they will change their minds and enter into all the fullness, and not settle for second best.

There are some battles in life that we must face alone. But it is not wise to become so independent that we do not have the sense to call on others to stand with us in prayer, counsel, and encouragement when we have testing times. As we have just seen, Moses had to learn that calling on others for help is not a sign of weakness, or defeat. It is a sign of strength and maturity. We are a body that is joined together for a purpose. Never let pride or fear prevent us from calling on others for assistance, of whatever type, in times of need.

CALL FOR ASSISTANCE

With regard to calling on others for help, I am reminded of an incident that will hopefully illustrate the last point.

It occurred one afternoon when I was on duty at a derby soccer match, which had a history of violence. The Police were stretched to their limits in personnel, and there were continual outbreaks of violence throughout the city. I had six officers under my supervision, and one of the areas for which we were responsible contained a pub full of local supporters.

It had one hundred squashed inside, who were in a boisterous and drunken state. Some of the customers had spilled onto the pavement outside, owing to the restricted space available in the premises. I considered it wise to remain in close proximity to the pub as it had all the makings of a flashpoint.

For a short time everything appeared to be going smoothly. Although the crowd inside was rowdy, singing their local soccer anthems, there was no violence. Sadly, the peace that we were enjoying came to an abrupt end.

In the distance I could hear further singing. I looked along an adjoining road and saw a crowd of rival supporters. There were two hundred in number, and took up the full width of the road, which was lined with shops. They had managed to separate themselves from the main bulk of supporters, who were being marshalled elsewhere by a police escort. As they approached the pub at which we were situated I could hear the popping sound of the shop windows being smashed, and I saw shoppers running for safety.

Unfortunately, some of the local supporters saw the same, and rushed into the pub to tell their friends. All one hundred of them then burst out onto the pavement. The seven of us stood between the two hundred away supporters, and the one hundred local supporters, who raced towards one another. A pitched battle broke out, with the whole area in complete mayhem.

Like most people, I have seen the film 'The Magnificent Seven' starring Yul Brynner and Steve Mcqueen. The film is very inspirational, and gives us all encouragement in what a few good men can achieve against many. Our situation was similar, in that there were seven of us officers against a combined group of three hundred.

However, that is where the similarity ends. The reason being is that I did not see myself as Yul Brynner, and I don't believe any of my fellow officers saw themselves as Steve Mcqueen at that particular point in time. In view of that, we did what everyone thought was appropriate in the circumstances. We yelled into our radios for assistance.

AVAILABILITY OF RESOURCES

Whether it be the detailed planning for a major event, the response to a sudden disaster, or simply the daily running of a Police station, the crucial factor in all these situations is what is commonly known in the Police as the 'availability of resources', by which is meant personnel. No matter how important the plan, or how necessary the need to respond to an emergency, there is nothing that can be done if the manpower is lacking.

When you take into account holidays, rest days, courses, sickness, extractions into departments etc., the number of officers that originally looked good on paper, suddenly begins to look pretty bare. Not only does this problem have consequences for middle to long term planning, but also it greatly affects the daily routine of Police work. Does this sound familiar with church life? All the more reason for developing collective responsibility, so that the tasks are spread.

The early church, like today, had many opportunities for growth. They responded to the prompting of The Holy Spirit to spread the Gospel message to other lands, and they also responded to the needs of the local community, both in spiritual and practical ways. In order to meet those numerous needs the leaders needed to know the availability of the believers with whom they were in contact, whether it be to help with the daily distribution of food to the needy, or the sending of believers to new churches that required assistance.

All the believers were together and **had everything in common**. *(Acts 2;44)*

The impression we get from this Scripture is that they were all fully supportive of one another, with each person playing their part, however big or small. **They made themselves available.**

FAITH AND WORKS

It is a useful exercise to examine our own lives to see how

many hours during a month we actually spend doing something specific for The Lord. Time spent in prayer and study is vital for our growth, but it is also helpful to do something practical with our faith.

> *I will show you my faith by what I do* ... **Faith without deeds is useless**. *(James 2;18-20)*

In family life there are many responsibilities, such as our professional work, daily chores, and commitments involving our children, which are all necessary. It is sometimes difficult to even find time for our wives or husbands. There is no doubt that modern day life is pressurised.

However, in it all, I feel sure that if we took a cool, calculated look at our lives, there will be some spare capacity of time we can set aside to do something specific, so that we do not let the months and years just roll by. It may even be just a commitment to telephone a person once a fortnight in order to encourage them. Every little helps, and as they say – "It's good to talk".

If we are wise stewards of our time, we will find it easier to engage in collective responsibility, and not allow the incidentals of life steal our time.

CHAPTER TWENTY-THREE

WATCHMEN

WHEN POLICE OFFICERS remain in the same area for a number of years it enables them to get a good personal knowledge of the inhabitants, and a genuine desire to keep the area as crime free as possible. In order to accomplish this, they get information about the local criminals, and gain intelligence as to their activities.

Various methods are used to target such criminals, and there is a flow of information between officers, and also through neighbourhood watch schemes, in order to prevent and lessen the threat of criminal activity. The Police and neighbourhood-watch volunteers guard and watch over their area. **Crime prevention is a collective responsibility.**

In olden times, towns and settlements would have watchmen on the walls, who would stand guard over the community, so that they could live in safety and not suffer invasion or theft. If an invader were to be seen, the watchman would sound the alarm. Today, we have that responsibility to one another, to be watchmen over one another's spiritual welfare, so that we can live in peace, and not experience theft or harm of any kind.

One of the chief slogans used by the Crime Prevention Panel is **'Watch out. There's a thief about'**. We constantly see the posters and stickers on billboards and vehicles. If the world is so concerned about theft, then surely we as Christians should also continually keep watch, and give the same warning. I certainly do not mean that we become neurotic about the situation, or engender fear in either others, or ourselves. I am simply encouraging us to be aware of what is happening around us. .

> *This is what The Lord says to me* **"Go post a watchman** *and have him report what he sees* ... **let him be alert, fully alert**.*"* (Isaiah 21;6-7)

A watchman will be alert in The Spirit, and will tell others what The Lord reveals to him. Most churches have a governmental structure containing elders, deacons etc. But it would be unfair, and unwise, to expect everything to emanate from these leaders. It is for everyone to seek the heart of the watchman. The newest believer may see something that has been overlooked by the eldership.

In addition to which, the aspect of being alert in The Spirit is at the core of having spiritual sons and daughters. We watch over them so that they do not come to harm. Scripture gives clear insight into the heart of a watchman.

> *The watchman shouted,* **"Day after day, my Lord, I stand on the watchtower**; *every night I stay at my post*.*"* (Isaiah 21;8)

A watchman is consistent, reliable, and trustworthy. A person who has a heart to disciple others will grow in the role of being a watchman. The two go hand in hand.

PRACTICAL APPLICATION

Both Matthew 25 and Matthew 26 contain teaching on keeping watch. The principle is given in chapter 25, while an opportunity to put it into practice is contained in the following chapter. This occurs throughout Scripture. The Lord God gives teaching and instruction, then provides a set of circumstances to put it into effect.

Jesus taught the disciples some of the principles of keeping watch just prior to the events at Gethsemane. Unfortunately, it proved to be a missed opportunity for them. Let us look at the sequence of events.

Matthew 25 contains three separate teachings. Firstly, the chapter begins with the Parable of the Ten Virgins where The Lord concludes the teaching by saying *'there-fore keep watch'*. Secondly, the following Parable of the Talents exhorts us to effectively use what we have, and not let it go to waste. Thirdly, the teaching regarding the Sheep and The Goats tells us of those who actively obeyed The Lord's exhortation by feeding, clothing, and looking after others.

There is a continuity of teaching, namely keep watch, effectively use the gifts and talents we possess, and also to remain obedient in continually looking out for one another. Jesus puts it into clear perspective.

*"I tell you the truth, whatever you did for one of the least of these brothers of mine, **you did for Me**."*
(Matthew 25;40)

It is interesting to note that verses 35-36 of the chapter have a natural and spiritual application.

"For I was hungry and you gave me something to eat, I was thirsty and you gave me something to drink, I was

> *a stranger and you invited me in, I needed clothes and you clothed me, I was sick and you looked after me, I was in prison and you came to visit me."*
>
> *(Matthew 25;35-36)*

There is the obvious practical and physical manner in which these needs can be met. But there is also a spiritual dimension to these needs. The hungry to be fed with The Word of God; the thirsty to be filled with The Holy Spirit; the stranger to be given hospitality; those who need clothing to receive salvation and put on the robes of righteousness; the sick to be healed; those in prison to be set free from their bondage.

This list of people in Matthew 25;35-36 is similar to that contained in Isaiah 61;1-4. These verses in Isaiah tell us that the purpose of The Anointing is to proclaim the Lord's favour to these people by restoring them.

WATCH AND PRAY

Matthew 26 includes Gethsemane, where The Lord said these words to the disciples – "Could you men not keep watch with Me for one hour? Watch and pray."To put this verse in context, it is important to remember what had happened in the previous chapter, when The Lord had only recently taught them concerning keeping watch, and effectively supporting one another.

In Gethsemane The Lord was looking for their support. He was hoping that they would have responded to His time of need in a positive and supportive manner. He had even put it in the clearest possible terms before his hour of need.

There would be future opportunities to serve and honour The Lord by supporting others, but here was an opportunity in the present to give Him their full support. As we have seen from the passage in Isaiah 21;6-7, a watchman is instructed to be alert. In His hour of need The Lord asked his disciples to be watchmen for Him, but they did not stay alert. They fell asleep. Have we also fallen asleep at times, and failed to watch and pray for a person in need?

SPIRITUAL SONS AND DAUGHTERS

Could you give a person one-hour a week in order to watch and pray? It may be a believer, or a non-Christian friend. Jesus experienced an hour of need. He asked his disciples to watch and pray for an hour. If we respond to one another in such a manner we will fulfil The Lord's exhortation. Our motivation is that as we keep watch over one another, we do it for our Lord.

> *I tell you the truth, whatever you did for one of the least of these brothers of mine,* **you did for Me**.
> *(Matthew 25;40)*

Spend an hour with that person in meaningful conversation and prayer. There will obviously be occasions when it is necessary to spend a lengthy time with an individual who has much to share, but it is also good to spend short quality time. The length of time does not determine our effectiveness.

> *As iron sharpens iron, so one man sharpens another.*
> *(Proverbs 27;17)*

Can you imagine the impact, if each member of a church faithfully gave an hour a week to watch and pray over the individuals that The Lord had put on their heart? This applies whether we are present with them in discipling, or praying separately. Imagine the harvest that would come from such sowing.

> **The watchman opens the gate for the shepherd** *and the sheep listen to his voice. He calls his own sheep by name and leads them out.*   *(John 10;3)*

The above verse shows us that the watchman not only protects and prevents harm to those in his care, but he has the privilege of preparing the way for The Lord. As we watch and pray over one another, we prepare the way for our Lord, The Good Shepherd, to come into the lives of those we are supporting. Just like the watchman who opens the gate for the shepherd, so we open the way for The Lord. It is a responsible position, but also a wonderful privilege.

WATCH AND SEE

Scripture also reveals that The Lord speaks to those who are prepared to watch and pray. A watchman will receive revelation directly from The Lord, which will not only affect his own life, but also that of others. I am sure we can all appreciate the impact this can have on our individual churches, and nation as a whole, as more people grasp the significance of having a watchman's heart.

> **I will stand at my watch** *and station myself on the ramparts;* **I will look to see what He will say to me**...*Then The Lord replied: Write down the revelation and make it plain on tablets so that a herald may run with it.*   *(Habakkuk 2;1-2)*

There is also a reward for those who are prepared to capture the essence of being a watchman. It will be a joyful role, because they will see wonderful things of The Lord.

Your watchmen *lift up their voices; together they shout for joy. When The Lord returns to Zion, they* **will see it with their own eyes**.   *(Isaiah 52;8)*

CHAPTER TWENTY-FOUR

GRACE

IN THE FIRST two parts of this book I have endeavoured to explain how we experience theft in our lives, and how it can be prevented. The latter part of the book reveals the means by which we can take back that which has been stolen from both others and ourselves through The Anointing of God.

But, before we go any further it is important to understand a vital truth, namely whatsoever we accomplish will always be by the Grace of God. Grace, which means 'the unmerited favour of God', is central to every aspect of our life.

In 1 Corinthians 12 & 14, Paul gives encouragement to eagerly desire spiritual gifts. Nestled between these two chapters, is 1 Corinthians 13, which deals solely with love. Paul wanted the Corinthian church to understand that although they were encouraged to abound in gifts, his chief desire was for them to have love at their centre. He knew the danger of becoming unbalanced in our approach, by concentrating on one area of growth. **Gifts have their full meaning and power when outworked in love.**

Bearing this principle in mind, I have placed this chapter at the centre of the book, because I do not want anyone to get the false idea that The Anointing is achieved by personal effort. Although there is a cost involved in dying to self, there needs to be the clear understanding that everything we achieve in The Lord is as a result of His Grace. Paul had some harsh words for the Galatian church, which had started out so well, but had then got caught up in believing that their faith was maintained by human effort.

You who are trying to be justified by law have been alienated from Christ; **you have fallen away from grace.** *(Galatians 5;4)*

Our spiritual journey begins with grace.

For it is by grace you have been saved, *through faith, and this not from yourselves,* **it is the gift of God**. *Not by works, so that no one can boast.*
(Ephesians 2;8-9)

As we continue along the way it is maintained by grace.

And **God is able to make all grace abound to you, so that in all things at all times,** *having all that you need, you will abound in every good work.*
(2 Corinthians 9;8)

The last verse of The Bible finishes with grace.

The Grace of The Lord Jesus *be with God's people.* *Amen*. *(Revelation 22;21)*

From the beginning to the end it is all about grace. Therefore, my sole intention in writing these few lines is that we continually remain aware of this key truth in our lives. There are so many good things happening, and many countries are either experiencing, or on the brink of revival. There is no doubt that we are in momentous times.

But it always is, and forever will be, by the Grace of God.

PART 3

TAKING BACK THAT WHICH HAS BEEN STOLEN

Nothing was missing; young or old, boy or girl,
plunder or anything else that had been taken.
1 Samuel 30;19

CHAPTER TWENTY-FIVE

FILLING THE TEMPLE

THE FIRST TWO parts of the book dealt with the nature of spiritual crime, and the need for prevention. The remainder will concentrate solely on The Anointing, and how to take back that which has been stolen. I can testify that an application of the following chapters will restore, rebuild, and renew.

John the Baptist testified of Jesus in the following manner.

> *The man on whom you see The Spirit come down and remain is* **He who will baptise with The Holy Spirit**. *(John 1;33)*

Ephesians 3;16-17 informs us that the Holy Spirit strengthens us with *power* in our inner being. When God fills us with His Spirit and power, it is not meant simply as a blessing, but it is also given for a purpose. Immediately before The Lord ascended into Heaven, He told His disciples what would result from being empowered by The Holy Spirit.

> *You will* **receive power** *when The Holy Spirit comes upon you, and* **you will be my witnesses**. *(Acts 1;8)*

When Jesus said these words, He was speaking of Pentecost, when they would be Baptised in The Holy Spirit. It can be described as not only an empowering, but also the gateway to the spiritual gifts, as recorded in 1 Corinthians 12;7-11. However, the gifts are not meant to be confined to the church environment. They are not introspective, but rather to be outward looking as part of our witness to the world.

BAPTISM IN THE HOLY SPIRIT

If anyone reading this is unsure about such matters, may I suggest a reading of Acts 8;14-17; Acts 10;44-48; Acts 19;1-7. It is clear from these Scriptures, and others, that The Baptism in The Holy Spirit is a separate experience to salvation, although they can both occur at the same time.

Such an encounter is not meant to be an end in itself. Ephesians 5;18 states – *be filled with The Spirit*, which in the literal translation means **be being filled with The Spirit**. It is in the continuous tense. There is little point in someone saying, "I was filled with The Spirit five years ago", if they are not living in the fullness of that experience in the present day.

The Baptism in The Holy Spirit can occur in a number of ways. There are various examples in Scripture. It does not have to be in a church meeting. A person can be alone in their room, in a group who are seeking together, or when someone lays hands on them, either individually or collectively. The Baptism occurs at a specific time, whereas to live in the daily fullness of what has occurred, depends on our daily relationship with Him.

Have you been in meetings when people have gone forward for prayer, to have a 'fresh touch' of The Holy Spirit, but after a few days they do not feel any different. The main reason for this is that they have relied on the experience alone. The fullness of The Spirit will never come about by the constant laying on of hands, but only by the developing of our relationship with Him.

You will appreciate that I am not saying anything detrimental about the laying on of hands. Quite the contrary. I partake in such matters myself. I merely wish to encourage us to be wise in these matters, and also to focus attention on The Person of The Holy Spirit, as opposed to the experience.

How do we remain filled with The Spirit? It is when our soul is in line with our spirit. The *rivers of living water (John 7;38)* that is present in our spirit does not encounter any obstruction, but is allowed to flow and saturate all parts of our being. The Lord knows our desires. In Luke 11;9-10 He encourages us to ask, seek, and knock. The passage of Scripture then goes on to tell us the outcome.

How much more will your Father in Heaven give The Holy Spirit to those who ask him.

(Luke 11;13)

IN ONE ACCORD

With regard to Pentecost, when the believers were first Baptised in The Spirit, have you ever thought what happened in the place where The Lord had told his disciples to wait? What were they actually doing? Were they praying, talking, sleeping, just sitting, or what? I would suggest that the disciples spent the time consecrating themselves to The Lord. (Consecration means to be set apart to God).

They repented, and settled any selfish ambition, personality conflicts and petty jealousies that had come to the surface in the past. They also spent time in individual and corporate prayer. They emptied themselves, ready to be filled with The Spirit. Following their Baptism in The Holy Spirit they went out into the street, and Peter addressed the crowd. He referred to Joel's prophecy and quoted directly from Joel 2;28-32. It is important to note that Joel 2;28 begins with the following statement.

And afterwards, *I will pour out My Spirit on all people*.

The two words *and afterwards* are very significant, because they obviously refer to something happening before God pours out His Spirit.

I will summarise what happened in the earlier part of Joel:

Return to Me with all your heart (Joel 2 v12):
Rend your heart (v13):
Call a sacred assembly (v15):
The promise of new wine (v19):
They will be full (v26).

What was prophesied in Joel is what occurred in the room where the disciples were waiting at Pentecost.

The reason that Peter referred to Joel's prophecy is that they had responded to the first part of the prophecy in their days of waiting. They had returned to The Lord with all their heart. They were a consecrated people waiting on God. When they were filled with God's Spirit they knew that the *'and afterwards'* had come. They knew that *'the vats were overflowing with new wine'*. (Joel 2;24). Both the first and second part of Joel's prophesy had been fulfilled.

ON GOING EXPERIENCE

Although Pentecost was a unique experience, The Lord
continued saturating believers in the Holy Spirit wherever
they met together.

> *After they prayed,* **the place where they were meet-
> ing was shaken.** *And they were* **all filled with The
> Holy Spirit** *and spoke the Word of God boldly.*
>
> (Acts 4;31)

The background to this verse is that the disciples
had encountered persecution and warnings from the
authorities, but they took no notice, and consecrated
themselves again to The Lord, asking for greater
boldness. God answered their prayer by literally shaking the place where they were met, and filling them
again with His Spirit. Although Pentecost was the initial outpouring of the Holy Spirit, it is evident that
the filling with The Spirit was a continuous experience. It is meant to be the same with us, both individually and collectively.

PARALLEL EXPERIENCE

There are certain similarities between what happened at
Pentecost and Solomon's dedicating of the Temple, when
The Ark of God was brought in.

> *All the priests who were there had* **consecrated them-
> selves** *... They were accompanied by 120 priests...They
> raised their voices in praise to The Lord...Then the
> Temple of The Lord was filled with a cloud, and the
> priests could not perform their service because of the
> cloud, for* **the Glory of The Lord filled the Temple
> of God**. (II Chronicles 5;11-14)

The people had consecrated themselves, they were united in worship, and The Ark which carried the Presence of The Lord, was being restored to its rightful place in The Temple. God responded by filling the place with His Glory. There are a number of spiritual principles contained in this Scripture for us in the present day.

Your body is a Temple of The Holy Spirit.
(1 Corinthians 6;19)

Permit me to ask – Is The Lord in the rightful place in our lives? Does He have pre-eminence? It was the heart of our Heavenly Father to fill The Temple with His Glory. His heart has not changed. In the time when Chronicles was written it was a physical Temple. At Pentecost we became that Temple.

I would suggest that the two accounts, namely II Chronicles 5, and Acts 1 & 2, are parallel passages of Scripture, which teach us what can happen to a people who consecrate themselves, and wait upon The Lord.

CHRONICLES	PENTECOST
120 priests gathered	120 Royal priests gathered
They had consecrated themselves	Disciples had consecrated themselves
They were united as one voice	They were in one accord
The Temple was dedicated	Body became temple of The Holy Spirit
Temple filled with God's Glory	People filled with The Holy Spirit
Priests could not minister	Believers appeared drunk

It is important to point out to any reader, who is unfamiliar with Scripture, that there is nothing significant about the figure of 120. The principle of consecration is the important point, and it does not matter how many persons are present. God pours out His Presence upon an individual alone in his room, and on a multitude of people.

PREPARING THE WAY

John The Baptist fulfilled prophesy. Isaiah prophesied this concerning him:

> **Prepare the way for The Lord**, *make straight...a highway for our God.* (Isaiah 40;3)

During my Police career I was on duty at a number of Royal visits, when either the Queen, or Prince Charles came to an engagement in our area. It is standard practice that before their time of arrival, the entire route of travel is cleared of any obstructions. This enables them to have a clear pathway.

A Police motorcyclist leads their cavalcade and there are outriders either side of their vehicle. The front rider travels ahead of the Royal vehicles, and radios to the outriders, informing them as to the state of the route. The all-important word they want to hear is "clear." The Queen or Prince then comes speedily through to their intended destination, not impeded by any obstructions.

If we do this for royalty, how much more ought we to do it for our Lord Jesus, who is The King of kings, and Lord of lords.

John The Baptist prepared the way for the coming of The Lord's ministry. Likewise, the disciples in the upper room made a clear pathway for The Presence of The Lord to come upon them. Let us follow the example of John and the disciples, and clear the way of anything in our lives that would hinder Him. We will then encounter the fullness of His Anointing.

CHAPTER TWENTY-SIX

THE ANOINTING

ISAIAH 61;1 states –

The Spirit of The Sovereign Lord is on me, because **the Lord has anointed Me** ...

The Anointing is being saturated in His Presence.

Whenever a Prophet, Priest or King entered service they were anointed. Each of these offices was an important function in The Israelite nation. They were anointed in order to receive God's blessing and equipping for their tasks. God gave the following instructions to Moses and Elijah respectively.

Anoint *Aaron and his sons and consecrate them so they may serve me as* **priests**.   *(Exodus 30;30)*

Anoint *Jehu son of Nimshi* **king** *over Israel, and* **anoint** *Elisha to succeed you as* **prophet**.
                                                              (1 Kings 19;16)

The Lord Jesus fulfilled each of the functions of Prophet, Priest, and King, and was also Anointed for service.

Jesus of Nazareth was a **Prophet**.   *(Luke 24;19)*
We do have such a **High Priest**.   *(Hebrews 8;1-2)*
He is Lord of lords and **King of kings**.   *(Rev. 17;14)*

Jesus was anointed for earthly ministry at His baptism. Peter refers to this incident when he is speaking at Cornelius' home.

Beginning in Galilee after the baptism that John preached, how **God anointed Jesus of Nazareth with The Holy Spirit** *and power, and how He went around doing good and healing all who were under the power of the devil, because God was with Him.*

(Acts 10;37)

It is important to say at this point that when we are born again, an Anointing takes place when we receive The Holy Spirit into our lives, and we become new creations. However, God wants us to walk each day in the fullness of that anointing.

Anointing and consecration, which mean to be set apart for God, are used together in scripture, as in Exodus 30;30 when Aaron and his sons entered the priesthood. However, it is not simply meant for those in leadership. It is for everyone, as we shall see later.

PREPARATION

Consecrate yourselves, *for tomorrow The Lord will do amazing things among you.* *(Joshua 3;5)*

An example of the importance of consecration can be seen in the above words that Joshua spoke to the Israelites. They were about to cross the Jordan River and enter the Promised Land. We all want to see amazing things happen among us. The principle still applies today. If we consecrate ourselves to God He will anoint us with His Presence and amazing things will happen.

Moses knew that it was vital to have the Lord's Presence in everything.

> *Then Moses said to The Lord,* **"If Your Presence does
> not go with us,** *do not send us up from here. How will
> anyone know that You are pleased with me and with
> Your people unless You go with us?* **What else will dis-
> tinguish me and Your people from all the other
> people?"** *(Exodus 33;15)*

The one thing that separates born-again believers from
every other religious group in the world is The Presence
of God. It can be compared to II Chronicles 5 that we
looked at in the previous chapter, when The Ark containing The Presence of God was brought into The Temple.
The Glory of The Lord then fell on those present. The
Anointing and empowering that will subsequently flow
will astound us.

> *Now to Him who is able to* **do immeasurably more
> than all we ask or imagine, according to His
> power that is at work within us.** *(Ephesians 3;20)*

ATTACHED TO THE SOURCE

The Apostle John gives us an insight into how to continue to live in The Anointing, namely to remain in Him.

> **The Anointing** *you received from Him* **remains in
> you,** *and you do not need anyone to teach you. But as*
> **His Anointing** *teaches you about all things and as*
> **that Anointing** *is real, not counterfeit, just as it has
> taught you,* **remain in Him**. *(1 John 2;27)*

Notice that this Scripture states that The Anointing
remains in us, and His Anointing teaches us all things. His
Spirit never leaves a believer, because we have the promise
that The Lord will never leave us, nor forsake us.
Therefore, when we continually consecrate our lives to

Him, that anointing is able to flow from our spirit and into our soul, without break or hindrance.

This is a parallel passage with John 15;1-9 where The Lord gives the analogy of the vine and the branches to His disciples. He encourages them to remain in Him, as branches cannot produce fruit unless they are attached to the vine. The Lord tells them in the clearest possible terms – *apart from Me you can do nothing*.

We have the confidence that The Lord will never leave, nor forsake us (Hebrews 13;5). But we are encouraged in 1 John 2;27 and John 15;1-9 that to remain operating in The Anointing we must not revert to operating out of our flesh, our old self. If that happens we are detaching ourselves from His direction. Although He does not leave us, our actions prevent us from being led by The Spirit. It is only when we remain in The Lord's ways that we encounter the fullness of The Anointing in our lives.

SPECIFIC INGREDIENTS

The anointing oil used in The Old Testament was sacred. Exodus 30;22-33 describes the ingredients, and how it was to be used to anoint the Tent of Meeting and its contents, including the Ark of the Testimony, in order that they were consecrated and holy. It was then to be used to anoint Aaron and his sons as they entered the priesthood. There was an instruction that no other oil was to have the same formula, and no other oil to be used as the Anointing oil. **It was sacred and unique**.

The Anointing oil was replaced at Pentecost with a new Anointing, when God poured out His Holy Spirit on His Church. Although it replaced the previous anointing oil, it was once again poured out on a priesthood. This time it was on a royal priesthood.

> *You are a chosen people,* **a royal priesthood**, *a holy nation, a people belonging to God.* (1 Peter 2;9)

That Anointing, which was first given at Pentecost, continues to flow today, and we can testify that the present day Anointing is also sacred and unique.

THE PRESENCE OF GOD

When the Israelites went from Egypt to the Promised Land, they carried with them The Tabernacle, which was where God would meet with them. This later became the Temple, a permanent structure. There is no longer the need for a Tabernacle, because God tabernacles inside us. He never leaves a born-again believer. He is with us always. There is also no need for a Temple, as we have become the Temple of the Holy Spirit (1 Corinthians 6;19). And as we saw earlier, the anoininting oil used in the Taberncle, and later in the Temple, has been replaced with the Anointing of the Holy Spirit in our lives.

It was a great honour and responsibility for those who carried the Tabernacle, and who later ministered in the Temple. The same applies today. Never let us take His Presence for granted.

The Anointing is not exclusive, and kept solely for those who hold office or position within the church. We are all included in the royal priesthood described in 1 Peter 2;9. God is not concerned with externals. He looks for what lies inside a person. David was anointed King because God saw his heart. Up until then he was just a shepherd boy. When the prophet Samuel was to anoint the new King he was told the following:

> *The LORD does not look at the things man looks at. Man looks at the outward appearance, but* **The Lord**

looks at the heart... *So Samuel took the horn of oil and* **anointed David** *in the presence of his brothers, and* **from that day on The Spirit of The Lord came upon David in power.**

(1 Samuel 16;7 & 13)

Notice that David was anointed, and from that moment the Spirit empowered him. The Anointing empowers and equips. When an individual or work for The Lord is anointed, there is a clear separation from the ordinary. There is no question of playing church, keeping up appearances, or going through the motions. Churches, and individual lives, are dramatically and visibly changed. The question we all must face is – How much do we thirst for The Anointing of God upon our lives, our ministry, our worship, our witnessing etc.?

As the deer pants for streams of water, so **my soul pants for you, O God.** *(Psalm 42;1)*

Exodus 30 records how the Israelites were given strict instructions as to the contents of The Anointing oil. They were not allowed to tinker with the ingredients. It is important that we learn a lesson from this account in Scripture. So often, churches and individuals want to receive The Anointing, but they try to tinker with the ingredients. They want to use some of the ingredients, but not all. Consequently they never encounter The Anointing that God has for them.

If we truly want The Anointing of God, whether as individuals or churches, then we will abandon our tinkering and experimenting with what satisfies ourselves. We need to count the cost, and pay the price by abandoning ourselves to The Lord. Not in part, but in whole.

CHAPTER TWENTY-SEVEN

PROPHECY AND FULFILMENT

THERE ARE THREE separate pieces of Scripture that progressively reveal different aspects of the Anointing. First the seeking, secondly the receiving, and thirdly the outworking.

THE FAST (The seeking)
Is not this the kind of fasting I have chosen
To loose the chains of injustice
Untie the cords of the yoke
Set the oppressed free
Break every yoke
Share your food with the hungry
Provide the poor wanderer with shelter
When you see the naked, clothe him
Not to turn away from your own flesh and blood.
(Isaiah 58;6-7)

THE ANOINTING
(The Receiving)
The Spirit of The Sovereign Lord is on Me
Because The Lord has anointed Me to

THE LORD'S MINISTRY
(The Outworking)
The Spirit of The Lord is on Me
Because He has anointed Me to

Preach good news to the poor	*Preach good news to the poor*
Bind up the broken hearted	*Proclaim freedom for the prisoners*
Proclaim freedom for the captives	*Recovery of sight for the blind*
Release from darkness for the prisoners	*Release the oppressed*
Proclaim the year of The Lord's favour	*Proclaim the year of The Lord's favour*
Comfort all who mourn	*Provide for those who grieve*
Bestow on them a garment of praise	*(Luke 4;18-19)*
(Isaiah 61;1-3)	

It is evident that the above three passages of Scripture are identical in theme and content. Is there a connection? Is there a reason for their particular order in scripture?

I. THE FAST (Isaiah 58;6-7)

This passage of Scripture deals with the type of fast that God has chosen. It is full of power and blessing. If you examine the verses at the beginning of the chapter, you will see that the fast that the people were conducting was in complete contrast to that desired by God. Their heart attitude was wrong, and they were just going through the motions. Have we ever felt like that?

It is the type of attitude that our Lord finds the most disturbing. He spoke these words to the Laodicean Church.

> *I know your deeds, that* **you are neither cold nor hot** *... because* **you are lukewarm** *I am about to spit you out of my mouth.* *(Revelation 3;15-16)*

The people, as described in Isaiah 58;1-5, were conducting a fast which was self-seeking, absorbed with their own desires, and stagnant. They could not understand why their prayers were not being answered. God's reply cut right through to the core of the issue.

> *You cannot fast as you do today and expect your voice to be heard on high.* (Isaiah 58;4)

However, to those that honour the fast that God has chosen, He has this to say.

> *Then you will call, and* **The Lord** **will answer**; *you will cry for help, and He will say:* **Here am I**. (Isaiah 58;9)

The reason that the fast comes first in the order of passages is that true fasting involves *consecration and self sacrifice*, a dying to oneself, and a handing over of oneself to the purposes of God. From this position of an emptying of self, comes the enabling of God to fill us with His Spirit, so that the fast becomes something which is living and vibrant, full of movement, powerful and outward looking.

An actual physical fast is not a condition of receiving the Anointing, but the ingredient of consecration is vital for continuing in its fullness. There is no formula, because each person is to make their own response to consecration. The central issue in all of this is our heart attitude, not how we individually go about it.

Who is prepared to be shaken by God, so that all that is not of Him falls away, so that all that remains, is of Him. To those who are prepared to be shaken, the first shaking that will take place will be that caused by the convicting power of His Spirit, as He establishes a consecrated life in the believer. To those who submit to His Lordship, and give full reign to His Spirit in their lives, a second shaking will then take place. This will be the shaking caused by the anointing power of His Spirit.

2. THE ANOINTING AND ITS PURPOSE
(Isaiah 61;1-3)

These verses are a prophetic declaration of what was to occur in Jesus ministry, and then in our lives.

It is not meant to be received as a blessing, and then become dormant. It is meant for ministry, and to be a continual life changing experience, both for the one who receives, and also for the lives we touch. Take another look at these verses in Isaiah 61, and see a sample of the type of people we are to reach. Then follow on in the same reading and witness the fruit of rebuilding, restoring, and renewing as we move in The Anointing. The Lord showed us the way, and what we can expect to happen.

3. THE OUTWORKING (Luke 4;18-19)

This passage records The Lord's first public message, when He got up in the synagogue, and read directly from the passage in Isaiah 61.

He declared in absolutely clear language what the people were going to see happen in His ministry, and also that He is the fulfilment of Scripture.

> *The Word became flesh and made His dwelling among us.* (John 1;14)

He took on humanity, but still received The Anointing for ministry.

Jesus therefore showed us that we all have need of that

Anointing, if we are to move in ministry. That is why He related back to the prophetic passage of Scripture in Isaiah 61, which outlines The Anointing. The next three years of His earthly ministry provided abundant evidence of the prophetic word being outlived.

CONTINUITY

An association can now be drawn between the three passages of Scripture. Isaiah 58 (**Consecration**) – Isaiah 61 (**Anointing**) – Luke 4 (**Ministry**). These principles are required throughout our entire lives. As stated earlier, it is not a one-off experience.

The Lord subjected Himself to the order of consecration, anointing, and ministry. He told Mary at the age of twelve that He must be about His Father's business.

For I seek not to please Myself but Him who sent Me.
(John 5;30)

He was consecrated throughout His life. He was later anointed at His Baptism, and then began His public ministry. Jesus always takes the lead, and shows us the way, because He is the Way, the Truth, and the Life.

The Anointing is for every believer, and not restricted in any way to those in full time ministry, or any other form of leadership. It is for each of us to seek, and it is irrelevant as to what age, church, or background we are from. In fact, there is a ministry that is common to each of us. We have a joint commission to reconcile the world to God. **He has equipped us for the task by the power of His Anointing.**

God reconciled us to Himself through Christ, and **gave us the ministry of reconciliation.**
(2 Corinthians 5;18)

Is there a clear Anointing on my life? Is there evidence of such an Anointing in my daily living and work for Him? If The Anointing is not there, then we labour in vain. It is reported that in the Welsh Revival, Evan Roberts would not even get up to preach unless he knew that The Anointing was upon him. Perhaps this is an opportune time to re-assess our lives, consecrate ourselves to The Lord, and seek His Anointing.

THE FRUIT

In the first part of this chapter I outlined the range of ministry that is common to the respective passages of scripture. The resultant fruit recorded in those scriptures is also identical.

Isaiah 58	Isaiah 61
Loose *the chains of* injustice	*For I, The Lord, love* justice
The Lord will strengthen your frame	*They will be called* oaks of righteousness
You will be like a well-watered, garden *like a* spring *whose* waters never fail	*As the soil makes the young plant come up, and a* garden causes seeds to grow, *so the Sovereign Lord will make righteousness and* praise spring up *before all nations*
Your people will rebuild *the* ancient ruins and will raise up *the age-old foundations; you will be called*	*They will* rebuild *the ancient ruins and* restore *the places long devastated; they will* renew *the*

Isaiah 58	Isaiah 61
repairer *of broken walls,* restorer *of streets with dwellings*	*ruined cities that have been devastated for generations*
You will find your joy *in the Lord*	Everlasting joy *will be theirs*
I will cause you to feast on the inheritance *of your father Jacob*	*They will* rejoice in their inheritance, *and so they will inherit a double portion in their land*

CHAPTER TWENTY-EIGHT

SPRINGS OF WATER

A PROPHETIC example of The Anointing, and its subsequent effect can be found in the life of Othniel, contained in Judges 1 & 3. The passage of Scripture relates to a time when the men of Judah went to fight the Canaanites. Caleb told the army that he would give his daughter Acsah in marriage to the man who captured the particular area they were attacking.

Othniel was successful, and he married Acsah. Some time later, Acsah approached Caleb with a request.

Do me a special favour. Since you have given me land in the Negev, **give me also springs of water**. *Caleb gave her the upper and lower springs.* (Judges 1;15)

Caleb, a man of faith and anointing, gave Acsah and Othniel springs of water. These springs can be seen prophetically as the overflow of The Holy Spirit. This theme continues in the New Testament where the Lord Jesus refers to Pentecost in such a manner.

Jesus said – If anyone is thirsty, let him come to me and drink. Whoever believes in Me, as the Scripture has said, **streams of living water will flow from within him. By this He meant The Spirit**, *whom those who believed in Him were later to receive.* (John 7;37-39)

The Lord asked – "If anyone is thirsty." Our response is the same as Acsah and her husband – **"Give me also springs of water that I may overflow."**

REFRESHED FOR BATTLE

The account of Othniel in Judges does not end in chapter one, when he received the springs of water. In subsequent years the Israelites stopped following God's ways, and got into trouble again. They were overpowered, and robbed of their land. They repented, and called out to God. He raised up for them a deliverer, none other than Othniel, who saved them, and restored that which had been stolen.

> **The Spirit of The Lord came upon Othniel,** *so that he became Israel's leader and* **went to war.** *The Lord gave Cushan-Rishathaim King of Aram into the hands of Othniel, who overpowered him.* **So the land had peace** *for 40 years until Othniel died.*
>
> *(Judges 3;10-11)*

The Spirit of God came upon Othniel and he went to war. When we call out to God to give us springs of water, what do we envisage? Do we simply want the blessing? It can be seen from the above passage that The Spirit of The Lord came upon Othniel in order to empower him to go to war.

Springs of water, which represent the anointing Holy Spirit of our God, is for action as well as blessing. We will then accomplish the same as Othniel in **rebuilding, restoring and renewing** that which has been stolen. You will notice that Othniel's actions brought peace to the land.

IMPEDING THE FLOW

It is important to know that The Anointing on our ministry can be lost. Samson disobeyed The Lord, and compromised his faith with Delilah. The Anointing and strength that God had given him was taken away.

> *Samson awoke from his sleep, and thought, "I will go out as before and shake myself free."* **But he did not know that The Lord had left him**. *(Judges 16;20)*

What a tragic situation. The words in Judges are devastating.

If Samson had spent time in The Lord's Presence he would have known that he was acting outside of His will. But Samson was intent on going his own way. This led to him losing The Anointing upon his ministry. He became bound, and thought he could once more break himself free. He realised too late that the source of his strength had been removed.

The above verse of Scripture illustrates that continued disobedience will ultimately lead to captivity or bondage of some kind. As we have seen previously, we are meant to be the captor, not the captive.

Samson did not appear to understand that there needs to be balance between the outward victory, and the inner victory. There is a Scripture that clearly illustrates this point.

> *I want to know Christ, and* **the power of His resurrection, and the fellowship of sharing in His suffering**, *becoming like Him in His death, and so, somehow to attain to the resurrection from the dead.*
> *(Philippians 3;10-11)*

The power of The Lord's resurrection reveals the outward victory, whilst the fellowship of sharing in His suffering reveals the inner victory. There is a danger of concentrating on one aspect, and neglecting the other. It is possible to dwell solely on sacrificial living, and neglect the miraculous, or alternatively to concentrate solely on the miraculous, and neglect the need for a sacrificial life.

This can also be seen in the fruit and gifts of The Holy Spirit. There are nine aspects to the fruit (Galatians 5;22-23) and nine gifts (1 Corinthians 12;8-11). This clearly illustrates balance. We are not meant to concentrate on one area, and neglect the other.

Samson knew the miraculous, but he only periodically lived a sacrificial life. His walk with God was unbalanced. He was too fond of going his own way, and eventually lost The Anointing on his life and ministry. Fortunately, Samson repented and The Anointing returned. But his life then ended.

Who knows what he might have achieved for God, had he not fallen into disobedience?

CHAPTER TWENTY-NINE

THE KEYS OF THE
KINGDOM

WHEN A POLICE OFFICER understands the power and authority that has been granted to him as a result of becoming an Officer of the Law, he performs his duty with confidence and assuredness. He knows that he has the authority of the Law to back up his actions. Likewise, as Christians, it is important that we are fully aware of the power and authority available to us. When we take positive action to prevent spiritual crime, or take back that which has been stolen, we make our stand in sure faith and boldness.

Our spiritual authority is based solely on the revelation of Jesus as both Lord and Christ. This revelation is the rock upon which we stand. Let us look at how, and when, this truth was established.

Before doing so, I would just like to refer back to my personal testimony at the beginning of the book. My reason for doing so, is that I want to reiterate that it was this revelation, concerning the Keys of The Kingdom, that enabled me to stand against the demonic attack that I was encountering.

You may find it helpful to once again read the relevant

portion of that chapter before going any further, in order to remind yourself of what happened. I have no doubt that The Lord not only strengthened me by giving me the means to fight back, but He also equipped me for the future. I have therefore come to appreciate the truth of the Keys in a way that not only rescued me, but also will continue with me for the rest of my life.

I would like to add, that although I gained a knowledge of this truth in a particular set of circumstances, I now appreciate its significance, and influence in all aspects of spiritual authority, and not simply in confronting the demonic. I am certain that this Scriptural precept will have remarkable impact on anyone who embraces its reality.

THE CONFESSION

Most people are familiar with the passage in Scripture that records the conversation that Jesus had with His disciples, concerning His identity. Peter responded with that wonderful truth.

> *You are* **the Christ**, *The Son of The Living God.*
> *(Matthew 16;13-16)*

Some time later, Peter addressed a crowd of people at Pentecost, immediately following the disciples being Baptised in The Holy Spirit. It is noticeable that it is the same statement that he had previously made directly to Jesus.

> *Therefore let all Israel be assured of this; God has made this* **Jesus**, *whom you crucified, both* **Lord and Christ**.
> *(Acts 2;36)*

Are these passages of Scripture linked in any way? In order to get the answer we need to look at the first occasion when Peter made his declaration. The Lord gave the following response.

> *On this rock I will build My Church, and the gates of hell will not overcome it. I will give you* **the Keys of The Kingdom of Heaven***; whatever you bind on earth will be bound in Heaven, and whatever you loose on earth will be loosed in Heaven.*
>
> *(Matthew 16;18-19)*

An examination of these words leaves us in no doubt whatsoever, that this was a truly remarkable promise to Peter. It was far more than a word of encouragement. This text raises certain questions. What are the Keys of The Kingdom? Why did Jesus give Peter the promise of receiving them? When were they given?

THE PROMISE

Matthew 16 records when Peter made his first declaration, and The Lord told him that He would give him the Keys. You will notice that the words used by Jesus were in the future tense. It was clear that it was not for that present time, but would subsequently happen in Peter's lifetime.

If it were something to be received in eternity The Lord would not have singled out just Peter, but would have said it directly to all the disciples who were present. Therefore, when such a statement is made, it is obvious that Scripture will record the time when it is fulfilled.

The lead up to the giving of the Keys came at Pentecost, when The Holy Spirit came to anoint the collective church. Following their Baptism in The Spirit, the disciples emerged from the upper room, and were faced with a crowd who had quickly gathered around them. Out of the 120 disciples, it was Peter who stood up to address the onlookers.

Have you ever wondered why it was Peter who took the initiative? Why not John, who seemingly was more stable in character, or Matthew who was perhaps better educated? Why Peter?

The answer lies in understanding the two separate confessions of Peter concerning The Lord. The first is recorded in Matthew 16, and the second in Acts 2. Both statements, made at separate times, testify of the same truth. They declare that Jesus is Lord, The Christ – The Anointed One.

The Holy Spirit therefore prompted Peter to speak to the crowd at Pentecost because of the revelation that he had previously received and the promise made by Jesus.

A revelation of that confession is the key to understanding the Keys of The Kingdom!

RECEIVING THE REVELATION

Before looking at the progression of events, it will be helpful to examine how Peter got the revelation in the first place. In order to do so it is necessary to first jump ahead, and then return to the passage under consideration.

Matthew 16;21-23 gives the account of Jesus beginning to explain to His disciples that He must go to Jerusalem, where He would be killed, but on the third day be raised to life. Peter tried to talk Him out of this course of action, and The Lord confronted him. This occurs in Scripture directly after Peter's confession, and caused a hugely different response from Jesus.

Although it is sometimes taught that the two events occurred the same day, it is worth noting that the subsequent portion of Scripture begins with – *from that time on … (v21)*. It therefore could have happened the same day, or a week or more later. There is no indication as to the time span. But how did Peter receive such revelation, and then within a short space of time appear almost devoid of spirituality? I believe that it is explained by understanding the different aspects of our spirit and soul. We saw earlier in chapters eight and nine that God relates Spirit to spirit. Therefore, God revealed this to Peter in his spirit? Jesus told Peter the following.

This was not revealed to you by man, but by My Father in Heaven.   *(Matthew 16;17)*

Now consider his attempt to dissuade The Lord from going to Jerusalem. Jesus pointed out to Peter that his motives were not God-inspired, but derived from man's thoughts. This is a complete reversal to the former statement.

You do not have in mind the things of God, but the things of men.   *(Matthew 16;23)*

What do you think was happening inside Peter which caused Jesus to highlight the contrast? He quite understandably did not want to lose Jesus both as his Lord and friend. He also did not wish to see Him come to harm. He may even have thought that all the wonderful experiences would come to an end.

But he was short sighted in only seeing The Lord's death, and not His resurrection. We can all sympathise with him, because we could well have acted in the same manner. However, if we examine Peter's reaction we will see that it was soul-orientated. His emotions and mental reasoning took centre-stage. He was not operating out of his spirit.

This illustrates the difference between a quickening in

our spirit which is birthed by The Holy Spirit, as opposed to acting on impulse that is driven by thoughts and emotions in our soul. Thankfully, Peter subsequently changed into someone who was consistently Spirit led.

RECEIVING THE KEYS

Having examined the origin of Peter's inspiration, let us now look progressively at the sequence of events concerning the Keys of The Kingdom, and in so doing it is helpful to divide The Lord's statement into three parts.

1. *On this rock I will build My Church, and the gates of hell will not overcome it.*

What 'rock' did Jesus have in mind? You will notice that He is very specific, stating *"this rock."* It is clear that Jesus was referring to the revelation and words used by Peter, and not the person of Peter.

This is confirmed by an examination of the Greek words used in the passage. 'Petra' is used to denote a mass of rock, while 'Petros' means a detached stone. In Matthew 16;18 petra is used metaphorically to describe Jesus, and the testimony concerning Him, while petros is used concerning Peter. The emphasis is therefore on the revelation and not Peter himself.

Some people get confused about this issue because Peter had originally been known as Simon. He was renamed as Cephas (or Peter), which both have the meaning of 'rock', as recorded in John 1;42. It is interesting that Jesus gave him this particular name. The word rock has the meaning of stability, solidarity, and strength, which were the opposite of Peter's testimony at that time. But The Lord had confidence in him, and knew what he would become one day.

What therefore caused Jesus to utter such a response to Peter? What was the rock? It was Peter's revelation that Jesus is The Christ. This was the foundation upon which The Church was to be built. It is to fully comprehend that Jesus is The Christ, The Anointed One, who is Lord over all things. **That revelation is The Key to establishing spiritual authority.**

All things were **created by Him** *and for Him...in Him* **all things hold together** ... *He is* **the head** *of the body, the church* ... *that* **in everything He might have the supremacy**. *(Colossians 1;15-20)*

Following His crucifixion, Scripture records that Jesus entered hell, where He made an open display of the devil, which further illustrated our Lord's supremacy. It is therefore important that we are clear on this issue. The Lord did not escape from hell – He completely defeated anything He encountered there. He entered and left at His own will.

To further reinforce the devil's defeat, He took the keys of death and hell. He then rose from the grave. Our Lord has overcome all things!

Do not be afraid. I am the first and the last. I am the living One; I was dead, and behold I am alive forever and ever! And **I hold the keys of death and Hades**. *(Revelation 1;17-18)*

Just think for one moment. Jesus holds the Keys of both Heaven and hell. He is Lord over all things. His name is above all other names, and at His feet all must bow, whether in this life or the age to come. His authority is undisputed. He also informs us what He will do with the Keys.

2. I will give you the keys of The Kingdom of Heaven.
This statement by Jesus explains why it was Peter who stood up amongst the 120 disciples, and spoke to the crowd at Pentecost. You will notice that it was a definite promise. If Jesus stated that He would do something, everyone knew that He would fulfil His word. There was obviously something very specific in Peter's words that caused The Lord to make such a declaration.

The promise was given to Peter as a result of his revelation that Jesus is The Christ – The Anointed One, who is Lord. The fulfilment of the promise occurred some time later at Pentecost, when The Holy Spirit directed Peter to speak, not only to the gathered crowd, but also ultimately to the world.

If you examine Peter's message in Acts 2 you will see that it progressively describes Jesus' life and ministry. He then brings it to a conclusion with the emphatic statement that **Jesus is both Lord and Christ** (Acts 2;36).

The first time that Peter made this statement, it had been directly to Jesus in the presence of a few disciples (Matthew 16;16). The Lord then entrusted him to declare this truth to the world at a future time. It can therefore be seen why it had to be Peter who spoke on behalf of the disciples at Pentecost. It was he who had first received and testified of the revelation concerning Jesus.

The Holy Spirit then directed Peter to speak to the crowd, and when he declared for the second time that Jesus is both Lord and Christ, the Keys were given. The two passages of Scripture in Matthew 16 and Acts 2 contain **revelation, promise and fulfilment** all combined together.

We have already seen in the first part of this chapter that the Keys of The Kingdom represent authority. At

Pentecost, Peter was given the authority to speak and act on God's behalf, and reveal the Gospel message to the world. It was built upon the truth that Jesus is both Lord and Christ.

Is access to the Keys reserved for just a few people? The answer is an emphatic "no". They are for everyone who has the revelation of Jesus, and the authority that He possesses. It is clear from Peter's message that the truth is open *for all*. (Acts 2;39).

Once we understand the spiritual authority that we have been given with the Keys of The Kingdom, then we will be able to exercise binding and loosing. However, it is always important to remember that when we exercise spiritual authority, it must be in accordance with God's will and purpose, and for His Glory, not something that we may think is simply a good idea!

3. Whatever you bind on earth will be bound in Heaven, and whatever you loose on earth will be loosed in heaven.

In order to understand the full significance of all that The Lord said to Peter, it is necessary to examine the meanings of certain words. The Greek translation of bind means to 'tie up'. The word loose is rendered 'release'. The Hebrew translation for the words is to 'forbid' and 'permit'. It can be seen that each of the translations incorporate an enforcing, or establishing of a certain rule or action.

It therefore has to be asked – what was Peter going to establish? In order to find the answer we need to look at what happened at the end of Peter's speech to the crowd. His message had convicted them, and they wanted to respond.

When the people heard this, they were cut to the heart and said to Peter and the other apostles, "Brothers, **what shall we do?** *"* (Acts 2;37)

Peter gave the following response:

"Repent and be baptised every one of you, **in the name of Jesus Christ** *for the forgiveness of your sins.* **And you will receive the gift of The Holy Spirit.** *"*

(Acts 2;38-39)

Peter's reply established the gospel message that salvation can only be obtained through Jesus.

ESTABLISHED FOR ETERNITY

Following on from Jesus promise to give the Keys of The Kingdom to Peter, He also told him about a further aspect of the authority that he would receive. He would have the ability to bind and loose. If The Lord told a person they were going to be given something, it was obviously meant for a reason, and for use. When Peter received the Keys he immediately established something not simply for that particular moment in time, but for eternity.

He established that the *rock* on which The Church will be built is the revelation that Jesus is the Christ – the Anointed One, The Lord of all. He settled for eternity that the only way that we can be saved is through Christ. The means to open Heaven's door is by using the key that has written on it – Jesus is Lord.

He revealed that spiritual authority, and the use of binding and loosing is through The Name that is above every other name. Peter bound the power of satan that had held the people captive, and loosed them from their chains. Three thousand were born again of The Spirit that same day.

Peter's message publicly established spiritual authority for every believer once and for all. He spoke these words on Heaven's behalf, because he had been given the Keys as the authority. They were not simply given to Peter. They are for everyone who receives, and operates in the same revelation.

Keys have two uses. They can be used to unlock and set free, but also to lock-up and imprison. There are too many people held captive. It is the devil who is to be bound, not people. We have been given the Keys for that purpose. The question we have to ask ourselves is – what am I doing with the Keys?

The Keys of the Kingdom, in the same manner as household or business keys, have a specific function. They are not meant as decoration to hang on someone's waistband. They are to be used for a specific purpose. Let us be challenged afresh to fully comprehend the magnitude of The Lord's authority that he has imparted to us.

Your Kingdom come, Your will be done on earth as it is in Heaven.

CHAPTER THIRTY

THE SOVEREIGN
WILL OF GOD

When Christians are about to take a step of faith on behalf of others, or themselves, they often ask the question – "How can I be sure that what I am doing is the sovereign will of God?" It all becomes clear when we realise that sovereignty is about an answer, not a question.

Sovereignty means *'supreme rank and power, and the right to exercise such power'*.

If uncertainty about the sovereign will of God persists in our life, it will have the effect of causing indecisiveness, and missed opportunities. Whereas a firm and sure knowledge of His will causes faith to rise as we encounter challenges. In order to help us have knowledge in this matter He has clearly stated His will in Scripture, as we shall see shortly.

We are all conscious and aware of occasions when bad things happen, or when someone is not healed, or not released from bondage or oppression. When that occurs we need to be careful that we do not misuse the expression 'the sovereign will of God'. It is so important that we do not use it as an excuse for lack of faith on our part, or that we develop a fatalistic approach to things. Although

He allows us to go through trials and tests in order that our faith is strengthened, we need to be abundantly clear that He is never out to harm us.

It was the sovereign will of God that Jesus was crucified and took upon Himself all our sins and sicknesses. He then made an open display of His victory over satan, and rose from the dead. It was a finished act. We therefore do not need to question whether it is God's will to save, heal, or deliver us from any form of evil. It is clear and settled. It happened once and for all at Calvary. In fact, it was God's will at the beginning of creation.

> *The Lamb that was slain from the creation of the world.*
> *(Revelation 13;8)*

SOVEREIGNTY EXPLAINED

What then is God's sovereign will? This is clearly described in Isaiah 61;1-3:

> *The Spirit of* **the Sovereign Lord** *is on me, because*
> *The Lord has* **anointed** *me*
> *To* **preach good news** *to the poor*
> *He has* **sent me to bind up** *the broken-hearted*
> *To* **proclaim freedom** *for the captives*
> **Release** *from darkness for the prisoners*
> *To* **proclaim** *the year of The Lord's favour*
> *The day of* **vengeance** *of our God*
> *To* **comfort** *all who mourn.*

Notice how this passage begins – *the Spirit of* **the Sovereign Lord**. The verse first makes the statement about The Lord's sovereignty. It then goes on to list ways in which that sovereignty is expressed.

Allow me to paraphrase the above Scripture.

God is sovereign over all things, and we encounter

His Anointing to do His will, which is:

To reveal a message of life and hope to the world;

We are sent, and therefore commissioned to rebuild, restore and renew that which has been broken and stolen;

To speak words of life into those who are held captive to sin and sickness;

To use our authority in Him to open the prison doors and bring release to those who are prisoners of doubt, depression, oppression and possession;

To openly declare to this world that the favour of God is available to all;

To reveal that the vengeance of our God is upon the devil.

There is coming a day when the devil will receive his final judgement. But in the meantime, when we accomplish all that the Lord God has empowered us to do, we actually proclaim and reveal His vengeance upon the devil's purposes. We can take comfort, and be at peace, that *'greater is He who is in us than he who is in the world'*.

HIS WILL EXPRESSED

Jesus began His earthly ministry by quoting this passage of Scripture (Luke 4;17-19). He made a public declaration that the world was going to see the content of Isaiah 61 fulfilled in His life. It is abundantly clear from an examination of The Gospels that The Lord accomplished all the categories listed in that chapter of Isaiah, which reveals the sovereign will of God.

I have come to do the will *of Him who sent Me.*

(John 6;38)

When Peter was at the home of Cornelius he informed

those present about The Anointing which was upon Jesus life, and the result that occurred.

> **God anointed Jesus of Nazareth** *with The Holy Spirit and power, and* **He went around doing good and healing all who were under the power of the devil,** *because God was with Him.*   (Acts 10;38)

The sovereign will of God is to defeat anything that has its root in satan, whether it is sin, sickness or affliction of various kinds. John testifies to the same truth in his Epistle.

> *The reason The Son of God appeared was to* **destroy the devil's work**.   (1 John 3;8)

FAITH

> *Without faith it is impossible to please God.*
> (Hebrews 11;6)

The heart of The Lord's Prayer is that God's will be done on earth as it is in Heaven (Matt. 6;10). Jesus wanted his disciples to understand that they also had a part to play in establishing God's sovereign will on earth. We can encounter the same anointing to do the same works.

> *I tell you the truth,* **anyone who has faith in Me** *will do what I have been doing. He will do even greater things than these, because I am going to The Father. And* **I will do whatever you ask in My Name, so that the Son may bring Glory to The Father.** *You may ask me for anything in My Name, and I will do it.*
> (John 14;12-14)

The key to understanding these verses is that we first

have faith. Secondly, in whatever we seek to do, we bring glory to The Father. Thirdly, our authority is in the Name of Jesus. He is The Word that became flesh. (John 1;1 & 14). Therefore, when we step out in faith, it must be in accordance with The Word of God.

It is obvious that Jesus only did the sovereign will of God. John then tells us that when we exercise our faith, and do the same things that Jesus did, we are also fulfilling the sovereign will of God. It begins with faith.

Anyone who has faith in Me *will do what I have been doing.* *(John 14;12)*

EMPOWERING

Paul, writing to the Romans explains that the same power and authority that occurred at the resurrection is at work in us.

And if The Spirit of Him who raised Jesus from the dead is living in you, then He who raised Christ from the dead will also give life to your mortal bodies through his Spirit, who lives in you. *(Romans 8;11)*

If we just meditate on this verse, our outlook on circumstances will dramatically change.

Peter testified that after Jesus ascended He imparted The Holy Spirit at Pentecost. He did not keep anything to Himself. He not only shared, but He poured out The Holy Spirit upon us.

Exalted to the right hand of God, He has received from The Father the promised Holy Spirit and **has poured out what you now see and hear**. *(Acts 2;33)*

Peter then declares what will be the result of The

Anointing being poured out, by quoting from Psalm 110;1. As stated earlier in the book, The Anointing is not simply meant as a blessing. It is an empowering for a purpose.

The Lord said to my Lord: **Sit at my right hand until I make your enemies a footstool for your feet**.
(Acts 2;34-35)

This is an ongoing work until the final day of judgement. We have a part to play in all of this.

The end will come, when He (Christ) hands over The Kingdom to God The Father after He has destroyed all dominion, authority and power. **For He must reign until He has put all His enemies under His feet**.
(1 Corinthians 15;24-25)

We therefore can see that every time we defeat the devil's work in our own lives, and that of others, we accomplish the sovereign will of God by bringing them to His footstool. The darkness is pushed back in homes, streets, cities, and nations so that His light comes. This is His will and purpose.

I am not suggesting that God only initiates things in response to our faith. He is obviously not reliant upon us having the same vision, because He engineers circumstances outside of our finite minds. But the wonder of it all is that He reveals and includes us in His purposes.

THE CREATIVE WORD

The God who calls things that are not as though they were. *(Romans 4;17)*

I am sure that He takes great delight when we, His creation, also become creative in the authority He has given us. This is why He has given us the measure of faith. Not to give us licence to act outside His will. But to give us a set of commands, with the accompanying authority to see them established.

Every born-again believer has access to the Keys of The Kingdom, and therefore has the authority in Jesus' Name to accomplish the sovereign will of God by rebuilding, restoring, and renewing that which the devil has stolen and destroyed. (Refer chapter 29.)

God has clearly revealed to us His Sovereignty in such things as creation; miracles down through the centuries; the resurrection of Jesus; the revelation of Christ being The Alpha and Omega, the beginning and the end. He is established as King of Kings and Lord of lords; sin and sickness have been dealt with once and for all in His sacrificial death at Calvary.

In addition to which, He has given us the Keys of The Kingdom to use His Name as the authority to bring all things to His feet. The same Spirit which raised Jesus from the dead is alive and at work in our lives. We have been commissioned to do the same works as The Lord; and He has given us His Word that clearly tells us what He wants us to do. There is nothing more that God could have done for us. He has done it all. **All He wants us to do is simply 'get on with it'.**

ROOTED

When we realise what we have been given, it does not cause us to become free-lance, or independent in any way. We know for certain the truth of Jesus words.

I am the vine; you are the branches. If a man remains

in Me and I in him, he will bear much fruit; **apart from Me you can do nothing**. *(John 15;5)*

It remains vital that we seek The Lord's guidance in order to carry out the sovereign will of God.

My sheep listen to my voice; *I know them, and they follow Me.* *(John 10;27)*

The Holy Spirit will then give direction.

He (The Holy Spirit) will bring Glory to Me by taking from what is mine and making it known to you. All that belongs to The Father is mine. That is why I said **The Spirit will take from what is mine and make it known to you.** *(John 16;14-15)*

The above verses emphasise the need to continually seek the direction of The Lord in our lives. But we do not need to keep asking His will about things that are clearly stated in His Word.

For example, He has given clear direction regarding such things as freedom from sin and condemnation, deliverance from bondage and sickness, Baptism in The Holy Spirit, gifts of The Spirit, and plans for us to succeed. These are fundamental truths which occur throughout The Bible, and yet you still hear people praying "If it be your will ..."in respect of these matters.

He has already told us His will. He now wants us to believe what He has said, and receive what He has promised. I believe that the prayer that God seeks from us is how best to carry out His will, not continually asking what is His will.

When someone is seeking salvation we do not pray "If it is you will for this person to be saved..."Whereas if someone is seeking healing you often hear the prayer, "If it be your will for healing..."But both sin and sickness were dealt with together at The Cross. We therefore do not have to question if it is His will.

As we have previously seen, some healing is obtained instantly, while on other occasions it occurs over a period of time. The actual timescale is irrelevant. The fact remains that God is sovereign over all sickness and it was revealed to the world 2000 years ago.

If we have the authority to tell someone they are saved after they have repented and asked Jesus to be their Saviour; then likewise we have the authority to speak to the sickness to depart in The Name of Jesus. There should be no doubt that it is His will. The main point to keep focussed upon is that He is sovereign over sin and sickness. It is not for us to question, "What if they are not healed?" This only negates our prayer and reveals unbelief.

UNBELIEF

> **When He asks, he must believe and not doubt**, *because he who doubts is like a wave of the sea, blown and tossed by the wind. That man should not think he will receive anything from The Lord; he is a double-minded man, unstable in all he does.* (James 1;6)

Our doubt and unbelief are so often the root cause of unanswered prayer. Disobedience, which stems from unbelief, is also an issue. Hebrews 3 & 4 encourage us to come into God's rest and promises through faith.

The reason that a section of the Israelites did not enter their inheritance is attributed to disobedience and unbelief. (Hebrews 3;18-19). It was God's sovereign will that they enter The Promised Land. But a twelve-day journey ended up taking forty years. His will never changed for the entire time. The fault lay with the people's attitude and actions. It is worth remembering that this portion of Scripture was written as a warning to Christians.

It has also to be said that in this life we will never be able to fully explain why some prayers are not answered, or why certain situations are not changed. In those cases we simply have to leave the matter rest. The finite mind can only partly understand the infinite.

Recently, my wife Irene and I lost two close friends to cancer. They were sixty. We were in faith for their healing, and although one of them lasted one year longer than the doctor predicted, the fact remains that they did not recover from the illness. But this in no way means that it was God's will that they were afflicted with cancer. If that were the truth, then it would mean in effect that The Lord was saying, "I took upon Myself all sicknesses for all mankind, but not in respect of those two." This would not make any sense.

The devil is continually out to rob us of our peace, and will use any circumstance we have to face. It would be quite easy to take the easy option of saying to ourselves, "What's the point in seeking the miraculous? What will be, will be". This is a fatalistic approach. It means that we have allowed the devil to steal our resolve.

HIS SOVEREIGNTY

I believe that the starting point of anything we approach in faith is the fact that God is sovereign over the situation. This applies to everything, whether it is sin, sickness, deliverance, or simply an ordinary situation we face in life. We first need to get that in perspective.

In earlier chapters we looked at the different aspects of our spirit, soul and body. I will therefore not repeat myself again. I would just like to add that this issue of sovereignty is a classic example of how the different aspects of our person function. Our spirit, where The Holy Spirit dwells, will continually remind us that God is sovereign over everything, because that is truth. Our soul, which includes our mind and emotions, will unfortunately operate on feelings, memories, and worldly perceptions. Our body will tell us if it is in pain or discomfort.

As stated before in the book. We have a choice to make. Do we listen to what comes out of our spirit, or our soul and body?

Our soul will say to us, "Are you sure about God's sovereign will? Is He really interested in this particular issue? What if it is not His will? What if you pray or take authority in His Name and nothing happens?" We end up asking ourselves so many questions that doubt and unbelief fill our minds, and we get dissuaded from stepping out in faith.

But there is also a work going on in our spirit. The Holy Spirit is speaking to us, and reminding us of Scripture. The faith that is present in our spirit mixes with the truth of His Word, and the leading of The Spirit. These seek to rise, but can be obstructed or diluted by what is happening in our soul.

Our minds need to be transformed, as described in Romans 12;1-2. When this occurs on a daily basis our soul gets in line with our spirit. This means that when we have something big to face we are already prepared, because our soul is renewed, and does not automatically think in terms of doubt.

When our minds are changed in this manner, according to The Word of God, we no longer question whether something is God's will. We know what He wants us to do, as we saw from an examination of Isaiah 61. In addition to which, we continually know and have reassurance in our spirit as to His sovereignty. This applies, irrespective of the outcome. This does not mean that we are like an ostrich burying its head in the sand, and refusing to face the issue. Quite the contrary. Allow me to explain.

THE WORK OF THE SPIRIT

Consider for one moment – What part does The Holy Spirit have in this matter of sovereignty?

The Spirit will take from what is mine and make it known to you. *(John 16;15)*

He (Jesus) is the beginning and the firstborn from among the dead, **so that in everything He might have the supremacy**. *(Colossians 1;18)*

Putting these two passages of Scripture together, we see that The Holy Spirit will continually make known to us the supremacy (sovereignty) of Christ. The 'what if' scenario therefore is no longer an issue when we live by The Spirit. This is because we have an inner certainty that The Lord is sovereign. We do not allow ourselves to be robbed of this fundamental truth, irrespective of circumstances, good or bad.

It is abundantly clear that the outcome of a step of faith on our part is not a test of God's sovereignty. His reputation is not at stake.

When we operate out of our spirit we encompass both aspects of sovereignty. Firstly, we have the faith and desire to establish His sovereign will over all that we seek to overcome; and secondly we have the peace and rest to accept those things that we cannot explain. We do not allow ourselves to be robbed.

IMPLEMENTING SOVEREIGNTY

Our understanding of the sovereign will of God is enhanced when we have a thorough knowledge of His Word. One person aptly put it – God said, I believe it, that settles it.

God stated the following.

My people are **destroyed from lack of knowledge**.

(Hosea 4;6)

The point I am seeking to make is that the sovereign will of God and our faith are meant to work in harmony. As stated earlier, He has given us the measure of faith for a reason. He could have created robots that were simply programmed to do what He said, and everything was pre-set and ordered. But He did the opposite. He created humans and gave us free will.

A parent takes great delight in seeing their children apply what they have been taught, and grow in confidence as they tackle matters of life. Our Heavenly Father feels the same about us. He rejoices when His people take Him at His word, and get on with establishing His will on earth as it is in Heaven. Our assuredness in this matter continues to grow the more we actually implement His purposes.

Because He has included us in carrying out His sovereign will He also leads us into 'appointed times'. We meet someone unexpectedly who had recently been on our mind; a seemingly random set of circumstances sudden come together to provide an opportunity; we are prompted to go to a particular place where there is an obvious need; or we have a great burden to pray for an individual.

What is happening in these circumstances? Surely it is God revealing His will to us. He then wants us to respond by stepping out in faith and action.

DAILY CHRISTIAN LIVING

What occurs in our daily Christian living is a combination of factors, but can essentially be summarised in three parts.

1. Part of the time we are taking the initiative by responding to the instructions already laid down in Scripture. Stepping out in such a manner does not mean that we do anything separate from Him. It simply means that we are obedient in carrying out the instructions He has already given us in His Word. For example, we do not have to wait to hear a direct word from God to show compassion to a neighbour or work colleague. He placed His love and compassion inside us at salvation. He has given us faith in order to put His Word into action.

2. While we are carrying out these general everyday things, it is important that we remain sensitive to The Holy Spirit, so that we can instantly respond to His guidance and direction. If we remain in this responsive attitude we will be aware of those appointed times, and be able to respond accordingly. We keep a listening ear.

3. In addition to these two areas, there is also the overall long-term sovereign will of God that is being accomplished. Scripture states that 'suddenly' something happens. What this generally means is that it had been the long-term sovereign will of God, and the different parts of the plan are then in place for it to happen.

I find it utterly amazing that He should include us in His plans and purposes. It is grace beyond measure. In addition to which, the manner in which we live has an effect on His sovereign will. The more we live according to His purposes we actually hasten The Day of The Lord. The Apostle Peter, writing about The Lord's Second Coming encourages us in the following manner:

> *Look forward to the day of God and* **speed its coming**.
> *(2 Peter 3;12)*

AUTHORISED

I will bring this chapter towards a close with an illustration, which hopefully explains what I have been endeavouring to say.

Suppose an employer gave an instruction to an employee "I give you authority in my name, and also hand you written instructions with regard to the weekly banking of the firm." But, at the end of each week the employee approaches him and asks, "What is your will concerning the weekly takings? Is it all right if I bank the money?" What do you think the employer would say?

He would quite rightly reply – "I have already given you my authority and instructions as to what to do. You do not need to ask if something is my will if I have already given it in writing. Of course you can seek advice as to the best way to implement what I have said. But have the instructions firmly fixed in your mind. Let there be no doubt. Believe that what I have told you is true. Then you will not need to keep asking about my will. Just do what I have already said. I employed you, therefore I trust you. Believe in me and believe in yourself. Have faith in my confidence in you. I will tell you if you get it wrong. But don't worry about making mistakes. You will learn from them. Let's just get on with it. Together we make a great team."

The Father's heart towards us is wonderfully expressed in the following Scripture. There is no doubt that that His sovereign will for us involves only good, not harm.

"For I know the plans I have for you," *declares The Lord,* **"plans to prosper you and not to harm you,**

plans to give you hope and a future. *Then you will call upon me and come and pray to Me, and I will listen to you. You will seek Me and find Me when you seek Me with all your heart."* *(Jeremiah 29;11)*

TESTIMONY

I will conclude this chapter by giving an up to date personal testimony.

For the past nine years I have been praying about a situation that I knew was contrary to the sovereign will of God. There had been no change for that entire time, but I knew that His will would one day be accomplished.

A week before writing these words I was giving this long standing issue some thought. (I would also add that not one day passed without it entering my mind at some point.) I started to pray, and then spoke in tongues. I confessed that it was time for a breakthrough. At the end of praying I had a conviction that something had happened, which created a greater sense of expectancy.

At that particular time I was about to send this book off to the publisher. But I had a prompting in my spirit concerning this matter of sovereignty. I then wrote the above chapter over a three-day period. On the day that it was completed I received a telephone call. It was wonderful news. The breakthrough had come after nine years of waiting. It was as if The Lord, in His grace and mercy, was confirming and reminding me that He is indeed sovereign over all circumstances, irrespective of time.

It was God's sovereign will for that entire nine years that the situation would change. Was He waiting for me to get my faith in line? By taking the action on that particular day, did I hasten the breakthrough? I had remained sure that it would eventually happen, but I did not know when. However, I knew in my spirit that something had happened that day when I prayed, and spoke in tongues. I had done those same things over the entire period, but I just knew that it was a significant time when I prayed that day.

There are often two schools of thought in respect of such matters. On one side there are those that believe that it was God's will nine years ago that it would happen on that particular day, and The Holy Spirit prompted me in my spirit that the time had come. The alternative view is that what affects the outcome of a day is mainly our faith, because The Lord has given us the authority to act in His Name.

I believe that there is a balance between these two views.

God most certainly has specific plans and purposes, but He also encourages us to walk in faith. If everything were pre-planned there would be no need for faith. I believe that the issue as to when something happens is a combination between His sovereign will, together with our faith and action. I mean this most reverently when I say it is teamwork. Such is the greatness of His love and grace that He includes us in His sovereign will.

The world would say that my hearing about the breakthrough, on the same day that I wrote the above words, was a mere coincidence. But I had believed for over three thousand days that it was the sovereign will of God for the situation to be changed. It seems rather strange that it should happen on the day that I completed this chapter.

Was this specific day planned nine years ago? Did it become God's will on that particular day? Was it simply my act of faith alone? Was it a mere coincidence? Or was it faith in harmony with the sovereign will of God?

I know what *I* believe.

CHAPTER THIRTY-ONE

PRINCIPLES FOR VICTORY

THE CROSSING of the Jordan was the beginning of a new era in the history of the Israelite nation. They were entering into their promised inheritance. The land which rightfully belonged to them was being taken back. The manner in which they entered, and began this task, obviously had profound meaning for what was to follow in the years ahead.

Three principles for victory were set in place as they crossed the Jordan, and as long as these principles were present they would have continual success. These were **'the Presence of God'**, **'obedience'** and **'steadfastness of faith'**.

We saw in chapter twenty-six that The Anointing is being saturated in His Presence. This is linked to an attitude of consecration and obedience. They are not meant to be short-term encounters, but a continual experience, by remaining steadfast in faith.

We will now look at some passages of Scripture that illustrate these principles.

The Lord said to Joshua, "... Tell the priests who carry The Ark of The Covenant, 'When you reach the edge of

the Jordan's waters, **go and stand in the river'...** *"*
When the people broke camp to cross the Jordan, **the
priests carrying The Ark of The Covenant went
ahead of them**. *Now the Jordan is in flood all during
harvest.* **Yet as soon as the priests who carried The
Ark reached the Jordan and their feet touched the
water's edge,** *the water from upstream stopped flowing ... So the people crossed over opposite Jericho.*
(Joshua 3;7-17)

1. THE PRESENCE OF GOD

The Israelites were shown the necessity of His Presence
going before them, and continuing to remain with them.
Notice that when they came to cross the Jordan, the
priests went first into the water carrying The Ark of The
Covenant, revealing that God's Presence was with them.
Joshua 3;15 tells us that as soon as the priests touched the
river, the water from upstream stopped flowing. Miracles
happen in the Presence of God! **When His Anointing is
present, the 'suddenly' occurs.**

2. OBEDIENCE

Secondly, they acted in obedience to God's command to
enter the river. Joshua had just reminded the Israelites of
God's promise to drive out the tribes who were occupying
the Promised Land. But in order for that to be fulfilled,
they first needed to cross the Jordan. This required them
to obey the command of stepping into the river.

When they took this positive action, they were not only
acting in obedience to God's instruction, but they knew
that if God gives direction, it is for a reason. They also had
the inner certainty that if they were obedient, something
was going to happen.

I am setting before you today a blessing and a curse – **the blessing if you obey the commands of The Lord your God** *that I am giving you today; the curse if you disobey the commands...*

(Deuteronomy 11;26)

3. STEADFAST IN FAITH

Thirdly, the Israelites remained steadfast in faith. This is illustrated clearly in the passage of Scripture by the fact that when they stepped into the Jordan, the water stopped flowing upstream. Therefore, the water must have taken a while to clear in front of them. They could have thought that nothing was happening, and even have stepped out of the river.

However, they remained steadfast in faith, and when the water cleared in front of them, they crossed over on dry ground. If they had stepped back out of the river would the miracle have happened?

How do we relate to these principles of first seeking The Presence of God, followed by acting in obedience to Him, and then remaining steadfast in faith? Would it be true to say that the first two parts are the easier, while the final part of remaining steadfast in faith is the hardest? The temptation is to step back out of the water because we believe that nothing appears to be happening.

The way in which The Presence of God, obedience, and steadfastness of faith combine together is another example of the importance of getting our soul in line with our spirit. We saw in earlier chapters how that God communicates with us Spirit to spirit. In our inner being (spirit) The Holy Spirit gives direction. Faith and obedience also rise from that place. However, problems arise if we think negatively, and thereby cause unbelief and disobedience to affect our soul. When this occurs, it is difficult to remain steadfast in faith.

AMAZEMENT

There are two examples in Scripture that record Jesus being amazed ('*marvelled*'). One relates to Him being amazed at faith, the other at unbelief.

Matthew records an incident when a centurion approached Jesus, and asked Him to heal his servant. He recognised The Lord's authority, and that He would only have to say the word for the healing to take place.

> *When Jesus heard this,* **He marvelled** *and said to those following Him, "I tell you the truth, I have not found anyone in Israel with such faith".*   *(Matthew 8;10)*

Mark 6;1-6 relates the time when Jesus returned to His hometown. He healed a few people, but did not perform any miracles because they questioned His authority. This is what is recorded at the end of His visit – **He was amazed** *at their lack of faith* (v6).

Do we cause The Lord to be amazed, and if so for what reason? Is it our faith, or unbelief? Faith is born in our spirit, whereas unbelief is formed in our soul. We have been given the measure of faith to respond to the Holy Spirit, who will teach, lead and guide us accordingly. Hebrews 3 & 4 warn us of the dangers of carrying any form of unbelief if we desire to enter the full inheritance that God has for us.

> *The message they heard was of no value to them, because those who heard* **did not combine it with faith**.
> *(Hebrews 4;2)*

It is worth bearing in mind that this was written to Christians. Therefore, when we tackle something let us rid ourselves of any unbelief, and **amaze** The Lord with our faith.

JERICHO

Joshua 3;16 records that the Israelites crossed over the Jordan opposite Jericho. It is significant that the word 'opposite' is used. Two nations stood in complete contrast. By crossing over at that location it also put fear into the inhabitants of Jericho, because they saw what was coming to confront them. There will always be a confrontation between the Kingdom of Light and the kingdom of darkness. Do we put fear into the powers of darkness because of our faith and action?

We all have our Jerichos to face at some time, or times, during our lives. It may be a personal conflict, or an issue affecting someone else. They are situations that we have to confront, and even battle over. When we approach such matters, what goes through our mind? Do we only see the high walls? Or do we have that inner conviction that says, "This city is going to be taken".

Over the last few years I have encountered a number of Jerichos. I have learnt that there is no point in trying to skirt around them. Jericho could not be avoided. It had to be faced and overcome.

When the Israelites attacked Jericho it was their first battle after entering The Promised Land, and the same three key principles of **the Presence of God, obedience, and steadfastness of faith** were again in evidence.

The armed guard marched ahead of the priests who blew the trumpets, and the rear guard followed **the**

Ark of The Covenant. ... **Joshua had commanded the people**, *"Do not give a war cry, do not raise your voices, do not say a word until the day I tell you to shout."* ... **The seventh time around**, *when the priests sounded the trumpet blast, Joshua commanded the people, "Shout! For The Lord has given you the city."*

(Joshua 6;9-16)

Firstly, the priests marched around the walls carrying The Ark of The Covenant, making a declaration to the people of Jericho that **The Presence of God** was with the Israelites. Secondly, the Israelites were **obedient** when they were told to march around the walls for seven days, during which time they were told to remain silent. Thirdly, they remained **steadfast in faith**. They did not get discouraged by the size of the walls, or the opposition within. They did not stop on the fifth or sixth day thinking that nothing was happening.

TAKE THE CITY

Is there an issue facing you at this time, or even a long-standing problem? Settle it in your mind that the city is going to be taken. See yourself, or even with others who are also battling with you, marching around the walls of the city. Continue to battle in prayer by remaining steadfast in faith until the walls come down.

Do not pray, and then talk negatively about the size of the problem. This will only negate your prayers. Joshua understood this could happen to the Israelites, so he told them to remain silent as they marched. He did not want them entering into negative conversation about the size of the walls.

Have you ever allowed yourself to be talked out of

doing something, which you knew was the right thing to do. It started off as a positive conviction, but it was subsequently influenced by a negative confession. This occurs when our soul is not in line with our spirit. Faith rises and remains when we are Spirit led. Whereas, negative thought and conversation about the size of the problem, or the length of time it is taking, will subsequently cause unbelief. We have a choice to make.

Whenever the elements of The Presence of God, obedience, and steadfast faith were present the Israelites experienced victory. If one or more of those elements were missing they experienced failure. This is clearly illustrated later in Joshua 9 where it records how the Israelites were fooled into signing a treaty with the Gibeonites. The reason for their being fooled is that they had not been obedient in seeking direction from The Lord. They had not gone into His Presence.

They did not enquire of The Lord.   *(Joshua 9;14)*

NEW TESTAMENT BELIEVERS

These key principles of The Presence of God, obedience, and faith can also be followed through scripture into the New Testament. Acts 10 tells us how on a certain day Peter went up onto the roof to pray. He had a vision from God that confronted his understanding of what was unclean.

While Peter was still thinking about the vision, The Spirit said to him, "Simon, three men are looking for you. So get up and go downstairs. Do not hesitate to go with them, for I have sent them".   *(Acts 10;19)*

As we have seen previously, a vision from God is birthed

in our spirit by The Holy Spirit, who then gives the leading and guidance for its outworking. Peter did not discount the vision, but travelled with these men to Cornelius' house, where he later preached a message. As he was preaching, the Gentile believers were baptised in The Holy Spirit.

Firstly, Peter was in the **Presence of The Lord** and received a vision. The Holy Spirit gave direction to Peter in his spirit. Secondly, he was **obedient**, and did not hesitate in going with the Gentile believers to Cornelius' home. He did not have unbelief in his soul that would have caused a conflict within him. He was sensitive to the leading of The Spirit and obeyed. Thirdly, Peter remained **steadfast in faith** on his journey to Cornelius' home.

He did not let any doubts pervade his thinking, which would cause him to change his mind and turn back. Upon his arrival he preached a message of faith. It was at this point that The Holy Spirit fell on those gathered. Peter had entered new territory by faith, as up to then he would not have associated with Gentiles by choice. The vision had enlightened him to the truth that the message was for everyone.

Everyone who believes …   (Acts 10;43)

PRISON DOORS OPENED

A second example of these principles is found in Acts 16, when Paul and Silas responded to the Macedonian call. Firstly, Paul like Peter had a vision from God. As we saw previously, the Holy Spirit births visions in our spirit. They come from **His Presence**. Secondly, Paul was **obedient** because we are told that they got ready at once, and left for Macedonia. Thirdly, they continually remained **stead-**

fast in faith, even in diverse circumstances.

Paul and Silas had an encouraging start. On the Sabbath they went outside the city gate to the river, where they expected to find a place of prayer. They met Lydia. Following this, they delivered a slave girl from an evil spirit. If we had been in their situation we would obviously think that we had received confirmation that we had made the right decision. However, they then got beaten and thrown in gaol. At this point, Silas might well have wondered whether Paul had heard right in his vision.

But this was not the case. Because, about midnight Paul and Silas were praying and singing hymns to God, and the other prisoners were listening to them. The earthquake occurred, their chains fell off, and Paul and Silas brought the gaoler and his entire household to The Lord. All this occurred because Paul had a vision from God; he was obedient, and then remained steadfast in faith. The result was a harvest of souls. Godly principles produce positive results.

If you are seeking an answer to prayer, or looking for a new direction in life, you may find it helpful to keep these principles in mind. And always remember – **don't step out of the water too soon.**

CHAPTER THIRTY-TWO

TAKE POSSESSION
OF THE LAND

I DO NOT WISH anyone to take offence or misinterpret what I am about to say, for I am not advocating the death penalty or vigilantism. But it is a simple fact of life that if all thieves were eliminated, they would no longer create a crime problem. Similarly, if you eliminate the opposition, then you no longer have to fight.

> *I pursued my enemies and overtook them;* **I did not turn back till they were destroyed. I crushed them so that they could not rise;** *they fell beneath my feet.* **You armed me with strength for battle;** *you made my enemies bow at my feet.*
>
> *(Psalm 18;37-39)*

Notice that there was a specific purpose in God giving King David strength. It was for battle. Paul continues in the same theme in his letter to Timothy.

> *God did not give us a spirit of timidity, but* **a spirit of power,** *of love and of self-discipline.* *(2 Timothy 1;7)*

Are we prepared to fight in order to have peace? There can sometimes be a certain confusion amongst Christians when it comes to the area of spiritual warfare. But if you look at some of the words used by King David in the above Psalm, we will have some direction in this matter. What happened in the physical has a spiritual application. He states that he *did not turn back till they were destroyed*. He did not stop there, because he then *crushed them so that they could not rise*. This is what is needed.

The Apostle Paul gives us some insight into how he led such a Spirit filled and self disciplined life. He ruthlessly dealt with anything harmful in his soul or body. He knew that the alternative is to provide the opportunity for it to rise again.

> *I beat my body and make it my slave.*
> *(1 Corinthians 9;27)*

DEALING WITH TRESPASSERS

Let us look at a further passage of Scripture, and examine how something which is not of God, is to be treated.

> *When The Lord your God brings you into the land you are entering to possess, and drives out before you many nations...and when He has delivered them over to you and you have* **defeated them, then you must destroy them totally**. *Make no treaty with them, and* **show them no mercy. Do not intermarry** *with* **them.** *(Deuteronomy 7;1-6)*

To put this passage in perspective, it is necessary to understand that the Hittites, and the other tribes, were occupying stolen land. They were trespassing. There is a spiritual analogy that can be drawn between this account, and our own experience. These tribes represent kingdoms, strongholds and sins in our lives that are taking up room that should be occupied by The Holy Spirit. The Lord does not wish to share that land with anyone else, for we are His treasured possession.

This raises the question – Is there anything unrighteous or harmful trespassing in our lives?

The above verses in Deuteronomy contain four separate instructions in how to deal with anything that is trespassing in our lives. Once the enemy has been defeated he must be totally destroyed: make no treaty with the enemy: show no mercy; do not intermarry. We will briefly look at the lessons we can learn from these four spiritual principles.

1. LORDSHIP

Those areas of our lives that are not under His Lordship, and part of His Kingdom rule, are to be defeated, and then utterly destroyed. The alternative is that we will continually have skirmishes, and not know real victory. If we have allowed sins, wrong attitudes, or strongholds to remain in our lives, they will continually rob us of our full inheritance. Being robbed as we go through life is a tragedy, but knowingly leaving a thief loose in our home is irresponsible.

2. NO COMPROMISE

Make no treaty or compromise with such things as sin, unbelief, or weaknesses that we wish to accept within ourselves. There is no point in trying to form a treaty with sin, for by its very nature it will always break a treaty. Peace will not come from compromise.

3. NO MERCY

Show no mercy with anything which seeks to trespass in

our lives. The devil continually seeks to steal, kill, and destroy. It is not a pastime, or minor part of his nature. This is for real. If he has such a determination, then surely we ought to be more positive in our actions.

4. NO MIXTURE

Have no mixture in our lives, by living with one foot in God's Kingdom, and the other foot in the world. The Israelites thought they could mix their inheritance with the way of life of the tribes around them. This proved disastrous.

The choice put before them was simple. Eliminate the thief from your midst, and you will enjoy peace and prosperity, or give him freedom and suffer the inevitable loss.

LESSONS FROM HISTORY

Someone once said, "History is the study of other people's mistakes". This prompts the question – Do we learn from past mistakes? Does history have to repeat itself? There is no doubt that the Israelite nation failed to learn lessons from its own history. They did not totally destroy the various tribes, and as a result they continually caused problems. Are we still experiencing problems from things that we should have conquered long ago?

The Israelites made treaties with the people around them, and you can appreciate what followed. These tribes became strong and numerous in their midst, and as we all know it is far more difficult to dislodge something when it is large. Do we have a similar history in our own lives? Have we compromised in certain areas, which have allowed things to escalate into big issues in our lives?

Some individuals have bad experiences in childhood,

and teenage years, which are not dealt with, and continue to grow as the years pass. Middle-aged people often carry baggage from the past. It does not have to be that way.

The surrounding tribes grew in large numbers, and Israel accepted them. They even inter-married. We can all see the inevitable consequence of acceptance of something that is unrighteous. The Apostle Paul had harsh words for the Corinthian Church, who had accepted a wrong relationship to continue in their midst. He knew that if one condoned such behaviour it would simply escalate. Paul gave them this advice.

> *Don't you know that* **a little yeast works through the whole batch of dough?** *(1 Corinthians 5;6)*

The Lord God caused Israel to face the issue they had brought on themselves.

> *Now therefore I tell you that I will not drive them out before you;* **they will be thorns in your sides** *and their gods will be a snare to you.* *(Judges 2;1-3)*

This initially prompted the people to repent. They suddenly realised that they had been the authors of their own misfortune. They learnt the principle of cause and effect. Do we have any constant thorns in our sides, and I do not mean mothers-in-law? Are there areas that we have put off dealing with, and as a result of which, they continually or periodically cause us discomfort?

God gave Cain true crime prevention advice. He could not have made it any clearer.

> *If you do not do what is right,* **sin is crouching at your door;** *it desires to have you, but* **you must master it**. *(Genesis 4;7)*

You can give the best crime prevention advice, but it is up to the individual to apply it to their life. Unfortunately, Cain did not heed God's warning.

PRIDE BEFORE A FALL

When the Israelites came out of Egypt they were untrained in warfare. During the following years they had to learn these skills. No doubt, certain individuals had been taught down through the years, and they were able to train others. It must have been quite daunting to enter this new phase in their lives. They had to make the transition from being slaves into warriors. To be able to make this change must have given them great personal satisfaction.

When the time came for them to take up arms they initially experienced victory. However, they let success go to their heads. They then acted outside the will of God, and disaster followed. When we engage in spiritual warfare it is not wise to have any form of triumphalism, because triumphalism is based on pride. Pride was the undoing of the devil.

Pride goes before destruction, *a haughty spirit before a fall.* (*Proverbs 16;18*)

The Israelites acted in a similar manner. They got caught up in pride, and then attempted to advance in their own authority.

Moses said to the people – "So I told you, but you would not listen. You rebelled against The Lord's command and **in your own arrogance** *you marched up into the hill country. The Amorites who lived in those hills came out against you; they chased you like a swarm of bees and beat you down."* (*Deuteronomy 1;43-44*)

Any soccer manager will tell you that a team is often the most vulnerable just after they have scored a goal. They get caught up in the euphoria of the moment, lose their playing pattern, and do not pay enough heed to their defence. The opposition often scores a goal soon afterwards. You hear the forlorn cry of the spectators saying, "We were robbed".

This is why as Christians we so often fall after a wonderful encounter with The Lord, or when we have seen a breakthrough or victory in a particular area. We get caught up in the experience, and not in Him. A consecrated heart prevents this happening. We will then avoid an arrogant attitude, which can open the door to all manner of things, and in so doing, leave us wide open to being robbed and defeated.

Many years ago I heard this good advice from a preacher: it is not wrong to receive a compliment, or get personal satisfaction from doing a good work. But when we lay our head on our pillow at night, bring these good things back to mind. Then hand them to The Lord, and say "You have the glory".

If this is done as a discipline each day, pride will not have an opening.

CHAPTER THIRTY-THREE

STRONGHOLDS

THERE ARE TWO different types of stronghold. The first is a **Person** to whom we can go to find security and peace.

> *The Lord is good,* **a stronghold** *in times of trouble.*
> *(Nahum 1;7 King James version)*

The second is a **place** that has been built contrary to the will of God. These are the strongholds that we are meant to destroy. They can affect individual lives, areas and even nations.

> **The weapons we fight with...have divine power to demolish strongholds.** *(2 Corinthians 10;4)*

Strongholds which are not of God are essentially committing the offence of trespass, because they are occupying land which should belong to God. We have been given the responsibility of pulling down these strongholds in both our own lives, and that of others in order to build something of The Lord in its place. It is unwise to leave anything in place that is contrary to our well being.

> **A wise man** *attacks the city of the mighty and* **pulls down the stronghold** *in which they trust.*
> *(Proverbs 21;22)*

The principle of pulling down and then building something in its place can be seen in what The Lord God spoke to the prophet Jeremiah.

> *Now, I have put My Words in your mouth. See, today I appoint you over nations and kingdoms to* **uproot** *and* **tear down***, to* **destroy** *and* **overthrow***, to* **build** *and to* **plant***.*   (Jeremiah 1;9-10)

Notice that the first work was to uproot and tear down, and to destroy and overthrow. It was only after this was accomplished that the prophet was told to build and plant. There is a sequence of events. There is order and purpose in all of God's instructions.

NEW BUILDING MATERIALS

When a stronghold has been destroyed in an individual's life, it is important that they are cared for, and not left isolated. Figuratively speaking, it would be like leaving someone surrounded by a pile of rubble, with no materials or plans in order to rebuild. Pulling down a stronghold is only half the job. We saw in chapter two that our goal is to **rebuild, restore and renew**.

The work is completed when something of The Lord has been rebuilt in the place formerly occupied by a stronghold. For example, where there has been the stronghold of doubt and fear, we need to build faith in its place, replace captivity with freedom, replace impurity with purity, replace anger and bitterness with forgiveness, replace continual despair about past mistakes, with success and a hope for the future.

I know from my own experience that there was a stronghold of failure in my life. I had to tear it down, and replace it with a renewed mind that confessed of who I am in Christ.

The Lord gave an illustration about what can happen when an empty space is created. Matthew 12;43-45 warns of seven spirits returning to occupy the house that originally contained one. It had been cleansed of the one, but it was left vacant. The same principle applies to strongholds that are pulled down. It is so necessary that something of The Lord is built in its place. Otherwise, the same stronghold or others will be built, and occupy the vacuum.

Best of all; let us *continually* build faith, hope, love, joy, forgiveness, peace etc. into our lives, so that there is no room for negative strongholds to be built.

It is unwise to hold onto sins and attitudes that provide the devil with building materials to construct a stronghold in our lives. Imagine if you left a pile of bricks and cement on your front garden, and then someone came along and started to build a tower in front of your window. Would you allow it to happen?

DELIVERANCE MINISTRY

I used a quotation in chapter four which is relevant to this present issue – "The biggest deception of all time has been committed by the devil. He has managed to convince people that he does not exist."

It is abundantly clear that there is a need for deliverance ministry in these days, in the same manner that The Lord cast out demons. After The Lord's resurrection He appeared to His disciples and commissioned them to go into all the world preaching the Good News with accompanying signs.

> *And these signs will accompany those who believe.* **In My Name they will drive out demons**.
>
> *(Mark 16;15-18)*

The early church continued in the same manner. Demonic influence did not happen purely in the time that The Lord was on earth.

> *The Apostles performed many miraculous signs and wonders among the people...Crowds gathered also from the towns around Jerusalem, bringing their sick and* **those tormented by evil spirits**, *and all of them were healed.*   *(Acts 5;12-16)*

An examination of Isaiah 61 reveals that part of the purpose of the Anointing is to proclaim freedom for the captives, and release from darkness for the prisoners. The words *'captives'* and *'prisoners'* illustrate the nature of someone tormented by evil spirits.

There can be a misconception that demonic activity is confined to certain countries. Have you heard people say, "That sort of thing doesn't happen around here." Scripture warns us that the devil is a deceiver. This is why we need to have discernment, which is one of the gifts of The Spirit, as recorded in 1 Corinthians 12;7-11.

During my time in the Police Force, I encountered situations and people that were affected by demonic activity. None of us should be naive about the devil's work. But there is nothing to fear for those who have Jesus as Lord of their lives.

> **Greater is He who is in you**, *than he who is in the world.*   *(1 John 4;4)*

DISCERNMENT

As has been mentioned in an earlier chapter, it is necessary to have balance. Some Christians go overboard in seeing demonic activity in every sinful situation in life. They are continually seeking to cast out demons, and by doing so, quite often put people into condemnation by the very nature of their actions. They are allegedly seeking to set people free, whereas they have the opposite effect of putting people into bondage.

The same can apply to strongholds. Not every sin or wrong attitude in someone's life is a stronghold. We need discernment and the counsel of God when dealing with one another, so that we recognise the difference between a simple act of sin that requires repentance, and the more serious situation where there is demonic activity, or where a stronghold needs pulling down.

Most sin in our lives does not occur because the devil is directly involved. Although all sin has its root in satan, it mainly occurs in us because there are remnants of our old nature still having an influence upon our thoughts and desires. If we blame every sinful or wrong act on the devil we are in one sense giving him fame, which he craves. What we need to do is continually experience our new nature having pre-eminence over the old.

It is an act of will on our part.

CHAPTER THIRTY-FOUR

ENTERING THE ENEMY CAMP

I HAVE BEEN to the enemy camp and I have taken back that which belongs to me.

Certain areas become renowned for their high rate of crime, drug supplying, violence, or simply for public disorder. Some people, for their own gain, try to make it as difficult as possible for the Police to perform their duties in such areas. They try to make them into no-go areas, and endeavour to create an atmosphere whereby the Police are entering a territory owned by others, who are not subject to the law of the land.

If the Police were to allow such a situation to persist, not only will they lose control of that particular area, but also what started out as comparatively small, will grow and spread elsewhere. The Police ought never to relinquish authority to others, and always be able to enter anywhere to enforce the law, in order to bring peace and order. The same principle applies in the spiritual realm, as we enforce the law and will of God.

Your Kingdom come, **Your will be done on earth** *as it is in Heaven.* (Matthew 6;10)

The Lord showed us the way to enter the enemy camp

in His earthly ministry. He did not compromise, but confronted sin, strongholds, sickness and demonic activity wherever He met them. The Lord never retreated. After His death on The Cross, He went down into hell where He made an open display of the devil. When He went into hell He did not stay there, for death could not hold Him, and He rose from the grave.

The Lord showed the devil that He had the power to enter at will, and leave at will, and took with Him the keys of death and hell. **You cannot be locked up if you hold the keys.**

I am The Living One; I was dead, and behold I am alive forever and ever! **And I hold the keys of death and hell**. *(Revelation 1;18)*

Jesus re-emphasised His authority to His disciples just before His ascension. During His earthly ministry they had already witnessed how He dealt with anything that was contrary to The Kingdom of God. They saw His Anointing, and how He walked with authority to confront and defeat the works of the devil. Jesus has given that same authority to all believers to enter the enemy camp, and leave at will.

All authority in Heaven and earth has been given to Me. *(Matthew 28;18)*

As we have already seen, Jesus holds the Keys of The Kingdom, and the keys of death and hell. He therefore has authority over all things.

The reason the Son of God appeared was to **destroy the devil's work**. *(1 John 3;8)*

RESTORATION

The prophet Samuel records how David and his men were away from their camp when the Amalekites raided it. The camp was destroyed, and their families taken captive. David enquired of The Lord what action to take. The Lord gave an emphatic reply.

> *Pursue them. You will certainly overtake them and* **succeed in the rescue**. *(1 Samuel 30;8)*

David obeyed The Lord, entered the enemy camp and defeated the Amelekites. He even brought back the Amelekite flocks – more than what was originally stolen. Nothing was missing. This would be a good principle to grasp in the spiritual realm.

> **... Nothing was missing**: *young or old, boy or girl, plunder or anything else they had taken.* **David brought everything back**. *(1 Samuel 30;18/19)*

Isaiah 61 deals with The Anointing of The Lord. It reveals how we use that anointing to take back that which has been stolen in our own lives, and that of others. In so doing, we **rebuild, restore and renew**. We have already seen in other chapters that the anointing is meant to be far more than just a blessing.

It is against God's justice for anything to be stolen from us. He has given us the power and authority to go and take it back, so that everything is restored to its rightful place. The central truth of restoration contained in this Scripture can be applied to any aspect of our life.

I would particularly like to encourage parents whose children are not following The Lord. 1 Samuel 30;18-19 are wonderful verses to keep at the forefront of your mind, when things appear to be going from bad to worse. Keep praying, confessing, and prophesying these words of God into their lives. **Do not give up until none are missing.**

KINGDOM RULE

You may be saying at this point – "I see the principle, but what is the enemy camp?" To fully grasp the meaning, it is first necessary to understand the meaning of 'Kingdom' and 'inheritance'.

Kingdom – The eternal spiritual authority of God, and the realm over which this sovereignty extends.

Inheritance – To receive property, a title, or the like, from a parent, or another person by legal succession or will. To succeed as an heir.

Kingdom essentially means 'anywhere that The King has authority'. Inheritance is that which a person receives from someone who has the authority to give. We therefore see that because Jesus is Lord of lords and King of kings, He not only has the authority to exercise rule over all things, but He also has the right to provide an inheritance.

Galatians 4;1-7 tells us that not only have we become sons and heirs of God, but we also have the full rights of sons, because of the inheritance we have received. In addition to this, Romans 8;16-17 informs us that we are co-heirs with Christ. Being an heir brings both blessing, and responsibility.

KINGDOM AGAINST KINGDOM

There are two Kingdoms operating 24 hours, each and every day. There is no 'time out', or agreement to have a truce for a specific time. There is a continual clash of Kingdom against kingdom. The ostrich has the ability to bury its head in the sand. We can often feel like doing the same, but unfortunately it is not an option.

It would be a tragedy, if we as Christians live in fear of the devil, or do not want to step out in faith, for fear of drawing his attention. This type of attitude would cause us to acquiesce, which literally means to accept, consent, or comply passively or without protest. As born-again believers we can be the most fearless, confident, and pro-active people on this planet, because we have a certain and sure promise.

Greater is He who is in you *than he who is in the* *world.* *(1 John 4;4)*

When we are in Heaven we will discover many things. However, it would be tragic if it is only when we reach there that we come to realise that the devil is insignificant compared to our inheritance in The Lord. We will discover that we had authority over him and his works, and that the only influence or harm he could cause us is what we foolishly allowed to happen.

Ephesians 1;22 confirms that all things have already been placed under Christ's feet, and therefore under our feet, because as we have already seen from Romans 8;16-17, we are co-heirs with Christ.

OUR STANDING IN CHRIST

God made Him (Christ) who had no sin to be sin for *us,* **so that in Him we might become the right-** **eousness of God.** *(2 Corinthians 5;21)*

For years I had very little perception of my standing in Christ. I had great difficulty in trying to grasp such verses as the above mentioned. Just consider the implications of that verse. We are the righteousness of God! How is this possible? The answer is found in the previous verse that states that we are Christ's ambassadors. It is because we are *in Him* that we are able to stand before God in righteousness.

Therefore, there is no reason for any Christian to have any lack of self-worth. The more we understand about the abundance of our salvation and inheritance in Him, the more confidence we will have to face whatever comes our way.

Ephesians 2;6 informs us that we are already seated with Christ in Heavenly places. Therefore we are able to look down on situations with faith and a sure hope for the outcome, as opposed to looking up with fear and foreboding.

Be strong and courageous. Do not be terrified; *do not be discouraged, for The Lord your God will be with you wherever you go.* (Joshua 1;9)

Joshua was about to cross the Jordan River, to take back the territory that belonged to Israel. He would have to enter the enemy camp, but he knew that he had the authority of God, and the promise that He would be with him wherever he went. The above words were given to Joshua for his encouragement, but are also recorded for our benefit.

Let us also remind ourselves of the verse that we looked at earlier in the chapter.

Nothing was missing ... *David brought everything back.* (1 Samuel 30;18/19)

The enemy had no right to take anything that did not

belong to him. David did not just accept the situation, and say to himself – "Ah well. That's life". Neither did he shrink back, and live in fear. He sought The Lord, and then resolutely conquered the enemy. Faith causes us to go on the offensive.

In conclusion, we see that the enemy camp is anything, or anywhere, which is not under God's Kingdom rule. This raises the question – Are we going to confront or acquiesce? There is no middle ground.

> *From the days of John The Baptist until now, the Kingdom of Heaven has been forcefully advancing, and* **forceful men lay hold of it**. *(Matthew 11;12)*

CHAPTER THIRTY-FIVE

STRATEGY

WE ARE NEARING the end of the book, and a fairly large number of topics have been covered. I hope that you have derived some benefit, and possibly further revelation. If you have a greater awareness and desire to tackle such matters, then it is important to have the right individual strategy in order to move forward.

In fact, the Bible begins with strategy.

In the beginning God created *the heavens and the earth. Now the earth was formless and empty, darkness was over the surface of the deep, and* **The Spirit of God was hovering over the waters.** *And* **God said, "Let there be light".** *God saw that the light was good, and He separated the light from the darkness. God called the light 'day' and the darkness He called 'night'.* **And there was evening and there was morning – the first day.** *(Genesis 1;1-5)*

In the above Scripture there are three stages that occurred in creation. A strategy took place. The principles that were present then also give guidance to us today.

1. *In the beginning God created. (v 1)*
When we set out to do a specific Christian work or ven-

ture it is vital that it is God created. If it is not of Him our efforts will prove fruitless. This does not mean that we become so cautious that we are afraid to make a mistake. We shall see in the following chapters that He encourages us to use our initiative. He is a creative God who delights in a creative people. But in the process of being creative we just need to be wise that it is not our own agenda that we are pursuing.

2. *The Spirit of God was hovering over the waters. (v 2)*
After something has been created there follows a sorting out period. A time when there can be a seeking of clarity and wisdom as to the right course of action. Although the concept or idea is formed, the actual manner in which it is to be outworked is still in a formless state. This is why it is necessary to keep praying so that we get the right direction and guidance. The Holy Spirit hovers over a work of God, caring for it, and taking it forward.

3. *And God said, "Let there be light"... And there was evening, and there was morning – the first day. (v 5)*
This is the stage when we get clear direction. Light comes into the situation. God gives us the starting point, and how to progress. In the same manner that God created the first day, we also can see that something of substance has begun.

As we continue in a specific work, it is so necessary that we discern when the next day has arrived. This may come within weeks, months, or even years. By remaining sensitive to The Holy Spirit we are able to recognise those times and make any adjustments, or change in direction, as the work evolves.

Sometimes, through impulsiveness or excitement, we try and jump onto the fourth day. But with God there is order. Day four cannot arrive until the completion of days one, two and three. Tragically, many good works have floundered because people tried to race ahead too fast, and disorder is created.

THE WHOLE OF THE GODHEAD
There is another aspect of strategy that is revealed in the first few verses of Genesis. Any work of God involves the whole of the Godhead – Father, Son, and Holy Spirit.

> *In the beginning God created...The Spirit of God was hovering...And God said, "Let there be light".*
> *(Genesis 1;1-3)*

The light that came into the world is Jesus. These are the words that He declared to the people.

> **I am the light of the world**. *Whoever follows Me will never walk in darkness, but will have the light of life.*
> *(John 8;12)*

We can therefore see that it begins in the Father's heart, it is covered by The Holy Spirit, and Christ is revealed. It is so good to have the assurance that when we are involved in something of God, the full resources of Heaven are with us every step of the way.

FACING THE OPPOSITION
Let us now look at strategy and its outworking.

One of the first things we need to understand is that if we operate under The Anointing of God we will face opposition. It is therefore important to have discernment in this matter, and not be naive. Knowledge of the enemy does not produce fear. Only lack of knowledge of our identity in Christ will produce this effect.

This is the reaction of the Philistines when David was anointed king.

> *When the Philistines heard that David had been* **anointed** *king over Israel,* **they went up in full force** *to search for him, but David heard about it and went down to the stronghold.* (2 Samuel 5;17)

Why did the Philistines react in such a manner? The reason is very clear. They knew that they could expect their kingdom to diminish as a result of David being anointed king, so they went *in full force* against him. The same principle applies in our lives. When we are operating under The Anointing of God, the devil realises that his kingdom is going to diminish further. He will attempt to steal our zeal and resolve and replace them with fear.

Some people may say to themselves at his point – "I think I will just stay as I am, and not get involved. It's less hassle. If I don't bother the devil, he won't bother me." This would be a tragic response, and in any case I do not believe that there is an opt-out clause in our salvation.

MAKE A STAND AGAINST INJUSTICE

The Philistines were set on robbing Israel of their land and possessions. Ever since David was a young boy he had the inner conviction and certainty that the Philistines were acting against God's justice. It grieved him when he saw Israel being subdued and robbed. He therefore made a conscious decision at an early age to make a stand against their theft and injustice.

You will notice that Scripture records that David went down to the Philistine stronghold. When he learnt that he was going to be attacked, he did not adopt a siege mentality, and become defensive in thought or deed. On the contrary, he went on the offensive.

There is a well known phrase which says something to the effect that the reason evil succeeds is because good people do nothing. David had an inner determination that he was not going to be such a person, who merely stood by and watched.

I am sure that we have all experienced those times when we encounter a situation that is unjust, and it troubles us. We have that inner nagging that the particular issue is just not righteous, and that something ought to be done about it. You may at this point in time be unsure of what to do in the circumstances. The solution is to seek, and wait upon The Lord for the right strategy in how to change that situation, then act. Do not leave it to somebody else. The more we bring God's light into all that is around us, the greater will be the retreat of darkness.

Quite often in our lives we face all manner of opposition, and sometimes, because of the pressure we are encountering, searching questions can come to mind, which are natural concerns. There is nothing wrong in enquiring. But we get ourselves into a knot when our probing turns into a questioning heart. There is a world of difference between asking a question in faith, as opposed to circumstances where we have contention filling our minds, which only creates confusion and doubt.

David faced a problem, but he knew how to get the answer. He asked in faith.

David enquired of the Lord.   *(2 Samuel 5;19)*

The Lord told David to attack the Philistine stronghold, and he achieved victory. It is not simply carrying on regardless, or attacking just for the sake of it. The Lord is interested in justice. The Philistines were acting against

His Justice. The Lord gave the command to continue.

But if we do not have His direction to continue, let us have the wisdom and judgement to hold fast until we get the confirmation, no matter how long it takes. We need a strategy, and in order to receive it, we enquire and wait upon The Lord.

DIFFERENT TACTICS

Sometime later, the Philistines resumed their offensive, and David again enquired of The Lord. The reply he received illustrates two important principles.

> **Do not go straight up,** *but* **circle round behind them and attack** *them in front of the balsam trees.*
> *(2 Samuel 5;23)*

Firstly, we cannot take victory for granted. Although we have confidence and faith that we can do all things through Christ, we constantly need to be aware that it is through Him, and not by our own strength. David did not move against the Philistines until he had enquired of The Lord. He did not think that all he had to do was turn up at the battlefield.

> *Trust in The Lord with all your heart and* **lean not on your own understanding** ... *and He will make your paths straight* *(Proverbs 3;5)*

Secondly, we do not make the assumption that we will use a strategy that worked on a previous occasion. David enquired of The Lord, who gave him a different strategy on the second occasion that he attacked the Philistines.

> **Commit to The Lord whatever you do,** *and your plans will succeed.* *(Proverbs 16;3)*

SPIRIT LED STRATEGY

Have there been occasions when we have confidently set out to pray about a certain situation, or even to wage spiritual warfare, but we have not seen the result that we had hoped? I would suggest that we have failed on occasions because we have put the cart before the horse. We have gone into battle without first seeking the strategy.

At those times we have basically operated out of our soul, and not waited for The Lord to speak to us in our spirit. Acting impulsively, although with good intentions, can be a block to us hearing correctly. The reason being is that impulse is generated from our mind and emotions, which are part of our soul. We see again the importance of getting our soul in line with our spirit.

What I have just said is obviously not to be confused with a quickening in our spirit when The Holy Spirit suddenly prompts us to pray about something, speak to someone, or take some course of action. This is quite different.

The particular type of strategy that I am referring to in this chapter is guidance and direction from The Holy Spirit in respect of a specific issue under consideration. When we set out to tackle such matters, the priority is to first enquire of The Lord, so that His Spirit can reveal to us the right strategy for each situation. This can happen in a variety of ways, such as His Spirit speaking directly to us, by His leading us to a passage of Scripture, The Lord using someone to speak into our situation, or a vision or dream. He may give us the same strategy as before, but it is vital that we enquire of Him. We can then pray, and act, with clear direction.

How do we approach the subject of other peoples' testimonies? What goes through our mind when we read or hear of how The Lord worked in their lives, or how they acted upon a revelation or teaching from His Word? I am sure that many of us have at some time said to ourselves – "I'll give that a try".

The only word of caution I would suggest to such an attitude is that we are not meant to flit from one thing to another, with whatever is regarded by some as the 'flavour of the month'. This will not produce maturity in the believer. There is nothing wrong whatsoever in giving something a try, but let it be done in faith. The purpose of receiving revelation is that it goes deep, and becomes a life changing word. One can liken it to the Parable of the sower in Matthew 13, whereby it is only the seed that went into the good soil that produced fruit.

PRAYER STRATEGY

The importance of seeking the right strategy has greatly altered the pattern of my prayer life. It may be a vision, a single sentence, or just one verse of Scripture that The Lord gives me as I wait upon Him about a particular situation, either affecting some other person, or myself. Having received the strategy, I pray with faith and assurance until the result is achieved.

On one occasion I was praying for a family member, and The Holy Spirit clearly told me to look at Isaiah 43;5. When He gave this Scripture to me I was unaware of its contents. Although I had read it in the past I was not able to recall the actual verse when The Spirit spoke to me. I immediately looked it up, and was greatly encouraged with what I read.

Do not be afraid, for I am with you; **I will bring your children from the east and gather you from the west**. *(Isaiah 43;5)*

The Lord showed me that I was not to fear about the future for this individual, but to continue to trust in Him, and that He would bring that person back to Him, into the place where they belong. Notice that the Scripture states that He was bringing them from one direction, to meet us coming from the opposite direction. The Holy Spirit then directed me to read the two verses immediately following the above-mentioned passage.

I will say to the north, "Give them up!" And to the south, "Do not hold them back". *Bring My sons from afar and My daughters from the ends of the earth – everyone who is called by My Name, whom I created for My Glory, whom I formed and made.*
(Isaiah 43;6-7)

The Lord revealed to me from these verses that I was to prophesy into the situation, calling the person back.

He began by encouraging me from verse 5 not to fear for the future, and then directed me in verses 6-7 to exercise faith, by taking authority over the situation in His Name. Whenever the Lord reveals a truth to us, He always provides the means to act upon it. He was giving me a lesson in how to take back that which the devil had stolen. It was against God's will for that person to be held captive, and He gave me the strategy to take authority.

STRATEGY FOR THE CAPTIVES

The Spirit of the Sovereign Lord is on me, because The Lord has Anointed me to ... **proclaim freedom for the captives**. *(Isaiah 61;1-3)*

The Sovereign Lord not only Anointed Jesus for His ministry, but He also pours His Anointing upon us for the same purpose, namely to defeat the work of the devil. You will notice from this Scripture that we are to *proclaim*. This is what occurred in the earlier passage in Isaiah 43;6-7, when it was prophetically proclaimed that the sons and daughters were to be released.

Make a clear decision – Are you going to let situations in life rule you, or are you going to rule over those situations in the authority that The Lord has given to us?

When we are praying for the unsaved or someone who has backslidden, the devil not only wants to hold the person captive, but also desires to keep us in captivity to doubt, and worry. Our worrying, and concentrating on the negative lifestyle of the individual will not bring them back to God. It is far better to have a clear vision of the individual coming out of captivity into freedom. Continue to prophesy and pray into that situation for however long it takes.

God gives life to the dead and **calls things that are not as though they were.** *(Romans 4;17)*

Hallelujah! We are in the hands of The creative God with whom nothing is impossible.

INDIVIDUAL STRATEGY

From my own past experience, and that of others, it seems evident that we so often rush into prayer, having no clear direction or vision. When such a situation exists, can we genuinely profess to be praying in faith? There is also no point in making excuses about the pace of modern day life, which we can blame for preventing us from spending time just waiting and listening to The Holy Spirit.

It is well worth noting that the main cause of modern day relationship problems is attributed to a lack of communication. This includes listening, as well as conversing. Have we lost the art of listening, both to our Heavenly Father, and others?

An example of listening and being sensitive to the leading of The Holy Spirit concerns Gareth and Dawn, who are close friends. In 1998 their twelve-year-old son, Paul-John, died as a result of a tragic accident. As you can well imagine, they were devastated. But they did not become bitter, and sought help from The Lord. He ministered to them in a remarkable way.

Soon after their loss, Gareth suddenly started to compose poetry about their son, with regards to both his life and death. Over the following year he completed thirty-five such poems. Paul-John had made a commitment to The Lord shortly before his death, and a number of the poems reflect the truth that they will one day see him again.

Up until that point in time Gareth, who was in his mid-forties, had neither written nor shown any interest in poetry. In fact, he has not composed any further poems since that initial year. It was as if he was given a gift for a season in order to help them through the most acute time. The poems became an integral part of their grieving, and have also been used to bring comfort and peace to other parents who have suffered the loss of a young child.

Their testimony is an encouragement to each of us to be open to The Lord's strategy, even when it is outside our 'normal' way of thinking, or acting. We have only to look at the many and varied ways that Jesus ministered to people while He was on earth, to realise that He does not follow a fixed plan that covers everyone. He responds to us with the right strategy for each individual.

HIS STRATEGY ALONE

You will recall from the end part of my personal testimony that I referred to the strategy that The Lord gave me in order to cope with the spiritual attack that I was encountering. The revelation about the Keys of The Kingdom was not only applicable to that particular period in time, but it is a truth that I will continue to apply. Some strategy is short term, while another is long term, and life changing.

The Lord's strategy can not only influence our own lives, but also how we minister to others. There are many different ways of tackling an issue in people's lives. Some examples are revealing a truth through Scripture, repentance, wise counsel, fasting and prayer, binding and loosing, confrontation of an unresolved sin, giving a good dose of grace and joy, or simply just making them feel loved.

What works for one person may not necessarily work for another. It is not wise to fall into the trap of thinking "It worked this way with another person". **Let us enquire of The Lord and get the right strategy for each person and situation.**

I fell into this trap some years ago. We had seen an absolute miraculous deliverance in a person. Two friends, quite separately, had been given a burden for an individual. One had a word of knowledge, while the other had a vision, and how to pray into the situation. We would fast for a day, once a week, and then meet up on the same evening to pray. There was such unity of purpose, and we prayed with clarity and boldness. Within a few weeks we saw absolute victory.

Some months later I encountered a similar situation in another person. Instead of seeking, and waiting upon The

Lord, I immediately prayed along the same lines as before. It was as if I was praying to a particular formula. Needless to say, I did not see the same result. I had not sought The Lord for His strategy for victory. Sometime later I realised that it is His Presence alone that changes lives and situations, not formulae.

STRATEGY FOR GROWTH

Similarly, many works for The Lord have floundered simply because the people concerned have not enquired of Him. They have not waited on Him long enough to receive the right vision and strategy to move forward. Consequently, they lack direction. So often in history, churches have lost ground and fallen into decline because they followed the earthly principle of "It worked this way in the past, so why should we change?".

Churches and individuals get locked into the traditions of men, which can rob us of present and future blessing. God's Word has warned us of such action.

> **See to it that no one takes you captive** *through hollow and deceptive philosophy,* **which depends on human tradition** *and the basic principles of this world* **rather than on Christ**. *(Colossians 2;8)*

Many great revivals and moves of God have died because the people did not keep looking afresh to God for direction, and got caught up in thinking "This is how it will always be." Whether in single, or corporate prayer, we need to be led by The Holy Spirit, who will give us the strategy in how to gain victory.

CHAPTER THIRTY-SIX

THINKING ON YOUR FEET

IN THE PREVIOUS chapter I referred to the strategy that involves the setting aside of time in order to seek life changing direction in one's own life, or that of others. However, when it comes to everyday issues, we do not have the luxury of time. We have to make on the spot decisions in work, and at home.

Although the choices are made quickly, they can not only affect the immediate, but can have long lasting consequences. In that sort of setting, how do we make wise decisions?

I believe that the answer is to live from our spirit, as opposed to our soul. I have covered this point in chapters eight and nine, so I will not repeat myself. However, I would just like us to consider for one moment – What course of action is going to prove the most reliable – impulse decisions from our soul, or Spirit led direction from our spirit?

As we saw in chapter eight, our spirit is inhabited by The Holy Spirit, whereas our soul contains our mind, emotions, heart, conscience, will, and intellect. The goal is to get our soul in line with our spirit so that they are operating in harmony. We listen first to the inner voice. Our decision making is then based on what is true, just, right-eous, and honourable. In so doing we will maintain a tes-timony of consistency.

You have probably heard the phrase: 'I used to be inde-cisive, but now I'm not so sure'. I know of someone who went for a job interview, during which he was asked, "Marking yourself out of ten, what number would you give yourself as regards decision making?" He replied, "Eight. No, second thoughts make it seven. No, definite-ly six." You can all guess the outcome.

Can you relate to this as Christians? I would suggest that it occurs most when our spirit and soul are in conflict. Is there a way forward, so that we are known as a people of clear minds, and resolute character, whose decisions have an impact in the home, church, and work, and whose strategy has a fruitful result? I believe that the answer is to get our soul in line with our spirit. **The inner voice becomes the loudest voice we hear, and we respond accordingly.**

The more we saturate ourselves in Him, the more our soul will get in line with the direction of The Spirit. This results in a renewed mind, emotions that are controlled, the right heart attitude, a clear conscience, a will that seeks first the Kingdom of God and His righteousness, and an intellect that instinctively knows the right choice. Our spirit and soul are in one accord.

THE ART OF BOXING

I do not run like a man running aimlessly; I do not fight like a man beating the air.

(1 Corinthians 9;26)

The above verse informs us that when the starting pistol fires, a runner sets his eyes on the finishing line. He does not wander around the track aimlessly, but keeps in his lane, heading directly forwards. Likewise, when a boxer is in the ring, there is little point in just beating the air. This sort of action does not win fights.

Have you ever felt like a boxer who has been forced back upon the ropes? When that situation occurs, it is no use for the boxer to merely fling his arms about, hoping to fend off the attacker. If his arms are flying about everywhere, he has dropped his guard, and is open to further attack, with more punishing blows being inflicted. In order to come off the ropes he needs to keep his guard up, and aim direct blows on the opponent. **He needs a strategy to come off the ropes.**

> **Take up the shield of faith,** *with which you can* **extinguish all the flaming arrows of the evil one.** *Take the helmet of salvation and* **The Sword of The Spirit, which is the Word of God.**
>
> *(Ephesians 6;16-17)*

This Scripture illustrates how we ought to keep up our guard, the shield of faith, and also to aim direct blows on our opponent (the devil) by using the Sword of The Spirit, the Word of God. This is the way to come off the ropes. Stand fast in our faith, and ask The Lord for a verse of Scripture. Then positively confess it in faith, and go on the offensive.

It is also worth remembering that when we are winning through in a situation, and see the victory in sight, we still need to keep up the shield of faith. It can be illustrated by the actions of a boxer who is getting the better of his opponent, but then becomes over confident, and lets his guard down. An opportunity opens up for his opponent to exploit, and from a position of attack he is forced back onto the defensive, simply because he let his guard down.

NEVER QUIT

Throughout our lives there may be times when we feel so battered and defeated, that we would like the towel to be thrown into the ring, to signal our desire to give up and quit. But we don't quit, because The Lord urges us to stand fast, and then move forward with the strategy that He gives. A boxing coach has to stay at the ringside shouting instructions, but our Lord is in the ring with us.

The One who is in you is greater than the one who is in the world. *(1 John 4;4)*

Have you seen a match when a boxer takes a heavy blow, and is knocked down? He hits the canvas and you think that he will never recover. The seconds are being counted out. But he does not quit, and manages to get a strength and determination to get back onto his feet, and resume the fight.

That is what can happen to us as Christians. We get knocked down either by affliction, or by stepping into trouble. But help is at hand, because when we are lying on our backs on the canvas, The Lord by His Spirit gives us the strength to get up and carry on.

Though a righteous man falls seven times, he rises again. *(Proverbs 24;16)*

A Christian is not defeated when he or she is knocked down. They are only defeated if they quit. The Lord will never quit on us, nor throw the towel in. Therefore, we do not consider quitting to be an option, because we have the assurance that He will never leave us, nor forsake us.

The strategy that The Lord gives us to defeat the enemy is accompanied on our part by a zeal and determination to see our opponent back away, and suffer defeat. Ask yourself – **Who should be against the ropes, and on the canvas, God's people or the devil?**

When a boxer wins a title he is awarded a belt, which is held together in the front by a large gold buckle. This displays that he holds the championship. We hear the phrase, "The undisputed heavyweight champion of the world". Christians are able to continually wear a belt, because Jesus has already won the fight on our behalf.

> *Stand firm then, with* **the belt of truth buckled round your waist.**   *(Ephesians 6;14)*

I have a bookmark in my Bible, produced by Easter Morning Inspirational Products. It is inscribed with the following words:

The next time the devil reminds you of your past, remind him of his future.

CHAPTER THIRTY-SEVEN

TAKE A RISK

YOU MAY THINK that what I am about to say completely contradicts all that has previously been mentioned on the subject of strategy over the past two chapters. However, I would ask you to bear with me, and it will hopefully come clear at the end.

The common phrase used when people leave one another's company is "Take care". I know of someone who does the opposite by declaring, "Take a risk". What percentage of Christians that you know, live truly radical lives? Would you agree that we view taking chances as almost unchristian? I would hasten to add that I am not talking about gambling, or anything surrounding that pursuit, which is self-destructive. I am referring to having an adventurous attitude, and abandoning the comfort zone of a safe and ordered existence, which is man-made.

Some may say at this point, "I have a pressurised job and work long hours, so when I come home I want to simply crash out on the sofa. I have a houseful of kids. I am either driving them somewhere, doing the laundry, or running the house. What little time I have to myself, I just want to relax". You may well ask – what opportunity do these people have to be radical?

In these sort of settings the people involved usually

crave ordinariness, because it means less pressure. It is a safe environment where minds quite understandably get conformed to simply surviving each week. There is not much room or desire for radical thought. This is not meant in any way to be critical. I am merely trying to be realistic about a current problem facing many households.

In addition to which, would you agree that we have all said the following, or something similar, at some time in our lives:

"After I finish this busy time in work, then I will have time to ..." "When the children are a bit older, then I will have more time to ..." "In the future I hope to ..." The problem is that we are always looking for that elusive free chunk of time that will allow us the freedom to concentrate all our efforts on achieving some goal. Unfortunately, it continually remains in the future, because the reality of life is that very few people have the luxury of large periods of free time.

I believe that being radical does not have to be determined by the length of time we have. It has more to do with our state of mind. **Five minutes of radical thought or action can have a considerable result.**

How often have you had a good idea at work, or church, but you have not mentioned anything because it is outside of conventional thought? Have you had an impulse to say something to someone at the school gates while you are waiting for your children, or in the queue at a supermarket? You keep quiet, but afterwards regret not taking the initiative.

We are robbed of opportunities because we have allowed our minds to conform to the pattern of the world of not getting involved, or taking a risk. Yet if you look at many inventions, changes in history, or individual lives being transformed, they often occur because people do the opposite of conventional thought. They take a risk. The world tells us it is wise to play safe, but God's Word informs us that the wise have a different outlook on things.

The wise make the most of every opportunity.
(Ephesians 5;15-16)

CREATIVE RISK

It could be said that God took the biggest risk of all time when He created us, and at the same time gave us free will. He could have created beings that were programmed to follow a pre-planned schedule. Let me ask you – if you were in God's place, would you have given us free will?

But He saw the wonderful union between Himself, and a people who sought out relationship with Him by their own decision. Of course His Spirit draws us to Him, but we still have a choice in the matter. Would you agree that God's actions were quite a risk?

But in fact it was no risk at all. Because creation needs its creator. Life needs the life-giver. We do not know the beginning from the end until we know The One who is The Alpha and Omega, the beginning and the end. Life only has meaning when we know The One who is the meaning of life.

RISKY LIVING

Matthew 25;14-30 records the Parable of The Talents. For anyone who may be unfamiliar with the passage, it describes a man who leaves his home to go on a journey, but before doing so he entrusts three servants with his property, giving them five, two, and one talent respectively. The two servants who had received five and two talents doubled their amounts, but the other servant simply buried his, and did not achieve any increase in its value.

When the master returned, he praised those who had gained a profit, but had harsh words for the one who had squandered his opportunity, for fear of losing it. The central message of this Scripture is that God wants us to use whatever we have, and in so doing it will expand. Anything good and wholesome, or any aspect of our lives that is talented or gifted, irrespective of whether it is in a small or large measure, should not be buried. It ought to be sown.

The last thing I would want to do is take liberties with The Bible, or distort any of its intended meaning, but I would like to share a perspective on these verses which has helped me.

What do you think was the governing factor in the mind of the servant with one talent? Would you agree that he was too afraid to make a mistake? He was bound up in fear, and consequently did not take a risk.

I am certain that The Lord wants each of us to 'have a go – take a risk'. He does not want us to be foolish, irresponsible, or act in an unrighteous manner. But I am sure that He wants us to be bold and radical. If the two servants with the five and two talents had been adventurous, and had lost them, I believe that the harsh words would still had been spoken to the servant who had simply played safe. He would have been proud of those who had been prepared to 'have a go'.

FEAR OF MISTAKES

Matthew 25;24-25 informs us that the servant with one talent was afraid. What made him fearful? He did not want to make a mistake, and thought that by being cautious, and returning the talent he would have pleased his master. The complete opposite was true.

How do we view mistakes? Do we regard them as sin? Would you agree that there is a difference between an act of disobedience, and a simple error of judgement? I believe that God does not view mistakes as sin. Throughout Scripture numerous verses inform us that He looks upon the motives of our heart. If we fail at something, let us listen to that 'inner voice' who will say "Well done. I saw your genuine desire, and I am proud of you for having a try".

Surely this is what happens concerning our relationship with our children. The matters that concern a parent the most are disrespect, and continual acts of disobedience. On the other hand, if they have a go at something and fail, we encourage them to try and try again. Their mistakes do not concern us, and we are proud of their efforts. If we act in this manner with our earthly children, how much more do you think this applies to our Heavenly Father?

SPIRIT LED OPPORTUNITIES

There are also specific promptings of the Holy Spirit when He guides us to those 'appointed times' with people. I have found that the Christians who are the most fruitful in this area are those who are the most radical on a daily basis. Could it be that The Lord knows that He can trust these individuals to be the most sensitive and obedient to His direction?

What point is there in giving these opportunities to those who would still be debating with themselves hours after the event – Is this God's will? Did I hear right? What if I am wrong? What if it does not work?

If you look at The Bible from beginning to end, it is full of characters that were prepared to take a risk. Abraham, Joshua and Caleb, Deborah, King David, Daniel, John The Baptist are just a few of the names that spring to mind. They were radical individuals who were not afraid to step out, and in consequence were used by God with regard to specific strategy.

The world often looks for men and women who are regarded as a 'safe pair of hands', especially with regard to forward planning and strategy. Our Heavenly Father takes the opposite view. He uses men and women who are not bound, and held captive by the fear of failure. Would you agree that we can all be guilty of wanting to see three angels, two lightening bolts, and five separate visions before we feel sure it is God's will to do something? Caution can be an excuse for unbelief.

Are you a person who likes to take a step forward from a place of security? Do you want everything in place and settled, together with clear sight of what is expected? For most of my life I had been in this category, until The Holy Spirit convicted me that I had more security in myself, than in God. The distinguishing contrast between a cautious Christian, and a radical, is that a radical's security is not in his or her own self, but in God. They have learnt to trust Him more than themselves.

NO RISK

The heart of the matter is that the issues in life that we regard as risks are in fact not risks at all. Laying hands on a sick colleague at work, giving your testimony to a person in a shopping queue, or stepping out in a spiritual gift is not risky living. It is simply following commands of Scripture. Although it is also important to be sensitive and obedient to those specific appointed times, the remainder of the time The Lord wants us to 'get on with it', as He has commanded us in His Word.

He has already empowered us by giving us The Holy Spirit. This is a completed work, and is not intended simply for church meetings, but for everyday encounters with people that we meet at work, on the street, in shops, or call at our home.

> **But you will receive power when The Holy Spirit comes on you; *and* you will be My witnesses *in Jerusalem...and* to the ends of the earth.**
>
> *(Acts 1;8)*

By way of personal testimony I can say that I have done a number of things in the last few years that I would formerly have regarded as taking a risk. The end result is that I have encountered The Lord's direction more in this small space of time than in all my previous Christian experience. I believe that part of the reason is that I am no longer afraid to make a mistake. This has brought release.

SUMMARY

I will now attempt to summarise these few thoughts on strategy, which I will place in three categories.

Firstly, there are times that require specific time set aside to pray and wait upon The Lord. This is not only for those who have a ministry in intercession, but also for everyone who is looking for strategy about a particular situation, or a new direction in life or ministry.

> **Do not leave *Jerusalem*, but wait *for the gift My Father promised*.**   *(Acts 1;4)*

Jesus spoke these words just before His ascension. The

disciples were obedient, and were subsequently empowered a short time later at Pentecost.

Secondly, we encounter those circumstances in life that require an immediate decision, and we do not have the luxury of time. We require the right strategy immediately, although we know that the resultant effect could be long lasting. The correct judgement will be made if our soul is in line with our spirit.

This is what happened in the case of Peter being invited to the home of Cornelius. Initially, Peter's mind and emotions were telling him not to associate with Gentiles, whom he regarded as unclean. But he listened to that inner voice in his spirit, and was obedient to the leading of The Holy Spirit.

> **While Peter was still thinking** *about the vision,* **The Spirit said to him...** *(Acts 10;19)*

Peter subsequently told Cornelius household that he came without raising any objection. If you think back to Peter's life, as described in the Gospels, it is clear that on many occasions his actions were governed by his emotions. But he later learnt to be led by The Spirit operating out of his spirit. His soul and spirit were in harmony.

> **I came without raising any objection.**
> *(Acts 10;29)*

Thirdly, there is the strategy that is given to those who are prepared to take a risk. The Lord knew that Philip was such a person.

PHILIP THE RISK TAKER

Philip appears four times in Acts. He was chosen as one of the seven who assisted in the distribution of food to the needy (Acts 6;1-6). He subsequently travelled to Samaria, where he brought *'great joy in the city'* because of his preaching and miracles (Acts 8;4-8). He later appears in Acts 8;26-40, which records his meeting with the Ethiopian eunuch. Lastly, he is mentioned in Acts 21;8-9 when Paul and Luke called at his home in Caesarea. He was an individual who got on with the task in hand, and was radical at the same time.

Philip was told by an angel of The Lord to go down the desert road towards Gaza. He was given no further information. Risky living would you agree? Why do you think he was chosen for the task? The key is found in Acts 6 which informs us of the criteria used to chose the seven to take responsibility for helping the poor.

They are known to be **full of The Spirit and wisdom**.
(Acts 6;3)

While he was walking along the road an Ethiopian passed him. Philip was prompted by the angel to stay near the chariot that was carrying the foreigner. *He then ran alongside.* Sometimes we can overlook seemingly ordinary words in Scripture. You will notice that in order for Philip to achieve an objective he had to accelerate from walking to running. He was not lazy, or expected the opportunity to come to him. **He was prepared to move at a faster pace to accomplish it.**

When he reached the chariot he heard the man reading Isaiah. Philip took the initiative and asked him if he understood the passage. He subsequently led the Ethiopian to The Lord and baptised him.

There is a very strong Christian community in Ethiopia, although they have suffered terrible persecution. Legend has it that the man, who became a Christian as a result of

Philip's intervention, is the same person who took Christianity to Ethiopia where there was a great revival. The Church that remains today is descended from that encounter on the Gaza Road.

It can be seen that, as a result of Philip's actions, he encountered an appointed time with the Ethiopian. The Lord had a strategy to take salvation to the country of Ethiopia, and used Philip to bring it about. When he set out on his journey Philip had no idea what would develop. When we take a risk we invariably do not know what will happen. There are also other occasions when we will never see the final outcome of our actions.

Philip's story does not end there, because in Acts 21;8 we read of him being referred to as *Philip the Evangelist*. Because he took that initial risk, he not only experienced that incredible appointed time, but he also discovered a gift within him – he was an evangelist.

Let me summarise Philip. Here was a person who was full of The Spirit, prepared to take a risk, even to chase after the chance encounter. He took the initiative that resulted in both the recipient and himself being blessed. He fulfilled an appointed time, which meant God's strategy for a nation being realised. In this process, Philip discovered a calling on his life, to be an evangelist.

He later had *four daughters who prophesied*. (Acts 21;9). They had seen something in their father's life that they wanted themselves. They too desired to be full of the Spirit and radical. Quite a testimony!

If we are prepared to take a risk, who knows where it may lead? The Lord knows. Hallelujah!

CONCLUSION

My purpose in writing these few aspects of strategy is to

hopefully reveal that each of our lives have purpose, and that there is no need whatsoever for any Christian to feel aimless, with no direction in life. The devil wants us to feel inhibited and over cautious. He does not want us to engage in purposeful, risky living because it threatens him. He would rather us be defensive in thought and deed. The last thing he wants to see is a church on the attack with zeal and direction.

I once believed that it was risky business tackling anything demonic, because I was unsure of my identity and authority in Christ. But The Lord revealed Himself to me, and gave me the strategy for victory, wiping away my fear.

We may fail at times, but we can never be failures. In addition to which, even when bad things occur, they can be turned around for our good. What happened to me six years ago was not pleasant, and it need never have happened. But The Lord has completely turned it around for my good.

We know that in **all things** *God works for the good of those who love Him.* (Romans 8;28)

This book is a testimony to the fact that:

... greater is He who is in me than he who is in the world. (1 John 4;4)

CHAPTER THIRTY-EIGHT

THE LAND OF INHERITANCE

MARTIN LUTHER KING'S final speech contained these words – "We have some difficult days ahead. But it really does not bother me now. For The Lord has allowed me to go up onto the mountaintop. I have looked over, and I have seen the Promised Land. I want you to know as a people that we will get to the Promised Land". Some years earlier He had given another famous speech entitled "I have a dream". He was referring to his vision of full human rights.

We each have a mountaintop. The Lord encourages us to look over and see the inheritance that He has given us, not only in eternity but also here on earth.

Joshua had a vision of the inheritance that The Lord had prepared for both the nation of Israel, and himself. In order for it to come into being, he crossed over The Jordan, and took possession of the land. In the course of time the Israelites won many victories, and many of the tribes had taken possession of their allocated land. However, for whatever reason, some tribes were not living in the inheritance that was there for them.

The country was brought under their control, but **there**

**were still seven Israelite tribes who had not yet
received their inheritance.** *So Joshua said to the
Israelites,* **"How long will you wait before you
begin to take possession of the land** *that The Lord,
The God of your fathers, has given you?"*

(Joshua 18;1-3)

Is this the question that The Holy Spirit is saying to us
in these days? **How long are we going to wait before we
decide to come into our full inheritance in The Lord?**

The Israelites did not seem to realise that the inheritance had already been given to them. It was lawfully their land, because God had given it to them. Even though the other inhabitants might seek to dispute ownership, they had no right to trespass or steal property that belonged to God's people.

At salvation we also came into an inheritance for both now and eternity. It is already ours, and we have a lawful right to live in its fullness and enjoy all the benefits.

Joshua fulfilled his calling, and is a testimony of faith in action. The book of Judges records what was written about him at the end of his life. Notice that it was not simply Joshua who had his own inheritance to possess, but the same applied in respect of each of the Israelites.

*After Joshua had dismissed the Israelites, they went to
take possession of the land,* **each to his own inheritance...** *Joshua died at the age of a hundred and ten,
and* **was buried in the land of his inheritance.**

(Judges 2;6-9)

Whatsoever The Lord gave Joshua to do, he completed. When Joshua died he was not buried in 'no man's land', or in defeat in the land of the enemy. He was buried in the land that he had faithfully claimed and taken for The Lord – *the land of his inheritance.*

Let us each have that same testimony.

CHAPTER THIRTY-NINE

GENETIC CODING

IN ORDER TO bring my testimony right up to date, I would like to share a further development that has occurred over the past year. It arose out of various medical examinations involving endoscopies, biopsies, and blood tests. The end result is that the specialist informed me that I have a genetic problem. In layman's terms I have one defective gene, and another gene is the worse for wear, coupled with high blood pressure and a high cholesterol count, even though I have a healthy diet.

The specialist attributes my condition to being inherited from my father, who died in his mid-fifties. In the natural, my present symptoms which are the same as my father, will cause heart disease or a stroke. Although it is seemingly bad news, The Lord had already prepared me for the prognosis.

The preparation occurred a few weeks prior to my hospital appointment, when I read an article in my daily newspaper. The writer was giving a moral perspective on a genetic issue. I took note of one point in particular, which read - 'it may be in your genes, but it does not have to be your future'. When I read this article I was unaware of any problem with my genes, but I remembered that phrase because I considered that it was quite a profound statement.

The results of the endoscopy, biopsy, and blood tests

confirmed that I had inherited a genetic defect from my father. When the doctor told me the news, the words of the article, that I had read only a short time earlier, came flooding back to me. I knew that The Lord had prepared me for the result.

I believe that He had guided me to that article about genetics, in order to give me further revelation about Him, and in so doing bring healing to my body. As the weeks passed, The Holy Spirit kept bring that sentence to my mind - it may be in your genes, but it does not have to be your future.

He was showing me that from a natural perspective the prognosis was not good. But my future is in Him, and that anything negative that I have inherited from my earthly parents does not have to govern my future. The reason being is that I have a Heavenly Father, and my life is now determined by a spiritual bloodline. My inheritance is in The Lord Jesus Christ, who died and shed His Blood for me, so that I am now adopted into a Heavenly family.

ADOPTION

God, The Father, predestined us to be adopted as His sons through Christ Jesus. (Ephesians 1;5)

The adoption that takes place in the Heavenly realm is far deeper than anything that we might perceive from a natural adoption on earth. When parents adopt a child they sign a covenant agreement to care and provide for their new son or daughter, and can love the child as much as if he was born to them. They can change his environment, and through many different ways, give the child a better start in life. However, there is nothing they can do to alter the effect of his genetic make-up.

But when we accept Jesus into our lives, and receive our spiritual adoption, we partake of a covenant relationship that is both eternal, and can effect us in spirit, soul and body in this present life. I therefore have a future that is governed from Heaven and not from earth, because I am His offspring - a child of God.

> *For in Him we live and move and have our being...We are His offspring.*   *(Acts 17;28)*

UNIQUE BLOOD

Just consider for one moment that point in time when The Holy Spirit conceived Jesus in Mary's womb. Have you ever thought - what type of blood did The Lord have? In His humanity he underwent a natural birth, and He was in bodily form, exactly the same as other men, yet of a divine nature. He was conceived by The Holy Spirit, who deposited the eternal seed of life itself into Mary's womb, and The Lord partook of humanity.

His genetic make-up, and the blood flowing through His veins were not contaminated. He had no defect what-soever. When His Blood was shed for our sins and sick-nesses, He was indeed the pure and spotless Lamb of God. This not only applied to Him being without sin, but also to the fact that His Blood was literally like no other.

> *You were redeemed...with the precious Blood of Christ, a Lamb without blemish or defect.*   *(1 Peter 1;18-19)*

HEAVENLY DNA

Our whole physical being is governed by the composition of our DNA. The human cell has 46 chromosomes, which are made up of long coils of DNA containing genes. However, the sex cell only contains 23 chromosomes. This is because, when the sex cells - the sperm cell (seed) from the man, and the egg cell from the woman - fuse together, one cell of 46 chromosomes is formed.

If there are different versions of the same gene at the point of 'fusing', they are called 'Alleles'. The dominant allele takes precedence over the recessive allele. One cell is produced out of this process, which is the creation of life. The DNA, blood type, and everything physical pertaining to the person is formed in that one cell, which continues to reproduce itself, and a living being is formed in the womb. The father's genes always determine the sex of the child.

I do not know what happened at the point of The Lord's conception in Mary's womb. It may have occurred by The Holy Spirit depositing the completed cell, or already formed child in the womb: or by The Spirit being the 'dominant' over any 'recessive' genes from Mary, so that anything impure was filtered. But what is clear to me is that Jesus' DNA, genetic composition, and blood was like no other.

The virgin birth was 'supernatural'. Jesus did not inherit any sickness or disease from any defective genes that may have been present in Mary. His genetic make-up was determined from Heaven. The natural order by which genes form life, subjected themselves to the supernatural order of Heaven. God is spirit, and does not have any genes or physical blood. But He spoke the word, and as He did at the creation of all things, life was formed.

The first man (Adam) was of the dust of the earth, the second man (Jesus) was from Heaven.
(1 Corinthians 15;47)

SPIRITUAL APPLICATION

If you follow on from this thought, and now consider what happens when we are born again. Jesus' Blood washes and cleanses us from our sins. The Holy Spirit enters our spirit and deposits the seed of life within us. We are reborn in our spirit. We are now of a different bloodline, which not only has a spiritual application, but also a physical effect. We are no longer subject to any genetic defect that we have inherited from our earthly parents. We have partaken of the very essence of life, because He is the giver of life, both in the spiritual and in the natural.

It is important to point out that our genes and blood do not literally take on a Heavenly form when we become a Christian. We essentially remain physically the same. It is only at our death, or when The Lord returns, that the perishable will be clothed with the imperishable, as described in 1 Corinthians 15.

But let us not underestimate what takes place in us when we accept Christ as our Saviour. We become inhabited by The Creator of all things while we are still on earth.

NEW FUTURE

At salvation we become a new creation. We not only encounter a spiritual re-birth, but it also means that our future, whether spiritually or bodily, is no longer determined by our earthly heritage. We are now subject to a different law. Although I have been a Christian since I was sixteen, it is only now that I am beginning to understand the sheer magnitude of what happens when we are born again.

> *Therefore, if anyone is in Christ, he is a new creation.*
> *(2 Corinthians 5;17)*

In the natural it was clear that the genes that I had inherited from my earthly father would have a determining influence on my future. However, I now have a Heavenly Father, and I am therefore of a different spiritual bloodline. Because of The Lord's wonderful grace, He has allowed us to partake of His divine nature. In the natural I have my father's genes, but praise God I do not have to be bound by anything earthly. It can best be illustrated by saying that a Christian has a Heavenly genetic make-up operating in their life. We are subject to a new set of principles, not only in eternity, but also while we are still on earth. This is why healing takes place.

> *As was the earthly man (Adam), so are those who are of this earth; and as is the man from Heaven (Jesus), so also are those who are of Heaven.*
>
> *(1 Corinthians 15;48)*

When Jesus was teaching His disciples to pray, He said the following:

> *Your Kingdom come, Your will be done on earth as it is in Heaven.* *(Matthew 6;10)*

I do not believe that it is His will that anyone has to live under the threat, or continual influence of sickness. The natural has to give way to the supernatural. I have faith in the creative Word of God, and believe that the defective genes are either repaired and restored, or that they will not cause ill health.

> *God gives life to the dead and calls things that are not as though they were.* *(Romans 4;17)*

I am confident that I will die in God's time, and I will not be robbed of years. I can therefore say with assurance - it may be in my (natural) genes, but it does not have to be my future.

RHEMA WORD

On the follow-up appointment with the specialist he told me that I had to take tablets for the remainder of my life. There was no alternative, because the genetic defects were the determining factor in the test results. It was emphasised that, because of my inherited genes, there was nothing I could do to get the results to the right level.

I initially took the advice, but stopped taking the medication after two weeks. I believed that The Lord had given me that word for a purpose. But I did not want to be foolish in the matter. The Lord had already saved my life and had given me a second chance, as I explained in my testimony at the beginning of the book. I did not want to throw it all away.

I decided that I would hold onto His Word, but also see the specialist the following year. I would have the same tests again, and if they had not changed, I would go back on medication.

The Greek has two meaning for The Word of God. The 'Logos' is the written Word of God; the 'Rhema' is the spoken Word of God into a situation. In serious health matters it is important to have real clarity before we step out in faith. If you are suffering from a debilitating, serious, or life-threatening illness, and have not received a specific Rhema Word about your healing, it would be wise to listen to the doctor's advice.

I only mention this, as many people become confused when they are in ill health, and falsely believe that their faith is on the line. The Lord will heal someone even if they are on medication.

TEST RESULTS

I have recently been for that appointment. The blood tests revealed that each of the categories that had formerly produced a poor rating, have dramatically changed to a good level. In consequence of this, there is no need for any medication. In addition to which, the other side issues are completely normal. I no longer need to see the specialist. The inherited genes from my earthly father have had to submit to my Heavenly genetic coding. I am healed. Hallelujah!

FAMILY LINE

It is very easy to look at one's parents and fear the worst, when negative traits are evident. This applies both in health matters and character. Most psychologists believe that our development is governed by either our inherited genes, or the environment in which we live, or a combination of both. My only point on this subject is that there is also a Heavenly order, which can alter the natural order of things.

We have all heard someone use the expression, 'it runs in the family', or 'it's a family trait'. Usually these phrases are used to describe a negative feature in someone. I would simply ask the question - Whose family are we talking about?

If there is a recognised aspect of character, health, or manner of living which is not right, then it does not have to stay that way. It is not inevitable that it has to pass from one generation to another. The line can be broken, whether in health or character.

There are even more serious implications when people feel under threat from a 'family curse'. Such individuals need to be assured that when we accept Jesus as our

Saviour we are a new creation. He dealt with the curse of sin and death on The Cross. Therefore, the effect of any unhealthy dabbling with unclean spirits, either by ancestors or themselves, does not have to affect their present life, or pass from one generation to another. The line can be broken, because The Name of the Lord Jesus is above every other name.

Obviously, not all genetic characteristics passed from our parents are bad. Use the positive aspects to their full potential. But also have the conviction that we do not have to accept anything negative. I hope this gives encouragement to those who feel threatened or intimidated by certain aspects of their family.

SUBJECT TO A DIFFERENT LAW

Some years ago I heard the following illustration that helps explain a miracle.

In many fairgrounds there is a ride called 'the wall of death'. It consists of a cylinder type compartment, where people stand with their backs to the wall. It then spins at a fast speed and the floor falls away. The riders remain pinned to the wall and do not fall, because of the centrifugal force that is generated by the spinning action. This particular law of physics causes objects to move away from the centre in an outward motion.

There are two laws at work. Gravity causes you to fall to the ground. You cannot stand in mid-air. But the centrifugal force superimposes itself upon the force of gravity.

This is what happens with a miracle. There is the natural law that determines a certain outcome. But when God superimposes His will on a situation, a supernatural act takes place.

The natural has to give way to the supernatural.